Praise for *Turn Right at Machu Picchu*

"Ebullient. . . . [An] engaging and sometimes hilarious book."

—*The New York Times Book Review*

"Like all great travelogues (and this is certainly one), *Turn Right at Machu Picchu* . . . should come with a fedora and a rucksack."

—*Men's Journal*

"Serious (and seriously funny) . . . smart and tightly written. . . . A rediscovery of Machu Picchu, the way Bingham did one hundred years ago."

—*National Geographic*

"In *Turn Right at Machu Picchu*, Adams proves an engaging, informative guide to all things Inca."

—*Entertainment Weekly*

"A story that hooks readers early and then sails along so interestingly that it's one of those 'can't put it down' books. What more could armchair adventurers want?"

—Associated Press

"Short of actually traveling to Machu Picchu yourself, it's the perfect way to acknowledge the lost city's 100th birthday as a modern-day tourist site."

—*The Christian Science Monitor* (editor's choice)

"With a healthy sense of humor. . . . Adams unearths a fascinating story, transporting his readers back to 1911, when Yale professor Hiram Bingham III hiked the Andes and stumbled upon one of South America's most miraculous and cloistered meccas."

—NPR.org

"[An] entirely delightful book."

—*The Washington Post*

"Adams deftly weaves together Inca history, Bingham's story, and his own less heroic escapade. . . . Those favoring a quirkier retelling [of Bingham's exploits] will relish Mr. Adams's wry, revealing romp through the Andes."
—*The Wall Street Journal*

"Mark Adams crisscrossed the Andes and has returned with a superb and important tale of adventure and archaeology. The Inca ruins at Machu Picchu are one of the world's enduring mysteries, and Adams has written such a bold, compelling account that I'm sure many of us will soon be trekking up those same outrageous mountains to see them for ourselves. It is a beautiful and profound world that he has entered, and his readers are immeasurably the richer for it."
—Sebastian Junger, author of *The Perfect Storm*

"In this book you will certainly learn more about Peru, Inca culture, half-sane pith-helmeted explorers of the twentieth century, zero-sane Australian travel guides of the twenty-first, and the mysteries of Machu Picchu than you ever knew before. But you will also learn more about Mark Adams, a hugely funny and thoughtful writer, diligent researcher, and unexpected man of action who climbs up from soft middle age to the dizzying, thin air of adventure. You will want to go with him."
—John Hodgman, author of *The Areas of My Expertise* and *That Is All*

"After reading Mark Adams's book, I did two things. First, I checked airfare to Machu Picchu. Second, I told my friends they had to read this amazing and entertaining tale about explorers, stolen treasures, Amelia Earhart, and the controversial professor who—according to new evidence Adams found—just may be the model for Indiana Jones."
—A. J. Jacobs, author of *The Year of Living Biblically*

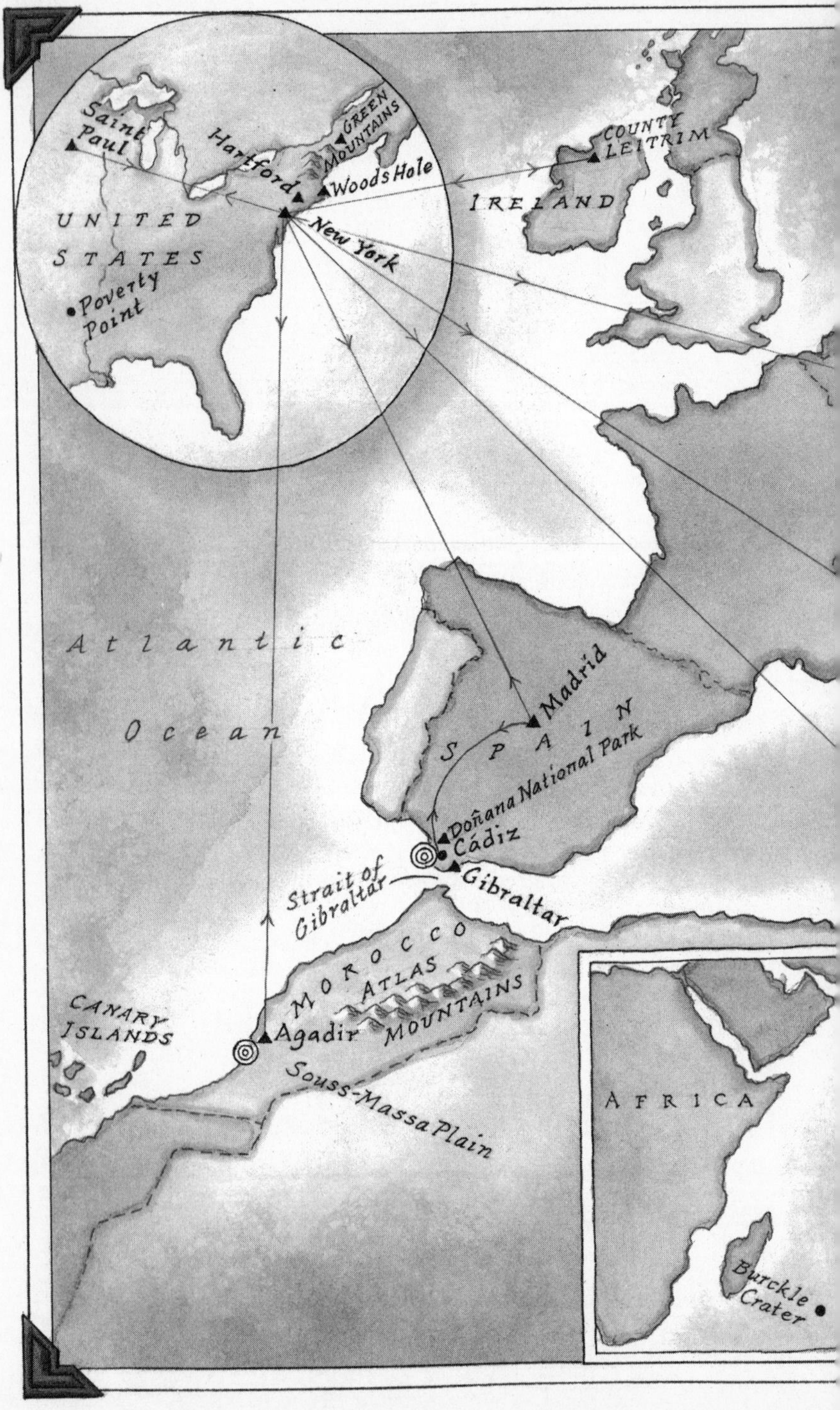
Saint Paul
GREEN MOUNTAINS
Hartford
Woods Hole
New York
UNITED STATES
Poverty Point
COUNTY LEITRIM
IRELAND
Atlantic Ocean
Madrid
SPAIN
Doñana National Park
Cádiz
Gibraltar
Strait of Gibraltar
MOROCCO
ATLAS MOUNTAINS
Agadir
CANARY ISLANDS
Souss-Massa Plain
AFRICA
Burckle Crater

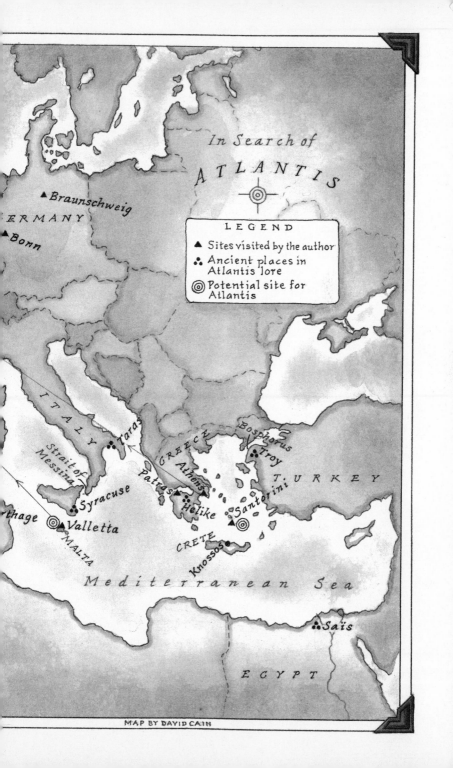

In Search of
ATLANTIS

LEGEND
▲ Sites visited by the author
⋮ Ancient places in Atlantis lore
◎ Potential site for Atlantis

▲ Braunschweig
GERMANY
▲ Bonn

ITALY
Strait of Messina
Taras
GREECE
Bosphorus
Troy
Athens
Patras
Helike
Santorini
Syracuse
TURKEY
Carthage
◎ Valletta
MALTA
CRETE
Knossos

Mediterranean Sea

Saïs
EGYPT

MAP BY DAVID CAIN

MEET ME IN
ATLANTIS

Across Three Continents in Search
of the Legendary Sunken City

MARK ADAMS

DUTTON
— est. 1852 —

DUTTON
— est. 1852 —

An imprint of Penguin Random House LLC
375 Hudson Street
New York, New York 10014

Previously published as a Dutton hardcover, 2015

First paperback printing, April 2016

The Library of Congress has catalogued the hardcover edition of this book as follows:

Adams, Mark, 1967–
Meet me in Atlantis : my quest to find the 2,500-year-old sunken city / Mark Adams.
pages cm
Includes bibliographical references and index.
ISBN 978-0-525-95370-8 (hardback) 978-1-101-98393-5 (paperback)
1. Atlantis (Legendary place)   2. Adams, Mark, 1967– Travel.   3. Explorers—Biography.
4. Plato—Influence.   5. Plato—Criticism and interpretation.   I. Title.
GN751.A38   2015
398.23'4—dc23

Printed in the United States of America
10 9 8 7 6 5 4 3 2 1

Designed by Nancy Resnick
Illustrations copyright © 2015 by Julie Munn
Map copyright © 2016 by David Cain

In memory of Kathleen McMahon Adams

Many cities of men he saw and learned their minds.
—Homer, *The Odyssey*

Lost and Found?

Near Agadir, Morocco

We had just met the previous week in Bonn, my new German acquaintance and I, and here we were on the west coast of Africa on a hot Thursday morning, looking for an underwater city in the middle of the desert. Our destination was an unremarkable set of prehistoric ruins. The shared interest—about the only thing we had in common—that had brought Michael Hübner and me together in Morocco for what felt like a very awkward second date was Atlantis. Hübner was certain he had found it.

Hübner was far from alone in this belief. I'd already met plenty of other enthusiastic Atlantis seekers who'd used clues gleaned from Renaissance maps or obscure Babylonian myths or unpublished documents from the Vatican Secret Archives to pinpoint its supposed location. There did not seem to be a lot of consensus. Morocco was the eighth country on three continents that I'd visited as I pursued those who pursued Atlantis, the legendary lost city. I'd become as fascinated by them as they were by their quest. I hadn't seen my wife and children for a month.

Hübner's unique search strategy was data analysis. He had scoured ancient literature for every mention of Atlantis that he could find and then plugged that data into an algorithm far too complicated for a math novice like me to understand. His results were clear, though. According to his calculations and the laws of probability, the capital city of Atlantis had absolutely, positively existed just a few hundred feet ahead at the nexus of GPS coordinates we were tracking. "It is very, very improbable that all these criteria are combined by chance in one area," he had already told me several times, his monotone voice betraying not the slightest doubt.

I wasn't so sure. Perhaps the defining characteristic of the landscape around us, the foothills of the Atlas Mountains, was its complete lack of water. Twice on the way here my driver had slammed on the brakes to avoid crashing into herds of camels crossing the road. The one thing that everyone knows about the legend of Atlantis is that it sank beneath the seas.

Hübner had a ready explanation for this aquatic discrepancy. An earthquake in the Atlantic Ocean, a few miles west of where we were hiking, had caused a tsunami that had flooded the Moroccan coast and then receded. The ancient story of this deluge had simply gotten garbled over generations of retelling.

A few months earlier, I would have said Hübner's explanation sounded crazy. Now it had a very familiar ring to it. I had heard a lot of location hypotheses that hinged on tsunamis and other improbable agents: volcanic explosions, mistranslated hieroglyphics, the ten biblical plagues, asteroid impacts, Bronze Age transatlantic cocaine trafficking, and the Pythagorean theorem.

All of these ideas had been presented to me by intelligent, sincere people who had devoted large chunks of their lives to searching for a city that most reputable scientists dismissed as a fairy tale. Most of the university experts I'd approached about Atlantis had equated the futility of searching for it with hunting down the specific pot of gold that a certain leprechaun had left at the end of a particular rainbow. Now I was starting to wonder if I'd been away from home too long—because the more of these Atlantis seekers I met, the more their cataclysmic hypotheses made sense.

Perhaps the second most famous attribute of Atlantis was its distinctive circular shape, an island city surrounded by alternating rings of land and water. At the center of those rings, the story went, stood a magnificent temple dedicated to the Greek god Poseidon. That innermost island, with its evidence of an advanced civilization suddenly destroyed by a watery disaster, was the proof that every Atlantis hunter most longed to find. Incredibly, this legendary island's precise measurements, as well as the dimensions of the temple and the city's distance from the sea, had been handed down from the philosopher Plato, one of the greatest thinkers in Western history. The clues to solving this riddle had been available for more than two thousand years, but no one had yet found a convincing answer. Hübner insisted that according to his own calculations, what we were about to see was close to a perfect match.

Hübner wasn't an especially chatty guy, so we trudged silently up the slope, the only sounds coming from our feet scraping the sun-baked ground and the occasional bleating of stray goats. Finally, the incline leveled off and we looked out onto a large geological depression, a sort of desert basin enclosed on all sides. I leaned against a leafless tree and wiped sweat from my eyes.

"You remember how I showed you the satellite photo, how it was like a ring?" Hübner said, waving his hand across the panorama. "That is this place here."

Of course I remembered. The image he'd shown me on his computer screen was like a treasure map leading to Atlantis; it was that photo that had convinced me to come to Morocco. I scanned the horizon from left to right and slowly recognized that we were standing above a natural bowl, almost perfectly round. In the middle was a large hill, also circular—a ring within a ring.

"On that hill in the center is where I found the ruins of the gigantic temple," Hübner said. "You can check for yourself the measurements. They are almost exact with the story of Atlantis." He sipped from his water bottle. "I would like to show this to you. Do you think maybe we should go down there?"

CHAPTER ONE

That Sinking Feeling

New York, New York

A few years ago, for reasons that presumably made sense at the time, a friend who worked at a popular women's magazine called to ask if I'd consider taking on an unusual writing assignment. Might I be interested in compiling a list of the greatest philosophers of all time and explaining, in easily digestible chunks, why their work was relevant to America's working mothers?

Having dropped the one philosophy course I'd signed up for in college, I knew little about the subject. But easy money is hard to come by for a freelance writer, and this job sounded like a cakewalk, so I set to work contacting professors at various reputable universities and asking them to rank their top ten philosophers. To my surprise, there was no disagreement about who deserved the top two slots on the list. Every professor I phoned or e-mailed named the ancient Greek philosopher Plato number one, followed by his protégé Aristotle.

I knew a thing or two about Aristotle, since he'd been one of the final entries in the lone Aa–Ar volume of a children's encyclopedia that my mother had purchased at the supermarket one Saturday to keep me quiet while she shopped. (I wrote many grade school papers on the differences between aardvarks and anteaters.) Aristotle's genius is still evident to a modern reader, and his work is very much in line with what most of us assume philosophy is. He talks a lot about ethics and logic. He was a master of classification who sorted messy subjects like language and nature into neat categories that we still use today. He's a little dull, but "invented deductive reasoning" is a pretty impressive accomplishment for anyone to list on his resume.

Aristotle's teacher, Plato, was in many ways his opposite. Where Aristotle's work is dry and rational like a science textbook, Plato's philosophy is entertaining and figurative. His writings unfold as dialogues between characters, some drawn from real life. It's not always clear if he's being serious or ironic. Yet Plato's influence has been so great that the eminent British logician Alfred North Whitehead once commented—in a remark that I must've heard a dozen times during my reporting—that Western philosophy "consists of a series of footnotes to Plato."

What had seemed like a quickie writing assignment stretched into weeks of research as I struggled to get a grip on Plato's engrossing but slippery ideas. One afternoon, while reading Julia Annas's introductory survey *Plato*, I came across a sentence so striking that I had to reread it twice before its significance sank in: "In terms of sheer numbers of people affected, probably the most influential thing Plato ever wrote was his unfinished story of Atlantis." In other words, the most impactful concept ever put forth by the most celebrated philosopher of all time was the famous tale of a lost civilization that sank beneath the waves.

That the story of Atlantis—much beloved by psychics, UFO spotters, and conspiracy theorists—should have sprung from one of history's greatest minds struck me, to put it lightly, as a little odd. It was like hearing that Wittgenstein had helped fake the moon landings.

Around this time the Ocean extension of Google Earth was launched. The Atlantis seekers almost immediately flooded the Internet with claims that they'd located it at the bottom of the

Atlantic near the Canary Islands. But what had initially looked like the street plan of a vast underwater metropolis turned out to be a grid pattern caused by ships' sonars. After a few days the excitement faded. I assumed the seekers turned their attention back to more important matters, like searching for Bigfoot.

I did not yet understand that Atlantis is a virus, and that I'd been exposed.

Starting in the late 1970s, a hugely successful movie trilogy was released that changed the lives of a generation of American boys. These three tales of incredible journeys, inspired by ancient myths and conflicts that transpired a long time ago in places far, far away, were cinematic catnip for preadolescent suburban youths with overactive imaginations and limited athletic skills. Some of my fondest childhood memories are of being dropped off with my best friend at the local Lake Theater and vibrating in our seats with anticipation. It didn't matter that the dialogue was hackneyed or that we knew good would triumph over evil in the end. Even today, reading the titles of those three film epics gives me a chill that Luke Skywalker's adventures never could: *In Search of Noah's Ark*, *Beyond and Back*, and *In Search of Historic Jesus*.

What made these movies, and their beloved stepsibling, the Leonard Nimoy–hosted television show *In Search Of . . .* , so enticing was their willingness to explore what were known then as "unexplained phenomena" by straddling the worlds of history and myth. My Catholic school education didn't allow for a lot of gray areas and ambiguities. Rather than declaring everything to be either true or false, these movies and programs left things open-ended. (*Could this thing that looks like a dirty tablecloth actually be the burial shroud of Jesus? Probably not—but maybe!*) A lot of what I watched was simply goofy— even at age ten I had doubts about anything involving Martians or communicating with plants. But usually, by the time the credits rolled I felt an uncontrollable urge to solve some mystery of my own. With enough hours in the library and one of those cool archaeologist's brushes, why couldn't I find Noah's ark or figure out the meaning of Stonehenge?

I should have known I had no natural immunity against a contagion as powerful as Atlantis, but the symptoms crept up on me slowly. Just as a couple who's thinking about having a baby suddenly starts seeing pregnant women on every street corner, I began to notice mentions of Atlantis online or on TV. The popular notion that Atlantis had sunk in the middle of the Atlantic seemed to have fallen out of fashion. I watched a BBC documentary that argued the Greek island of Santorini had been the original Atlantis, then saw a Discovery Channel special that strongly suggested the lost city had once been located in Antarctica. Months passed. Another writing assignment took me to a banquet for people who'd achieved incredible medical results through alternative health therapies. As a conversation starter I mentioned my new interest to my tablemates and nearly started a fistfight between a homeopath and an aromatherapist. One knew beyond the shadow of a doubt that Atlantis had been in the Bahamas while the other angrily insisted that only an idiot would search anywhere but the Mediterranean.

The more I became intrigued, the more apparent it became that searching—*actively* searching—for Atlantis, a discipline sometimes referred to as Atlantology, is something of a growth industry. Using clues embedded in Plato's dialogues, Atlantologists had variously "located" his lost island empire in Scandinavia, Alaska, Indonesia, and just about every country that touches a large body of water. A few arguments were even made for landlocked, mountainous countries such as Bolivia, which seemed a little ambitious considering that whole sank-into-the-sea aspect. According to the most thorough tally I could find, more serious hypotheses about the location of

Plato's lost civilization had been proposed in the last ten years than in the previous twenty-four hundred, going all the way back to the days when Plato walked the streets of Athens.

Virtually all these possible sites had been found by energetic amateur sleuths. Serious historians and archaeologists, when they deigned to consider Atlantis at all, have always tended to treat Plato's tale as a fiction invented to illustrate his complex political philosophy. At least the polite ones did. One specialist in archaeology and ancient history had written an entire book that treated the urge to find Atlantis as a sort of mental disorder.

And yet, almost universally believers and nonbelievers both agreed that Plato had done two things that made a real Atlantis seem believable. First, he embedded dozens of precise details in his story, including measurements, landmarks, and its position relative to other known places—the same sorts of particulars that have been used to find other lost cities. Second, Plato claimed repeatedly that the story was true and had been passed down to him from very reputable historical sources. This assurance only raised more questions. Was his pledge of veracity a clever philosopher's trick to make a fantastic tale sound more realistic, or did he really believe that Atlantis had once existed? Was it possible that Plato believed the story but had been given false information? No original manuscripts of Plato's works exist. Could his writing have been corrupted with errors over the centuries through the process of being transcribed by hand, over and over? Or had Plato, as some believed, hidden a coded message in his works that might be deciphered?

Because Plato is the only known source for the Atlantis tale, people had been debating the truth or falsity of the city's destruction since his death in 347 BC. Academics typically gave the last word to the levelheaded Aristotle, who is quoted as having dismissed Plato's sunken kingdom with the words, "He who invented Atlantis also destroyed it."

Proof that the Atlantis tale was true wouldn't just make for a great episode of *In Search Of*. . . It would also help solve some of ancient history's greatest mysteries. The details of its sudden destruction may help explain a bizarre chain of natural catastrophes and apocalyptic famines that caused several advanced Mediterranean societies to collapse suddenly at the end of the Bronze Age. Some believed, with good reason, that the details in Plato's Atlantis tale were closely related to stories in the Old Testament.

The virus continued to incubate. I set up an e-mail news alert for "Atlantis and Plato." About once a week I'd receive notice that someone had devised a new location theory, as often as not pinpointing someplace like the Great Pyramid or the Bermuda Triangle.

The day after the devastating Fukushima tsunami in Japan—descriptions of which eerily echoed the "violent earthquakes and floods" that Plato claimed destroyed Atlantis—I was sitting in my office when Atlantis news alerts started pinging like a pinball machine. Evidently, someone had found the lost island for real this time, or at least serious media outlets around the world were treating the latest discovery as news.

I was torn. The logical, Aristotle half of my brain told me that it couldn't be possible, that any search for Atlantis was bound to be the wildest of goose chases. The daydreamy, Plato half of my brain said that nothing was beyond imagining. Perhaps this was something I should look into further, I thought. I searched out a passage I'd underlined in Plato's *Meno*, in which the characters discuss the limits of knowledge. One philosopher says to another, "We shall be better and braver and less helpless if we think that we ought to inquire than we should have been if we indulged in the idle fancy that there was no knowing and no use in seeking to know what we do not know."

Bumper sticker translation: If you don't ask questions, you'll never find any answers.

CHAPTER TWO

Philosophy 101: Intro to Plato

Lowenstein Academic Building, Fordham University

When I first read that Plato was the source of the Atlantis myth, I imagined the Atlantis I knew from Saturday morning cartoons: a city of hyperintelligent beings who dwelled beneath the waves in air-locked bubble houses powered by magic crystals. It turned out that Plato's original version is a bit more complicated and a lot more interesting.

The Atlantis tale unfolds in two parts, stretched across a pair of Plato's later works, the *Timaeus* and the *Critias*. Few non-Atlantologists without PhDs are familiar with these dialogues, and for a good reason: They are extremely weird. They are also, however, closely related to Plato's most famous dialogue, the *Republic*, which would finish first in a poll to determine the most influential philosophical work of all time. The *Republic* is logical and forceful and covers a lot of ground—not many books can be called foundational texts of both Christianity and Fascism—and is packed with brilliant, radical ideas.

The *Timaeus*, a dialogue that Plato wrote as a sort of sequel to the *Republic*—and which introduced Atlantis to the world—is messy and confusing. It contains mathematics, cosmology, natural sciences, an explanation of why time exists, possibly ironic musings on what types of animals humans transform into after reincarnation, and, as the philosopher Bertrand Russell drily noted, "more that is simply silly than is to be found in [Plato's] other writings." The *Critias*, which provides most of the details used to search for Atlantis, reads like a Greek myth rewritten by a middle schooler whose grade depends on using lots of numbers and adjectives. It ends unresolved, halfway through a sentence.

Two painful attempts to plow through the *Timaeus* and *Critias* convinced me that I needed a guide. Enter Brian Johnson, who was teaching Introduction to Plato at Fordham University. I was swayed by his near-perfect ratings on RateMyProfessors.com, which included encouraging comments such as "Philosophy can be reallllly boring, but he makes it interesting." Johnson invited me up to his tiny, windowless office on the eighth floor of a high-rise on Manhattan's west side. He was slim, bespectacled, and cheerful. We purchased gigantic coffees in the university cafeteria and retired to the silence of the philosophy department.

One reason why the *Timaeus* is so confusing, Johnson explained, is that it was the product of a rather daunting assignment Plato had given himself—to formulate a theory that explained pretty much everything in existence, known and unknown. "There's no such thing as a cosmic book that you can open up and it explains the laws of nature," Johnson said. "Plato's concerned about the grounds for knowledge. He's looking for regularity in a chaotic world. In the *Timaeus* there's this attempt to associate all things with numbers," Johnson said. "He's trying to give a theological account that provides something like the geometric logic of nature." According to tradition, over the entrance of the university Plato founded in Athens, the Academy, were posted the words LET NO ONE IGNORANT OF GEOMETRY ENTER HERE.

For Plato, the earth is a globe that rotates because that is the most perfect shape and the most perfect motion. Everything in the natural world can be broken down into four elements: fire, air, water, and earth. These elements are in turn composed of four geometric solids: four-sided, six-sided, eight-sided, and twenty-sided. A fifth, twelve-sided polygon represented the universe. Johnson pulled an animated diagram of the Platonic solids up on his computer screen. They looked like the multifaceted dice from *Dungeons & Dragons*. These five solids, according to the *Timaeus*, can be subdivided further into two types of triangles, both of which have measurements that correspond to the Pythagorean theorem: $A^2 + B^2 = C^2$.

The *Timaeus*, with its emphasis on a world created by a single god, was hugely influential in the development of Christian and Islamic ideas. The speaker Timaeus explains how the cosmos was fashioned from chaos by a single demiurge, or Divine Craftsman. This creator is good, and therefore the world is good. This will sound familiar to anyone raised in a modern religious household, but it was a fairly radical departure from the traditional Greek pantheon of gods who drank, fought, engaged in various sexual hijinks, and capriciously meddled in the affairs of mortals. Unlike the Old Testament God, Plato's Divine Craftsman does not create the cosmos ex nihilo. He uses a set of ideal blueprints but must work with the imperfect materials the universe has presented to him, which is why the world often falls short of mathematical perfection.

Plato's odd choice to sandwich his theories about the creation of the cosmos between the two halves of the Atlantis tale has been discussed and debated almost since the moment he died. So has the question of whether he meant the story to be true or not. I mentioned to Johnson that Aristotle had famously dismissed the story, and he nodded in agreement. Aristotle spent twenty years studying at Plato's Academy, which was the world's first university. During and after his time there he seems to have rejected many of Plato's ideas. According to one melodramatic bit of ancient gossip, following Plato's death, his star pupil was angry at being passed over to replace his mentor as the head of the institute. One later writer, Johnson told me, said Plato had referred to Aristotle as "the foal that kicks its mother when it's had too much milk."[1]

I was curious to know if stories like that of Atlantis were common in Plato's writings. "There are things about it that are typical," Johnson said. "It's a story within a story. It's a way of Plato distancing himself from making it literal. It allows Plato a little free range." The philosopher was certainly fond of inserting myths into his dialogues. The *Republic* ends with the Myth of Er, about a soldier who comes back to life on his funeral pyre after dying on the battlefield. "He claims to have seen the transmigration of souls," Johnson said. "You get to pick your next life." According to this myth, those who choose to live justly go to heaven, while those who seek money or power are condemned to misery.

"One thing I noticed is that Plato stresses over and over that the Atlantis story is true," I said.

"You've probably heard about the Noble Lie."

I had. This was Plato's mandate in the *Republic* that in order to maintain the class structure necessary for an ideal society, the rulers would need to tell the lower caste that the system had been put in

---

1 A logical question to ask here is, do we know what Plato's students at the Academy thought of Atlantis? The answer is yes—sort of. Aristotle, in addition to his famous quip about Plato having invented the lost island, also echoed a key point from the Atlantis story in his *Meteorology*, a work probably written before Plato's death, when he stated that "outside the Pillars of Heracles the sea is shallow owing to the mud, but calm, for it lies in a hollow." A member of the next generation of Academy students, Crantor, seems to have taken the view opposite Aristotle's. (We can't know for certain because like the writings of so many of the ancients, his original works have been lost and live on only in citations made by later writers.) According to the fifth-century-AD writer Proclus, Crantor—whose status as the first scholar to write extensive commentaries on Plato's works is not in dispute—may have sent envoys to Egypt in an attempt to verify Plato's original sources.

place by God. In this way the wisest would continue to lead and the others would be satisfied with their station in life.

"Maybe when he insists on the truth of Atlantis, that itself is sort of a Noble Lie," Johnson said. He reached for his thick *Collected Works of Plato* and scanned the pages with his index finger. "One other thing that seems typical is that the story resolves itself through natural disaster. Here it is, in the *Laws*." The *Laws* was one of Plato's final works, an attempt to draw up a blueprint for the society he'd outlined in the *Republic*. It's infamous for being even harder to comprehend than the *Timaeus*, and mind-bendingly dull. "Even people who study ancient philosophy tend to dip in and out of the *Laws* rather than reading the whole thing," Johnson admitted.

Johnson read aloud. "The human race has been repeatedly annihilated by floods and plagues and many other causes, so that only a fraction of it has survived."

That sure sounded a lot like Atlantis. In the *Timaeus*, an Egyptian priest tells his Greek visitor, "There have been, and will be again, many destructions of mankind arising out of many causes; the greatest have been brought about by the agencies of fire and water, and other lesser ones by innumerable other causes." Might it have been a story Plato made up to show an idealized state, like the one he proposed in the *Republic*, that was corrupted and thus had to be punished by the gods?

"Here's a hypothesis that could be wildly wrong," Johnson said, closing the book. "It seems like the Atlantis myth does cash in on some ideas from the *Republic*. Have you bumped into this idea of the Golden Age?"

I had. The Greeks were great believers in the Good Old Days. For Plato, who was a bit of a snob, this would have been an imaginary time when Athens was ruled by wise aristocrats rather than a mob ignorant of geometry.

"I gather that Atlantis was supposed to be like his philosopher-kings model and that it was destroyed by natural disaster," he said.

In the *Republic*, Plato proposes that the best possible leaders would be philosopher-kings, monarchs who ruled wisely because they had been trained in the philosophic arts, especially mathematics. "Plato says that the ideal state cannot last. He seemed to think its own downfall is built into the very structure of nature."

Johnson had a fascinating poster on his wall that at first glance looked like the concentric circles of Atlantis. I was disappointed to learn it was actually a re-creation of a map from the movie *Time Bandits*. I seemed to recall the movie beginning with a boy's fascination with ancient Greece and leading through a long, complicated journey based on possibly unreliable source materials. I couldn't remember if it had a happy ending.

"I'm guessing Atlantis isn't discussed much in professional philosophy circles," I said.

"It isn't. Insofar as it is referenced, it's going to be to ask, what philosophy can we extract from this myth?"

"So do you think it's possible that Atlantis ever existed?" I asked. I didn't mention anything about actually going to look for it.

We sat in silence while Johnson formulated an answer. He had the sympathetic look on his face that teachers use when they don't want to discourage classroom discussion, even though the students obviously haven't understood the assigned reading. The five Platonic solids rotated merrily on his computer screen.

"I guess I'm open to the idea," he said, finally. "So long as it's reasonable."

CHAPTER THREE

"Disappeared in the Depths of the Sea"

Saïs, Egypt (ca. 600 BC)

This is a detective story, one that starts in ancient Greece and follows a twisting path through (to list just a few locations) Pharaonic Egypt, Nazi Germany, and contemporary Saint Paul, Minnesota. And as with any good detective story, it helps to assemble all the available evidence in one place.

The story begins in the *Timaeus*, which takes its title from the character of that name, whose elaborate musings on the nature of the universe have kept philologists busy for two millennia. As was common in Plato's dialogues, some of the speakers are historical figures whom Plato knew personally. Socrates, who in real life was Plato's beloved philosophical mentor, sets the scene by reminding everyone that the previous day he had given a speech on the ideal city, a reference to the *Republic*. He asks his three companions—Timaeus, Critias, and Hermocrates—to each tell a story to illustrate his ideas. Hermocrates suggests that Critias should start by sharing "one that goes back a long way."

Critias, a relative of Plato, prefaces his tale by saying it is "a very strange one, but even so, every word of it is true." To stress its veracity, Critias explains that he heard it from his very old grandfather, who heard it from his father. The original source was unimpeachable: Solon, one of the great statesmen in Athenian history and Plato's great-great-great-great-grandfather. The story Critias tells his friends recounts a great moment in the history of Athens, "the most magnificent thing our city has ever done."

Following so far? Two historical figures, Socrates and Critias, have a presumably invented conversation about a supposedly true story passed down by one of Plato's ancestors. Let's proceed.

Long ago, Critias tells his friends, Solon paid a visit to the Egyptian city of Saïs. He was greeted as an honored guest by priests who were scholars of ancient history. One day Solon began to speak with his hosts about figures from Greek antiquity, but one of the Egyptians interrupted him and said, "O Solon, Solon, you Greeks are never anything but children, and there is not an old man among you." The priest explained that Greek society had been repeatedly wiped out by floods or fire, while Egypt had been spared these disasters. The collective history and culture of the Greeks had been all but erased many times, leaving behind only an illiterate band of survivors on each occasion. Therefore, the priest told Solon, the Greeks had no memory "that the finest and best of all the races of humankind once lived in your region." The Egyptians, having avoided such catastrophes, had maintained in their temples records of the great or noble acts of all peoples, including those of the Athenians.

Before the most devastating of all floods, the priest explained, the laws and military deeds of Athens had been the greatest ever known. This was in the far distant past, nine thousand years ago. The most glorious Athenian deed of all, the priest continued, was its halting of a vast sea power called Atlantis. Atlantis had insolently attacked all of Europe and Asia, and its empire was larger than Libya and Asia combined. Atlantis was situated on an island in the infinite Atlantic

Sea, located in front of the straits that the Greeks called the Pillars of Heracles.[2] Without provocation, Atlantis had conquered all lands up to Egypt and Tyrrhenia. It sought to subdue and enslave Egypt, Greece, and all other countries within the Mediterranean. But the noble Athenians, deserted by their allies, fought on alone and defeated the invaders, thus freeing all those "within the boundaries of Heracles."

Plato, via the priest, has spun a classic story of heroism—the virtuous underdogs defeating the powerful, evil empire. *Star Wars* in sandals. But then Plato adds the twist that has made the Atlantis story immortal. After the Athenian victory, the priest continues, "there occurred violent earthquakes and floods; and in a single day and night of misfortune all your warlike men in a body sank into the earth, and the island of Atlantis in like manner disappeared in the depths of the sea. For which reason the sea in those parts is impassable and impenetrable, because there is a shoal of mud in the way; and this was caused by the subsidence of the island."

Then, just as the story is heating up, Critias pauses to tell Socrates that actually, Timaeus should speak first, because his tale deals with the creation of the entire universe. Timaeus, a Pythagorean philosopher from Italy, takes over the dialogue by asking a very Platonic question—"What is that which always is and has no becoming; and what is that which is always becoming and never is?"—and then commences to explain at length Plato's kaleidoscopic scientific

---

2 *Heracles*, occasionally spelled *Herakles*, is the Greek name for the mythical hero, a son of Zeus, famous for his strength. The Romans incorporated him into their own pantheon, changing his name to Hercules. Historians and classics scholars generally agree that the Pillars of Heracles that Plato refers to are the narrow Strait of Gibraltar at the mouth of the Mediterranean Sea between Spain and Morocco. If you look up Pillars of Heracles/Hercules in Wikipedia, you'll see a photo of the Rock of Gibraltar. Among Atlantologists, however, the debate over where Plato intended these pillars to be situated is far from settled. For simplicity's sake, when I use the term *Pillars of Heracles* (other than to cite Plato's use of the name), I'm referring to those at Gibraltar.

speculations about the order of the cosmos and how at the atomic level everything is composed of tiny triangles.[3]

We're only part of the way into the Atlantis story—we haven't even gotten to its supernatural creation—but already Plato's character is giving an account that a TV judge would call unreliable, considering that it would need to have been transmitted absolutely error-free through six generations from Solon to Plato. Unfortunately, Plato also contradicts himself on its source. In the *Timaeus*, Critias claims to be speaking solely from memory and complains of having lain awake all night trying to remember the story's details as he's heard them from his grandfather. In the *Critias*, however, the speaker Critias says that he possesses Solon's original notes from his conversation with the Egyptian priest at Saïs.

Even if we take the leap of faith and assume that Solon did write Dictaphone-perfect notes of his conversations in Saïs, there is the question of whether the priest himself was a reliable source. He tells Solon—whom most experts agree really did visit Egypt—that the great events of antiquity had been inscribed in Egyptian temples. The temples were certainly real; Saïs has long since vanished, but researchers are still digging out archaeological clues in the area where it once stood. It seems certain, though, that Solon neither spoke the Egyptian language nor read hieroglyphs. Thus, the absolute best-case scenario is Plato having two-hundred-year-old, third-hand information, relayed by a priest who might have wanted to impress his distinguished visitor. Not exactly evidence you'd want to bring before a grand jury.

Then there's the question of what defined accurate information

---

3 Though the *Timaeus* and *Critias* were evidently planned as the first two parts of a trilogy, Plato seems to have never written the dialogue for Hermocrates, who in real life was a Syracusan general famous for helping repel an Athenian invasion.

in Plato's day. Recorded history in the fourth century BC was a fairly recent invention. Herodotus, celebrated as the "father of history" by Cicero, began compiling his historical narratives based on firsthand accounts more than a century after Solon died. Prior to that time, events had been recorded in stories passed down orally, such as the *Iliad* and the *Odyssey*. Plato himself was ambivalent about the relatively new technology of preserving information through writing. In his dialogue the *Phaedrus*, he has Socrates discredit writing as inferior to memory because it cannot be probed by questioning and so offers "the appearance of wisdom, not true wisdom."

The quality of Plato's evidence for Atlantis may be debatable, but he did not stint on the quantity. In the sequel to the *Timaeus*, the *Critias*, the eponymous speaker once again takes up the story he says originated with Solon. This time Plato puts so much detail into his character's mouth about the lost island kingdom that a curious reader naturally starts to wonder where it all came from.

Critias starts with a recap, adding some specifics: Roughly nine thousand years have passed since war broke out between those who lived outside the Pillars of Heracles and those who lived within; Atlantis sank and "became an impassable barrier of mud to voyagers sailing from hence to any part of the ocean." He explains that some of the names of great men from Athenian history have been passed down from long ago but that most of the details of their deeds had been erased by the intervening catastrophes the Egyptian priest described. The only survivors of these disasters were illiterate mountain dwellers who were too preoccupied with trying to survive to be concerned with the events of the past, which is why the story of Atlantis was forgotten.

Here, Critias starts dropping hints that only a classics professor who dabbles in numerology—or an Atlantologist—would look at closely. Nine thousand years ago, Critias explains, all of Greece had been fertile, but floods washed much of its soil into the sea, leaving behind "the mere skeleton of the land." Simultaneously, "there were earthquakes, and then occurred the extraordinary inundation, which was the third before the great destruction of Deucalion." The flood of Deucalion is a Greek myth, probably based on a historical event, with many parallels to the tale of Noah's ark, most notably that a good man is spared the watery wrath of an angry god by building a wooden vessel. Nine thousand years before Solon's time mammoths and saber-toothed cats still walked the earth; for now, let's just say the date is important but problematic.

Way back then, the Acropolis of Athens, the rocky hill atop which the Parthenon was later constructed, was much larger and more fertile than the skeletal ruins–covered outcrop seen on posters in Greek diners. The warrior class of Athens lived there communally, in simple buildings on the north side of the hill. A single spring provided sufficient water, but it was smothered by the debris of an earthquake. Athens's population of military-aged men was kept steady at about twenty thousand. Then, in a single night's storm, all the topsoil from the Acropolis washed into the sea.

That's an awful lot of detail for Plato to have invented and we haven't even gotten to the really strange stuff yet.

As for Atlantis, Critias says, we don't know what it was really called, since all the names in the original story were long ago translated into Egyptian, which Solon then translated into Greek. This is a key point: Atlantis wasn't actually called Atlantis by the citizens of Atlantis. Here, Plato really starts piling on the specifics. Atlantis was under dominion of the god Poseidon. Atlantis was beautiful. At its center was a large, fertile plain. Near the plain was a short mountain on which dwelt Cleito, the mortal mother of Poseidon's children. Around this hill Poseidon cut a series of concentric circles—two of land and three of water, laid out perfectly equidistant from one another as if shaped "with compass and lathe." (Remember that: three concentric circles of water.) Poseidon installed two springs, one hot and one cold. Cleito bore Poseidon five sets of twin sons, so the island was divided into ten districts with each son receiving dominion over one. The finest of these belonged to Atlas, who inherited his mother's lands in the central plain. The second-best allotment was given to Atlas's twin, Eumelos, who was called Gadeirus in the language of Atlantis. His plot faced the Pillars of Heracles, opposite the land that Critias said was now known as Gades, probably in his honor.

Atlantis was the wealthiest kingdom ever known, Critias continues, and what few things it could not provide for itself it obtained through trade. Atlantis was rich in orichalcum, a glistening metal whose preciousness was second only to gold. Fruits, flowers, and domesticated grain crops flourished, and the island's lush plants supported abundant wildlife, including many elephants.

At this point Plato starts to sound less like a philosopher than a zealous urban planner. A canal was dug that pierced the three circles of water so that ships could pass to the center; it measured three plethra (three hundred feet) wide, one plethron (one hundred feet) deep, and fifty stades (at six hundred feet to the Greek stade, a little under six miles) long. Bridges were constructed over the rings, and smaller water passages large enough for a single warship to pass were dug next to each bridge. Atlantis's interior island measured five stades across, or about three thousand feet in diameter. Around it was constructed a stone wall. Stone for building was quarried from beneath the central island and other zones—this stone was white, black, and red. (The tricolor stone: remember that.) The space where stone had been removed was used as harbors for ships, with stone roofs. The walls around the outer rings were decorated in brass and tin; the wall around the central citadel "flashed with the red light of orichalcum."

Just think: Solon or one of his assistants was scribbling all this down. Wouldn't his hand get tired?

In the innermost circle of the concentric rings, the kings of Atlantis built a spectacular palace, "a marvel to behold for size and for beauty." There was also a shrine to Poseidon and his wife, Cleito, which was surrounded by a wall of gold. This temple was one stade long and half a stade wide (approximately six hundred by three hundred feet) and had "a strange, barbaric appearance." The walls and ceilings were covered in precious metals and ivory; inside, gold statues had been erected, including a roof-scraping Poseidon guiding a chariot led by six winged horses. A beautifully crafted altar stood outside the temple. Nearby were two springs, one hot and one cold; their overflow was used to irrigate the grove of Poseidon, in which grew "all manner of trees of wonderful height and beauty."

Atlantis was a busy maritime port; its large navy sailed in triremes, warships pulled by oars. A wall fifty stades (about six miles) from the outermost ring of water ran around the central circles. Inside the wall lived a densely populated mercantile society whose ports "kept up a multitudinous sound of human voices, and din and clatter of all sorts night and day."

The capital of Atlantis abutted an oblong plain that measured three thousand by two thousand stades, or approximately 340 by 230 miles. The island sloped southward toward the sea, and the central plain was surrounded by mountains that "were celebrated for their number and size and beauty, far beyond any which still exist." (The plain, the mountains—those will come up again.) These peaks protected the island from strong northerly winds. A great canal was excavated around the entire plain. Water trickled down from the mountains into a grid of massive irrigation channels that crisscrossed the plain, spaced one hundred stades (eleven miles) apart. Atlantis had two growing seasons per year.

The plain was divided into sixty thousand districts, each of which

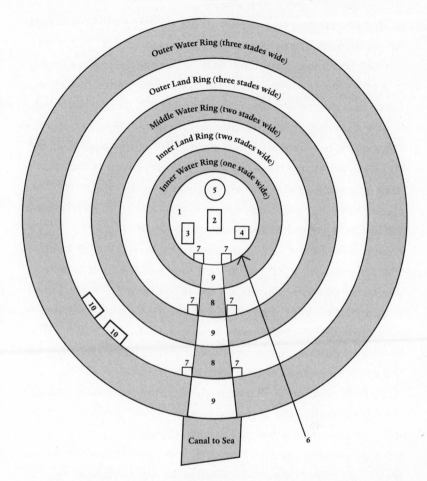

KEY:

1. Central Island (five stades wide)
2. Temple of Poseidon and Cleito
3. Royal Palace
4. Hot and Cold Springs
5. Grove of Poseidon

6. Stone Wall Decorated with Orichalcum
7. Towers and Gates
8. Covered Channels
9. Bridges
10. Docks Carved from Rock

was led by a military commander who was expected to raise at least twenty men, including ten armed soldiers, four sailors, four horses, and four horsemen. The Atlantean navy had twelve hundred ships.

(One can almost imagine Timaeus counting on his fingers and giving Socrates the side eye.)

The ten kings of Atlantis ruled according to the laws of their father, which had been inscribed on a pillar of orichalcum in the Temple of Poseidon. The kings gathered every fifth and then every sixth year to determine if any of them had violated the sacred laws and to take part in the ritual capture of bulls that had been set free in the temple. They caught the beasts using only staffs and ropes ("but with no iron weapon"), then slaughtered them on the pillar as a sacrifice. The kings put on magnificent blue robes for a ceremony in which they passed judgments and swore to rule fairly. Above all, the kings vowed never to war among themselves. If one of their number should attempt to overtake the kingdom, all the rest promised to join forces against the insurrection. They understood their great material fortune and saw their wealth as a burden.

Over the generations, though, the Atlanteans became debased, filled with "avarice and unrighteous power." Zeus could see that the Atlanteans must be punished for their waning virtue. So he hailed the gods to their pantheon, from which all the world could be seen. "And when he had called them together, he spake as follows—"

There, Plato breaks off the story abruptly, as if someone has kicked the plug out of the phonograph. Whether Plato terminated the story abruptly for dramatic effect or because Aristotle had just arrived with his lunch order is impossible to know.

CHAPTER FOUR

Mr. O'Connell's Atlantipedia

County Leitrim, Ireland

Getting philosophy professors to rank their top ten thinkers had been surprisingly easy. Getting academic specialists to discuss searching for Atlantis proved to be somewhat more difficult. Brian Johnson had been correct; those philosophy professors who wrote about it tended to dismiss it outright as a clever invention, a literary device created by Plato to illustrate his political ideas. Julia Annas, perhaps America's preeminent expert on Plato, decreed that it has been "convincingly established" that the story was fictional. A symposium held at Indiana University devoted to the topic "Atlantis: Fact or Fiction?" had awarded the title to the latter in a knockout. Most of the e-mails I sent and re-sent to addresses ending in *.edu* went unanswered. One prominent archaeologist whom I contacted wrote back to inform me that no serious scholar would ever entertain the idea that any part of the Atlantis tale had been real, and that I was foolish even to inquire about such things. Her definitive sign-off was ominous: "I hope you listen, for the sake of your reputation as a writer."

I couldn't blame academics for being wary. Any online search for information about Atlantis quickly sucks one into a wormhole of conspiracy theories and magic portals to untapped dimensions. Anyone with credentials who dared to entertain the possibility of Atlantis having existed was probably inundated by weirdos.

As I typed Atlantis-related search terms into Google, one glaring exception came up again and again, a site called the Atlantipedia. It was comprehensive, with hundreds of entries, all of which were written in an evenhanded style, offering dry commentary where appropriate. (Of one theorist who suggested that the Atlanteans had access to space travel, lasers, and cloning, the site's author noted, "A cynic might be forgiven for attributing his outlandish views to his unrepentant support for the use of marijuana.") The tone was skeptical but not dismissive. The range of subjects was exhaustive. Several feasible location theories were presented and dissected. The Atlantipedia, it emerged, was the work of one person, an Irish retiree named Tony O'Connell.[4]

I e-mailed Tony and asked if he might be open to answering a few questions. He suggested a list of books to read and invited me to come over to Ireland and stay with him as long as I liked. "The simple fact is that these theories cannot all be right and quite possibly all are wrong," he cautioned. "Take it slow or your head will spin."

A month later, as Tony and I drove west from the Dublin airport, he explained over the sound of the windshield wipers how he'd gotten involved in Atlantology. Years before, he had owned a small trucking dispatch company in Dublin, an all-consuming job that required him to keep track of thousands of details. One early morning while he and his longtime boyfriend, Paul, were working late in the warehouse, a gang of robbers entered and held guns to their necks. Afterward, Tony had a revelation. "I was sitting atop a forklift and I realized, I can't do this anymore." He left the city for a tiny village in

---

4 Tony O'Connell's site is atlantipedia.ie. There are other unaffiliated Atlantipedias.

County Leitrim, which is probably best known for being Ireland's least-populated region. When Tony's mother began to suffer from dementia, she moved in with him. "As she descended into madness I decided that I needed a distraction," he told me. He had the idea of compiling an Atlantis encyclopedia.

The more evidence Tony amassed about the various location theories, the more he became convinced that Plato's story was probably true. And the more he learned about the subject, the more he felt able to narrow down the area in which Atlantis might have existed.

Tony lived about a mile outside of a village that consisted of two pubs, the ruins of two medieval abbeys, a grade school, and a visitors center that never seemed to be open when I passed by. He and Paul (who had moved in for a while with his own ailing mother) lived in a house that had until the 1950s been the station for a narrow-gauge railway line. Their home was cozy, with two bedrooms upstairs and a small office on the ground floor that held Tony's impressive Atlantis library. The kitchen smelled of spices and cigarettes, since Paul was a passionate cook and smoker. Tony did most of his Atlantis-related work in the front room, tapping away on a laptop perched atop a coffee table as the BBC News played on the television, muted. He was round and bald and walked with a limp from gout. A mischievous gleam in his eye hinted that he might be pulling someone's leg and made you hope that it wasn't yours. He raised his eyebrows above his wire-framed eyeglasses whenever emphasizing his doubts about something. When he laughed, which happened often, his whole body shook. He reminded me of an off-duty department store Santa Claus.

Like most men of a certain age, Tony had a daily routine that varied only slightly. Tony and Paul kept almost opposite hours. Tony got up early. Paul, who was a couple of decades younger, was a night owl and usually woke in the afternoon, when Tony brought him breakfast in bed. After dinner, Tony usually dropped Paul at one of the two local pubs; Paul carried a reflective vest and penlight for his 2:00 A.M. walk home. His mortal enemy, a nasty Doberman, lived a few doors down. "If you decide you'd like to go for a walk, you'd best go in the other direction," Paul warned me, lighting another cigarette to steady his nerves.

Tony usually conducted his online Atlantis business in the mornings while drinking a mug of tea and wearing his bathrobe, which gave the impression that he was puttering about on the web. Later, I'd log on to the Atlantipedia site and find that he'd written three new entries while I was in the kitchen eating my morning muesli. The Atlantipedia served as a sort of clearinghouse for amateur, and occasionally professional, Atlantologists. "Some person has identified Mesopotamia as an island surrounded by two rivers," he called out one morning from the living room. "Not the Mesopotamia where Iraq is, which might make some sort of sense. It's the one located in Argentina."

Late each morning, Tony and I drove over to the small city of Carrick-on-Shannon to do a little shopping and run some errands, like placing horse racing wagers for Paul at the off-track betting office. One day we stopped by the local registry so that Tony could pick up the paperwork for a civil partnership. After twenty-odd years as a couple, Tony and Paul were making things official. Once our tasks were completed, we'd stop for a coffee and slice of cake.

When I had initially asked Tony why he thought the Atlantis story was true, he had pointed me to a fascinating scholarly essay by a former NASA scientist, the late A. N. Kontaratos, which cites twenty-two instances in which Plato attests to the veracity of the Atlantis story.

"Solon was a very important lawmaker, a very just man, and highly regarded," he told me at the coffee shop, whose jazzy decor made it seem as though we were discussing lost cities on the set of *Friends*. "Plato using him would be like you writing a book and invoking Benjamin Franklin as your source. You wouldn't do it if it wasn't true. I think the most powerful argument is when he expresses reservations—like he does about the ditch around the plain." Critias pauses his description of the enormous channel carved by generations of Atlanteans to explain that while he knows that its incredible proportions seem unrealistic, he's only passing along what he was told. "No one's ever going to express reservation about his own argument," Tony said. "That's counterproductive."

On the other hand, Tony noted, "no one ever asks if Solon made it up. Or if the Egyptians made it up to impress their visitor. You've got to tread very carefully."

But though Tony believed that the core story—that a large maritime power had waged a war against the eastern Mediterranean—was true, almost everything else should be viewed with skepticism, most particularly numbers and measurements, such as the claim that Atlantis had been larger than Libya and Asia combined. Libya in Solon's day was the coastal strip of North Africa from the Atlantic Ocean up to Egypt. Asia was Asia Minor, or modern Turkey. The Greeks of Plato's era had no methods to measure large areas of interior land. Greek sailors followed the coast and navigated by landmarks and other recognizable features, as in Herodotus's advice, "When you get eleven fathoms and ooze on the lead, you are a day's journey out from Alexandria."

"Plato wouldn't have known how big Atlantis was," Tony scoffed. "He was remembering things discussed as a child." Tony also wasn't convinced that Plato was talking about physical size. The ancient Greek word he used, *meizon*, can be translated as "greater." Most readers took that to mean the island of Atlantis was enormous, so large that it had nowhere to fit except in the middle of the Atlantic Ocean. Tony argued that by *greater* Plato might have been speaking of the military power of Atlantis.

I asked him for his thoughts about the location. Again, the translation of a single word was the source of much speculation.

"Plato mentions an island *before* the Pillars," Tony said. The Greek word Plato used was *pro*. "Was that inside or outside? I have to depend on the English translation, so I'd be wary of that. We only have Plato's works. Anything else isn't evidence. People get an idea and they just find a theory to match. They've drawn up these checklists and conveniently leave out anything that might work against their theories. It doesn't work to get nine out of ten things to match up but the tenth is no good."

Kontaratos, the NASA scientist, had listed helpful criteria for finding what he termed "a potential resting site for Atlantis," the basic elements of which were

1. Atlantis must have been located someplace where an island exists or once existed.
2. The island must have once sunk, entirely or partially.
3. The island must agree with Plato's description of Atlantis's "distinct geomorphology." It should have concentric rings of water, mountains, and a large plain.
4. The island must have been home to "a literate population with metallurgical skills."
5. The island must have suffered a cataclysmic natural disaster.
6. The island must have been "routinely reachable from Athens."
7. The island must have been at war with Athens when the cataclysm occurred.
8. The island must have been situated "just outside" of the Pillars of Heracles.

9. The island must have been destroyed around 9600 BC.
10. The island must have been as large as a continent or connected to a body of land of that size.

It's a very sensible-sounding checklist, but as I was slowly learning, every single one of these criteria was open to interpretation. Kontaratos, for example, argued that the rings of Atlantis were inspired by a semicircular earthworks in Poverty Point, Louisiana, a landlocked spot in the northeast corner of that state. How would news of this structure, which wasn't exactly "routinely reachable from Athens," or even New Orleans, have traveled to the Mediterranean? Kontaratos believed it had been brought back by European seafarers who had traveled up the Mississippi River to mine a deposit of high-grade copper found near Lake Superior.

"The name *Cyprus* means 'copper,'" Tony said, referring to the mineral-rich island off the coast of Turkey, well-known to Athenians of Plato's time. "Why bother going all the way up the Mississippi?"

Meizon and *pro* weren't the only ancient Greek words up for philological debate. Some Atlantologists were arguing that the word *island* in the original Greek, for example, might signify something other than land surrounded on all sides by water. A surprising number of theories were based on the notion that the Greeks applied the name *Pillars of Heracles* to any number of narrow channels around the Mediterranean, and therefore Plato wasn't necessarily referring to the Strait of Gibraltar. Tony thought that the term might not represent an actual place but rather the furthest limits of Greek exploration during Plato's lifetime.

Over the days and various desserts, Tony and I discussed the pros and cons of the leading theories and how they stacked up against Plato's story. After a week, I'd narrowed my list of candidates down to four.

The most popular theory by far was what's known as the Minoan Hypothesis. This was the idea that Plato had been inspired by the massive eruption of the volcano at the center of the Greek island Thera, now called Santorini. Like Atlantis, Santorini has a circular shape, almost like a bull's-eye. In the 1960s, archaeologists had uncovered there an entire lost city buried for thirty-five hundred years beneath a thick layer of ash. This city was filled with extraordinary artworks and architecture and had evidently been home to a technologically sophisticated people with close ties to the Minoans of Crete, who had built the spectacular Palace at Knossos. But Tony wasn't convinced. "Remember, Plato said it was an earthquake, not a volcano," he said, his raised eyebrows punctuating his doubts. The Thera eruption had almost certainly caused a tsunami, though, a logical explanation for the floods that sank Atlantis. A few scholars had even connected the Thera eruption with the biblical plagues recorded in the book of Exodus. Some theorists had made a big deal about the similarities between Minoan artworks with a bull motif and Plato's description of the bull-killing ceremony practiced by the kings of Atlantis. Tony was dubious. "Stories about bulls are all over the place," he said. "We have them here in Ireland."

Another location that had recently gained in prominence was the coast near the city of Cádiz in southern Spain. Geographically, it seemed a better match than Santorini, since it was located just outside the Pillars of Heracles at Gibraltar and in the Atlantic Ocean. Plato had even mentioned it by name. The area was rich in copper, which could account for the orichalcum mentioned in the *Critias*. Historians generally agreed that another famous lost city, Tartessos, had once existed in the vicinity. Tartessos might have served as the model for what Plato called Atlantis. The region had a well-established history of earthquakes and massive tsunamis. Satellite photos seemed to show large shapes, including concentric circles, buried beneath what was now a swampy nature reserve. "But it doesn't exactly have a sign saying WELCOME TO ATLANTIS, with the population and elevation numbers, does it?" Tony said, crossing his arms. There also was no large island in southern Spain, and Plato had been clear about Atlantis being an island.

Malta was a perfect candidate for Atlantis. It's an island, located due south of the Strait of Messina between Sicily and Italy, one of the many possible locations for the Pillars of Heracles that Tony identified. Malta is an ancient maritime culture, home to some of the oldest and least understood ruins on Earth, including some extraordinary stone temples older even than those of Egypt and Athens. Many of these were now submerged due to centuries of rising sea levels. Archaeological evidence has shown that Malta's entire population vanished without explanation long before Plato was born. It's a generally mysterious place. Malta even has intriguing grids of trenches etched into its rocky surface, which might have inspired Plato's ancient irrigation canals. But Malta has no mountains and is nowhere near large enough to have contained the enormous plain that Plato described, nor to have launched a million-strong navy.

The final candidate was a dark horse, Morocco. I probably wouldn't have considered it at all if Tony hadn't called it the most convincing hypothesis he'd seen to date. Michael Hübner, a computer programmer in Bonn, had made a list of geographical details in the *Timaeus* and *Critias*—fifty-one in all—and had used sophisticated statistical analysis to plug them into a mapping program. The result he came up with was indisputable, by the numbers anyway. Virtually every clue that Plato noted—the rings, the earthquakes, the elephants, the location outside the Pillars of Heracles—coincided with the relatively obscure Souss-Massa plain on Morocco's Atlantic coast, about one hundred miles southwest of Marrakesh. But virtually no archaeology had been done in the area.

"I haven't been able to satisfy myself about two things," Tony told me. "You start with Plato's description for these mountains." (From the *Critias*: "The surrounding mountains were celebrated for their number and size and beauty, far beyond any which still exist.") "It was almost as if Plato was writing a travel ad," Tony said. "The only ones that would count are the Himalayas, the Alps, and the Atlas. You look at those and look at the prevailing winds from the north. You should be able to limit the possibilities to a manageable few, but I keep going in circles on that."

Tony's other sticking point, one that I'd noticed most theories glossed over, were the impassable shoals left behind after Atlantis sank. "Let's take the word *impassable*. It would have to take into account the tides. The draft of triremes I gather was only about a meter. That would make it impassable for part of the day but not all day. It would have to be a place with very little tidal effect—like the Mediterranean." Tony likened such dangerous shallows to the banks of Syrtis (now Sirte in Libya, best known today as the hometown of Muammar Gaddafi). "The shoals to me sound like liquefaction," Tony said. Liquefaction is the process by which an earthquake converts wet soil into something like quicksand. Anything built on this suddenly unstable ground is likely to collapse or sink.

Tony believed that clues to the location of Atlantis might even be found outside of the *Timaeus* and *Critias*, a possibility I hadn't considered. "Plato was talking about serious matters—when the earth was washed away from Greece," he said. "You should study the deluge stories and look for the common elements." Most ancient cultures seemed to have a Great Flood myth. The Deucalion flood, which the Saïs priest says came after the greater cataclysm that sank Atlantis, is strikingly similar to the Noah's ark story and the Mesopotamian flood epic of Gilgamesh; in all three versions pious men are instructed by gods to build floating vessels in order to survive an inundation. Where exactly all of that water might have come from remained one of the great mysteries of antiquity. "One scenario that does make sense is an asteroid or comet in the ocean—that could've sent a giant tsunami around the world," Tony said, adding quickly, "Obviously strange things have happened." I sensed that linking the Atlantis story to ancient myths, gigantic flying projectiles from space, and possibly the book of Genesis would not make mainstream academics any more likely to respond to my e-mails, but Tony had been at this game a lot longer than I had. I made a note to look into it.

"In the end, you have to go back and read Plato again," Tony said. "Be happy that what he's written has some degree of credibility. From that you can form a theory. The mountains, the plains, and the shoals—those are the challenges."

"The beginning is the most important part of any work," Plato wrote in the *Republic*. Spain. Malta. Greece. Morocco. It was a start.

One night Tony and I broke our routine and drove to the village, stopping at both pubs for a pint and a little *craic*, a term that as far as I could tell referred to the unique Irish gift for free-flowing conversation. (During the span of a single pint with Paul and Dai, a friendly neighbor from down the road, the topics swerved from a famous snooker match in which the champion had worn his spectacles upside down, to the problem of Polish handymen emptying local rivers of fish, to the time Paul dressed up as Cruella De Vil for Halloween, to the debate over whether it was sacrilegious to grill sausages during a pilgrimage up a mountain associated with Saint Patrick.) I had, admittedly, been a little curious what Tony's neighbors—residents of an overwhelmingly Catholic country that hadn't legalized divorce until 1995—might think about living near a gay couple whose elder member was a storehouse of information about Atlantis. They had very strong feelings indeed about both topics. Several people told me that we were standing in *the very pub* where the publishing party for the hardcover *Atlantipedia* had been held, evidently a legendary blowout rivaling Truman Capote's Black and White Ball. Everyone was eager to talk about Tony and Paul's upcoming civil ceremony. "Tony O'Connell, gettin' married at your age, are ye?" teased one local matron, who boasted that she owned two signed copies of the *Atlantipedia*. "Paul's finally making an honest man of ye?" asked another. "A real May-December romance 'tis, just like in the movies."

By the end of the week, my head was stuffed with Atlantis information and the rest of me with pie, cake, soda bread, full Irish breakfasts, and Guinness. Before dropping me back in Dublin, Tony took me to see Newgrange, one of the world's great megalithic monuments. Someone had managed to incorporate it, like almost all impressive pre-Hellenic structures, into an Atlantis location theory. "Your man Ulf Erlingsson"—a Swedish geographer who argued that Newgrange and its nearby structures were the temples that inspired Plato's story—"estimated that it was 99.98 percent likely that Atlantis was in Ireland," Tony told me. Tony was as proud an Irishman as one could hope to meet, but he wasn't in the least convinced by Erlingsson's argument. "He goes on and on about the concentric circles on a stone basin found near here," Tony told me as we walked through the exhibits at the Newgrange museum. "Ah, there it is." He pointed at a carved bowl with an image of circles, perhaps the size of an LP record, carved onto its side.

"There's your 99.98 percent proof of Atlantis," Tony said. "Pathetic, isn't it?"

CHAPTER FIVE

Amateur Hour

Nininger City, Minnesota (ca. AD 1882)

For someone who professed such deep respect for numbers, Plato certainly used some head-scratching ones in his Atlantis story. The dates don't match up even remotely with ancient history. Solon likely visited Egypt not long after 600 BC, which means that by the priest's reckoning, Atlantis and Athens were destroyed around 9600 BC. Historians believe that Athens was first settled sometime in the fourth millennium BC and did not grow to a size anything like that of a city—let alone a city with twenty thousand soldiers—for another two thousand years. The founding of the first Egyptian dynasty has been dated to approximately 3150 BC. Were these exaggerations invented by Plato on purpose, or were they the work of some sleepy Byzantine transcriber?

Plato wrote that the Atlanteans had twelve hundred triremes, or oared warships. Triremes don't turn up in historical records until the seventh century BC. It's possible that either Plato or Solon was using a modern term to describe older boats. The Atlantean army's ten thousand chariots are harder to explain. Chariots seem to have emerged in Mesopotamia around 3000 BC; domesticated horses date to the fifth millennium BC. Plato estimates the combined forces of

Atlantis to include about 1.2 million men, who are improbably defeated by those twenty thousand guardians of Athens. By comparison, Herodotus estimated that the massive army and navy that Xerxes of Persia brought to Greece in 480 BC was more than a million men strong, a number now believed to be greatly inflated. During the D-day sea invasion of Normandy, 156,000 Allied troops crossed the English Channel.

As Tony O'Connell had explained, perhaps the most fantastic figures in the Atlantis story are the dimensions Critias somewhat sheepishly gives for the enormous channel surrounding the plain:

> The depth, and width, and length of this ditch were incredible, and gave the impression that a work of such extent, in addition to so many others, could never have been artificial. Nevertheless I must say what I was told. It was excavated to the depth of a hundred feet, and its breadth was a stade [approximately six hundred feet] everywhere; it was carried round the whole of the plain, and was ten thousand stades [more than eleven hundred miles] in length.

Some have argued that the Atlanteans were technologically sophisticated—an argument that has sparked some outlandish theories about their prehistoric airships, radios, and microwave ovens. But no one, to my knowledge, has suggested that the Atlanteans had access to backhoes and bulldozers. The canal described by Plato would require the removal of ten billion cubic meters of earth. The Panama Canal project involved excavating 120 million cubic meters of earth.

In part because these numbers seemed so incredible, speculation about the location of Atlantis remained a pretty low-interest field for almost two thousand years. Then in 1492, Christopher Columbus sailed west and found a sizable land mass roughly where Plato had said (according to a popular interpretation) one would be. As fleets of European explorers followed, theories soon abounded that the largest and most sophisticated New World cultures, such as the Mayas and Aztecs of Mesoamerica, were descendants of an Atlantean diaspora. Brilliant naturalists such as France's Comte de Buffon and Prussia's Alexander von Humboldt seriously considered possible links between Native Americans and the peoples of Atlantis.

These hypotheses were essentially intellectual parlor games, though. No one looked very hard for Atlantis until the late nineteenth century, when an unusually dedicated amateur archaeologist decided to search for Homer's mythical city of Troy, using the evidence of the original story. And then he found it.

Skepticism from experts about using ancient stories to find lost civilizations isn't exactly new. As I dug in to the canon of Atlantology, I repeatedly came across instances of historians and classicists condescendingly referring to the idea of a real Atlantis as "euhemerism." The term comes from the Greek philosopher Euhemerus, who hypothesized that some myths—in particular those of the Greek gods—had been based on historical events. (The residents of Mount Olympus, he believed, had been inspired by ancient Greek kings.) The third-century-BC geographer Eratosthenes—who served as chief librarian of the Library of Alexandria—may have been the first scholar to throw cold water on euhemerism when he quipped that "you will find where Odysseus wandered when you find the cobbler who sewed up the bag of winds."

More than two thousand years later, in the middle of the nineteenth century, the relatively new field of archaeological excavation was not yet the sole province of academic professionals when the German businessman Heinrich Schliemann took an interest in it.

Schliemann was a self-made millionaire and self-taught historian who read Homer's epic myths the *Iliad* and the *Odyssey* as history and thus believed that the Greek hero Achilles truly had battled the Trojan Hector and that the beautiful Helen—later famous as "the face that launched a thousand ships"—actually had been kidnapped from Sparta and taken to Troy. When Schliemann read that Achilles had dragged the dead body of Hector around the walls of Troy in revenge for the death of his friend Patroclus, the German was convinced not only that those walls had once existed, but also that they might be found and excavated. As Plato had with Atlantis, Homer had described Troy in enough detail to identify it if located: a prosperous city of temples and fine homes, located near a river and the Hellespont between Greece and Turkey, surrounded by an imposing high wall with a gate that was located near two springs, one warm and one cold.

In his book *Minotaur*, the modern archaeologist Joseph Alexander MacGillivray quotes George Grote's "universally accepted" twelve-volume *History of Greece* on the subject of Homer as history circa 1850: "Though literally believed, reverentially cherished, and numbered among the gigantic phenomena of the past by the Grecian public, it is in the eyes of modern inquiry essentially a legend and nothing more." Schliemann disagreed. He was convinced that Troy would be found at the village of Hissarlik, farther north than most searches had been conducted. In 1871, he hired a hundred laborers, who tore into the site and uncovered thousands of artifacts. Over three seasons Schliemann claimed to have found a building he identified as the palace of King Priam; the Scaean Gates, the spot where Hector prophesies Achilles's death in the *Iliad*; and a large cache of gold objects, which Schliemann smuggled out of the country. The headline over a story in the December 29, 1872, *Chicago Daily Tribune* was typical of the enthusiastic press reaction: HOMER VINDICATED.

Schliemann followed his work at Troy with another spectacular

success, this time in Greece. Amid the remains of a hilltop fortress at
Mycenae, in the northeastern part of the Peloponnesus, Schliemann
searched for the palace of King Agamemnon, who according to
Homer had led the Greeks into battle against the Trojans to reclaim
Helen, his brother's wife. Here Schliemann found even greater rel-
ics, including five skeletons wearing gold death masks.

Schliemann was a gifted promoter but a flawed archaeologist.
His accounts of his discoveries were filled with inconsistencies and
falsehoods, and some of the most important antiquities he claimed
to have found may have been planted by himself and his wife. In his
rush to discover what he assumed was the original Troy, Schliemann
ordered his workmen to dig and dynamite their way down through
several layers of stone building remains. This archaeological refuse
turned out to be the evidence of multiple other settlements, including the actual ancient city of which Homer had sung.

Schliemann's work set a precedent, though. He had poked a hole
in the wall between Greek myth and history, so carefully constructed since Plato's time. Amateur archaeologists around the
world realized that they might not even have to leave their desks in
order to locate a lost city. All one needed was a familiarity with the
classics and a fertile imagination.

One of those most inspired by Schliemann was history's first great
Atlantologist, the progressive Minnesota politician Ignatius Donnelly. To say that Donnelly also left behind a complicated legacy
would grossly undervalue the variance in opinions about his work.
One account of his life proclaimed him the "greatest uncelebrated
man in American history." Another labeled him "quite possibly the
greatest failure who ever lived."

Born in Philadelphia in 1831, Donnelly moved west at the age of
twenty-five with plans to cash in on a speculative land boom in the

go-go Minnesota Territory. The planned community he cofounded, Nininger City, failed when the Panic of 1857 brought on an economic depression. Donnelly rebounded from bankruptcy to become Minnesota's lieutenant governor at twenty-eight and a US congressman at thirty-one, serving as a radical Republican who supported women's suffrage, education for newly freed slaves, and immigrants' rights. By 1880 he was finished politically and back in Nininger City, living in his grand house amid the empty acres of his failed real estate investment. In a diary entry written on his forty-ninth birthday he wrote, "All my hopes are gone, and the future settles down upon me dark and gloomy indeed."

Just a few weeks later, Donnelly scribbled optimistically in his diary that he'd begun work on a book he was planning to call *Atlantis*. His inspiration is unknown, though it's possible he was influenced by the success of Jules Verne's 1870 novel *Twenty Thousand Leagues Under the Sea*, in which Captain Nemo leads Professor Aronnax to the very impressive submarine ruins of Plato's lost city. If one considers the *Timaeus* and *Critias* as a single entity, it would not be an exaggeration to call Donnelly's book the second most important work in the Atlantis canon. One leading chronicler of the search for Atlantis described the work, eventually titled *Atlantis: The Antediluvian World*, as the "New Testament of Atlantism," companion to Plato's Old Testament.

In the book's first sentence, Donnelly explained that he aimed "to demonstrate several distinct and novel propositions." Chief among them was that Plato's Atlantis was real, not a myth. Donnelly's version of Atlantis was a utopia, "the Garden of Eden," and wellspring of all the world's great civilizations: Egypt was the oldest Atlantean colony. Technologies that emerged during the Bronze and Iron Ages, and even later—"it is not impossible that even the invention of gunpowder may date back to Atlantis"—had emerged from an original Atlantean source, as had the alphabet, paper, and agriculture. When

Atlantis sank beneath the waves, the victim of a catastrophic global flood, a few of its inhabitants paddled and sailed away to create "the Indo-European family of nations, as well as of the Semitic peoples," and possibly others.

It would be hard to overstate the impact that this introductory chapter to Donnelly's book had on future Atlantology; in a sense it created the template for all later location theories. Tony O'Connell writes in the *Atlantipedia*, "It is quite possible that without the impetus created by Donnelly's book, Atlantis would have remained a relatively obscure subject." Donnelly was the first great Atlantis fundamentalist, in that he believed that Plato's story was factually accurate outside of the supernatural elements like Poseidon. Plato said Atlantis was in the ocean opposite the Pillars of Heracles; therefore, it had once existed in the middle of the Atlantic Ocean, he theorized. (Even more than Plato, Donnelly is responsible for the general belief that Atlantis sank into the Atlantic.) Fantastic-seeming dates and measurements, like the nine thousand years or thousand-mile-long trench, only buttressed Donnelly's faith that the society of Atlantis had been exceptionally advanced. The story of the inundation of Atlantis had been passed down by escapees, which, Donnelly explained, is why cultures from Europe, Asia, and the Americas all share flood myths.

The early 1880s were a rich era for popular science; some of the very secrets of nature that Plato had tried to imagine in the *Timaeus* were finally revealing themselves to inquisitive, industrious men. Names such as Schliemann, Thomas Edison, and Charles Darwin appeared regularly in newspapers. Donnelly, setting an example for future Atlantologists, was clever enough to salt his tale with the scientific fashions of the day. He even provided a thing rare in Atlantis studies—scientific evidence. In 1860, the US Coast Guard had compiled its first comprehensive charts of the Gulf Stream, the circular current that flows clockwise around the North Atlantic. Why did it flow in this manner? "The gulf stream flowed around Atlantis, and it still retains the circular motion first imparted to it by the presence of that island," Donnelly explained. Recent bathymetric surveys had confirmed the existence of a large volcanic mountain range situated beneath the waves running almost straight down the middle of the Atlantic. For Donnelly, this was obvious evidence of a sunken continent. The islands of the Azores archipelago were the only visible remains of mountains that had once loomed above the doomed civilization.

"Portions of the island lie but a few hundred fathoms beneath the sea," he wrote in his conclusion. "A single engraved tablet dredged up from Plato's island would be worth more to science, would more strike the imagination of mankind, than all the gold of Peru, all the monuments of Egypt, and all the terra-cotta fragments gathered from the great libraries of Chaldea."

Reaction to *The Antediluvian World* was rapid and enthusiastic. The local *Saint Paul Dispatch* credited Donnelly with having written "one of the notable books of the decade, nay of the century." William Gladstone, the prime minister of Great Britain and a renowned classics scholar who had published a massive study of Homer, sent Donnelly a letter of qualified congratulations. "I may not be able to accept all your propositions," he wrote, "but I am much disposed to believe in an Atlantis." Donnelly responded with an appeal to have a Royal Navy vessel make further soundings in the Atlantic. Gladstone politely declined his request.

Donnelly also sent a copy to Darwin, who replied with a note saying he'd read the book "with interest, though I must confess in a very skeptical spirit." His tepid response was typical of the scientific establishment and inaugurated the pattern of condescension and contempt for amateur Atlantis scholarship that has thrived ever since. Donnelly's theory directly contradicted Darwin's own ideas of evolution. *The*

Antediluvian World, with its thesis that "Atlantis perished in a terrible convulsion of nature," was horribly out of scientific fashion.

No modern denunciation of Atlantology is complete without a section vilifying Donnelly. Not without reason, he is frequently cited as a cautionary tale in the uses and abuses of euhemerism, and his faith in the instant gratification of catastrophism—the school of thought that natural history had been a series of cataclysms, such as Noah's flood—is often contrasted with Darwin's saintly gradualism (i.e., the earth was many millions of years old and had experienced geological change at an imperceptibly slow pace). But experts also single him out for having committed the much more grave offense of "diffusionism," sometimes upgraded to the more evil-sounding "hyperdiffusionism." In his book *Frauds, Myths, and Mysteries: Science and Pseudoscience in Archaeology*, the anthropologist Kenneth Feder defines *diffusionism* as the presumption that "cultures are basically uninventive and that new ideas are developed in very few or single places. They then move out or 'diffuse' from these source areas."

Donnelly's faith that all great cultures and most advances in human history can be traced back to a large continent that sank midway between Europe and North America is the spine of his argument. It is also the element that is most likely to drive historians nuts. In his otherwise evenhanded account of Donnelly's Atlantis theory, Feder calls his diffusion argument "a confusing morass of disconnected claims and ostensible proofs." And yet for more than a century *The Antediluvian World* had been the most influential work, outside of the *Timaeus* and *Critias*, in the Atlantological universe. This seemed like something that deserved a closer look.

CHAPTER SIX

Lost City Meets Twin Cities

Saint Paul, Minnesota

When I arrived at the Minnesota Historical Society in downtown Saint Paul, I was slightly alarmed to be greeted by Ignatius Donnelly himself. Actually, it was a two-dimensional Donnelly, a slightly larger-than-life cardboard cutout of the former congressman sporting a top hat and resembling Babe Ruth out on the town. Tracing the trail of Donnelly's theory had led me to the office of Patrick Coleman, the acquisitions librarian for the historical society. Coleman looked like a Broadway casting director's idea of a state librarian—tall, white-haired, tie askew. His office was as comically perfect as a stage set, too: precarious piles of ancient hardbound books, sepia maps of Minnesota on the walls, a large framed photo of Walter Mondale atop his desk. I'd come across a recent newspaper article in which Coleman had been asked who the most interesting person in Minnesota history was, and without hesitation he'd answered Ignatius Donnelly. Surely there was a good reason to pass over Bob Dylan and F. Scott Fitzgerald?

"Donnelly has gotten a reputation as a kook," Coleman told me, his head framed by two stacks of leather-bound books on his desk like a priest hearing confession. "That's really a misrepresentation of his ideas. He had the best private library in Minnesota, maybe the best library in the state, period." Some of the remnants of that collection were in the piles in front of Coleman. Shortly before his death at age sixty-three in 1901, Donnelly had married his twenty-year-old secretary, who outlived him by sixty-three years. "I was a teenager when she died," Coleman told me. "She had some books from his library that had his corrections in them. I paid $75 for those over there." He pointed to a two-volume collected works of Shakespeare that Donnelly had used to write *The Great Cryptogram*, his magnum opus of Shakespeare scholarship. "I was living in a really sleazy apartment in Minneapolis and had them on top of my $2 black-and-white TV with a tinfoil antenna," Coleman said. "Some thieves broke in, removed the two volumes, and took the TV instead." Coleman later had them appraised at $1,600.

Coleman grew up in a politically active family—his brother is the mayor of Saint Paul—and he originally admired Donnelly for his liberal views. Donnelly was a radical progressive during America's Gilded Age, a time "much like today, when money and power were concentrated in the hands of a few people," Coleman said. Over time, Coleman came to admire Donnelly for the breadth of his knowledge. "In the nineteenth century you didn't need a geology degree or an astronomy degree to write about those things," he said. This was true. Polymath politicians like Thomas Jefferson are celebrated for their wide interests. Donnelly, because his Atlantis theories have not aged well, is now mocked for his. "It was the end of an era when you could be a Renaissance man. Now you have to specialize."

To demonstrate, Coleman offered to show me what remained of the library from Donnelly's own prairie Monticello. Actually, he clarified as we strolled through the sunny atrium, "the Minnesota Historical Society has his *library* in storage." The actual room, that is. When Donnelly's abandoned house at Nininger was being demolished, a team "went out and took the paneling off the walls and sent it here." Coleman said that for years, clever booksellers would go hunting on Donnelly's abandoned estate, stop to eat lunch, and fill their empty knapsacks with volumes from the once-great collection. What the historical society owns of Donnelly's books, still hundreds on almost as many topics, is whatever was left behind.

We cut through an administrative area and descended two flights of stairs. Coleman pulled out a key card and swiped it to open a locked steel door. Inside was a sterile-looking storage room filled with metal shelves. "Some people's libraries you can't tell whether the books have ever been opened," Coleman said, reaching for a volume of Irish history. "These books have been *read.*"

Inhaling the scent of nineteenth-century paper and glue, I gathered up an armful of books and took them upstairs for a closer look. What became obvious over two days of reading Donnelly's tiny marginalia confirmed the opinion of a Minnesota historian who'd written that Donnelly "wrote with the impulsive force of a man defending a cause rather than the caution of a scientist seeking the truth." Donnelly wasn't merely attempting to sew up a bag of winds; he was a bag of winds. He knew the result he wanted and rummaged through his sources searching for only those facts that fit his needs, without pausing to note any reasonable doubts. In his hands, pyramids stretching from Egypt to Peru to India to Mesoamerica indisputably share an Atlantean source despite their having been built in hugely different styles over thousands of years. The use of bronze, mummification of the dead, similarities in language—Donnelly assembled every available scrap of evidence to support his diffusionist idea of a benevolent ur-Atlantis spreading its wisdom to the far corners of the globe.

With his tendency to pile up page after page of proof without ever stopping to ask if there was a reasonable explanation as to why he might be wrong, Donnelly set the pace for much of future

Atlantology. Too often, coincidence is transformed into evidence, which is taken as proof. A typical example: Circumcision was common among the peoples of the eastern Mediterranean, so they must have inherited the practice from their wise common ancestors in Atlantis. How do we know? Because the Atlantean king Uranus, noting the horrors of "one of the most dreadful scourges of the human race"—syphilis, presumably—"compelled his whole army and the armies of his allies to undergo the rite." Modern life insurance statistics show that Jews are healthier than average. Ergo, Atlantis was real.

Donnelly probably hoped that he was writing a book that would draw comparisons to Darwin's *The Voyage of the Beagle*. Reading *The Antediluvian World* reminded me more of a book I'd once purchased at a yard sale that amassed hundreds of tiny clues to prove that Paul McCartney had died at the height of the Beatles' fame and had been secretly replaced by an exact double.

After two days with Donnelly I badly needed a drink. As luck would have it, Coleman was giving a "History Happy Hour" talk in downtown Saint Paul on the topic of Donnelly's life. I offered to help him carry his visual aids. The Minnesota sky, playing along with the deluge theme, was dark hours before sundown. Coleman grabbed a box of Donnelly's old books, I picked up the congressman's cardboard doppelgänger, and we ran through the downpour to Coleman's Subaru. The location of the talk was the sumptuous Victorian home of Donnelly's onetime boss, Minnesota governor Alexander Ramsey. As a roomful of damp people sipped beers and munched on mini hamburgers, Coleman stood in front of a gigantic fireplace and talked about Donnelly's political adventures in Minnesota. Then he turned to Atlantis. "I've been fighting this idea my whole life that Donnelly was a kook," he said with more resignation than the first time I'd heard him use the slur. "He had this weird, wonderful, and creative mind that couldn't be curtailed. And I'll bet anyone here right now that someone's on a boat in the Mediterranean with a copy of Donnelly's *Atlantis*, looking for the lost city."

Most of the happy hour attendees seemed to be hearing about Donnelly for the first time, but there were some devotees in the crowd. When Coleman quoted Donnelly's famous line from the Populist Party platform of 1892—"From the same prolific womb of governmental injustice we breed the two great classes: tramps and millionaires"—I noticed at least two people mouthing the words along with Coleman, as if reciting a prayer. No one snickered when Coleman talked about Donnelly's progressively less successful literary works, including *Caesar's Column*, a dystopian science fiction novel that takes place in 1988, and *Ragnarok: The Age of Fire and Gravel*, a sort of sequel to his Atlantis book, in which he amped up the catastrophism to propose that ancient myths had been inspired by a comet striking the earth.

Finally, Coleman addressed what he called Donnelly's "black helicopters" opus, *The Great Cryptogram*, presumably the source of much guffawing and drink spilling at humanities department cocktail parties. This book, which followed *The Antediluvian World* by six years, marked Donnelly's shift from revisionist historian to all-out conspiracy theorist. It was Donnelly's attempt to decipher the code embedded in what he named "the so-called Shakespeare plays." His theory posited that Sir Francis Bacon, the English statesman and philosopher whose prodigious career included serving as lord chancellor, helping develop the empirical method in science, and authoring dozens of influential essays and books—including the utopian classic *The New Atlantis*—had also managed to secretly write the collected works of Shakespeare. If composing the greatest dramas ever written in English weren't enough to occupy a man's time,

Bacon also, according to Donnelly, embedded them with subtle clues about his true identity.

When Coleman finished his talk, I walked up to the front of the room to take a look at Donnelly's copy of the First Folio of Shakespeare's plays. The volume lay open to a pair of annotated pages. Each had dozens of numbers scribbled on it, occult-looking calculations, underlined passages, and chaotic notations in the margin. For all I could tell, these pages demonstrated beyond a shadow of a doubt that 9/11 was an inside job and that Paul McCartney's secret twin brother really had written "Helter Skelter."

It was a reminder that if you bent the facts enough, you could convince yourself of anything.

CHAPTER SEVEN

Secrets of the Wine-Dark Sea

On the Mediterranean

I n 1982, a Turkish sponge diver named Mehmet Çakir surfaced from a plunge near a rocky promontory off Kas, on Turkey's southern coast, with a confusing bit of information to report. About 150 feet down on the seafloor, he'd spotted a pile of unusual "metal biscuits with ears." Çakir's captain, who had recently attended a briefing about the emerging field of underwater archaeology, quickly understood what the objects were: oxhide ingots, slabs of copper cast in uniform shapes for easy sea transport. What Çakir had found was a Bronze Age shipwreck that dated to approximately 1300 BC. *Scientific American* later named the Uluburun wreck one of the greatest archaeological discoveries of the twentieth century.

What made the discovery so extraordinary was the cornucopia of goods the boat had been carrying when it presumably smashed against the rocks. Over the next decade, divers pulled seventeen tons of artifacts from the site. The cargo had originated in ports all around the eastern Mediterranean. The boat was Syro-Palestinian, built of Lebanese cedar and operated by the ancestors of the Phoenicians who lived along the Levant. Its ten tons of copper had been mined in Cyprus. One ton of tin, the other element essential in the manufacture of bronze, had likely originated in Afghanistan. Elephant ivory and ostrich eggs had journeyed from Africa. Mycenaean pottery had come from the Greek mainland. Gold and silver jewelry, including a gold scarab inscribed with the name of the Egyptian queen Nefertiti, dated to the reign of Tutankhamen. Here in one spot was ample evidence of a highly advanced ancient trading network that spread across three continents.

For modern geographers, the Uluburun provided rare material evidence of where people were traveling, and why, in the time before Golden Age Greece. The Uluburun sank around 1300 BC, before the transition from oral transmission to written records took place. At that time the Mycenaeans ruled the Aegean Sea and traded widely in the area between Sardinia, Egypt, Asia Minor, and the Levant before their empire collapsed mysteriously during the late twelfth century BC. Exploration of the western Mediterranean beyond Sicily and Sardinia seems to have been spearheaded by Phoenician traders who passed through the Pillars of Heracles at Gibraltar sometime between 1100 BC (according to legend) and 800 BC (according to archaeological evidence). There they founded the trading colony of Gades mentioned by Plato in the *Critias*, which grew into the Spanish city of Cádiz. It's probable that sailors from Iberia had met traders from the coast of Sardinia even earlier, exchanging information along with their goods.

Little is known about early Greek attempts to explore the western Mediterranean. This gap is important to the search for Atlantis for two reasons. One, the likeliest spot for the Pillars of Heracles is the Strait of Gibraltar. If the story of Atlantis really was transmitted via Solon's visit to Egypt, the information could have reached the priests of Saïs through the same trading network that assembled the Uluburun cargo. Two, it's possible that Plato picked up stories from sailors in Syracuse, one of several distant lands he visited on a long journey after Socrates was sentenced to death in 399 BC for the crime of corrupting Athens's youth. In the ancient Mediterranean, Syracuse was a key meeting point for East and West.

As Duane Roller points out in his fascinating book *Through the Pillars of Herakles*, the Greeks had no word for *exploration*. Expeditions were launched to gather intelligence for military or trade purposes. Such valuable proprietary information was likely to be closely guarded; the Carthaginians are reported to have drowned anyone who attempted to locate the Pillars of Heracles. Any information travelers collected came from the residents of foreign lands, whose languages would have been difficult to translate and easy to misunderstand. Information passed along orally was transmitted in the form of stories. Thus accounts of fantastic voyages across the "wine-dark sea" to distant lands such as those in the *Iliad* and the *Odyssey* might combine essential geographic data with supernatural elements.

In the *Odyssey*, Odysseus is trying to reach his home city of Ithaca (which, like many of the Greek places Homer names, actually existed) when he is blown for nine days to the land of the lotus-eaters. Here the inhabitants lived on the sweet fruits of a flowering plant "so delicious that those who ate of it left off caring about home." Homer may have been describing the Tunisian island of Djerba, where date palms grew plentifully and still do.

The pioneering Greek geographer Pytheas sailed shortly after Plato's death on a journey that took him to the British Isles and beyond. He reported traveling so far north that the sun never set; claimed to have seen impassable frozen seas; and six days beyond Scotland discovered a mysterious distant island named Thule, which may have been Norway or Iceland. Christopher Columbus later claimed to have stopped in Thule on his way to encountering the New World.

Pytheas was widely disbelieved when he returned home. Later historians cast doubt on his claims, those of Thule especially. The eminent Greek geographer and historian Strabo, who believed that Plato's Atlantis was a true story, accused Pytheas of having lied outright about Thule's existence. More than a century later, the respected historian Pausanias wrote credulously about the satyrs who lived in distant lands. "In modern times it is perhaps easier to be more dismissive of promiscuous red-haired men with tails than a frozen ocean," Duane Roller notes, "yet in antiquity the former was believed rather than the latter."

We do have a few snippets of information that indicate some Greek exploration to the west was going on. Homer, who probably composed his works in the eighth century BC, describes Odysseus passing through Scylla and Charybdis—likely the Strait of Messina—sailing for the west until approaching the Oceanus, a deep-flowing river that encircled all the lands of the earth and marked the boundary of the world. Around 630 BC, a sailor named Kolaios from the island of Samos claimed to have been blown by a powerful easterly wind through the Pillars of Heracles and into the great sea beyond. According to Herodotus, Kolaios returned home with a vast fortune in silver from a land called Tartessos. Herodotus also related the story of the pharaoh Necho II (ruler of Egypt from 610 to 595 BC), who dispatched an expedition of Phoenician sailors to circumnavigate the African continent, departing southward through the Red Sea. During their third year at sea, Herodotus wrote, they "rounded the Pillars of Heracles" and sailed for home. "On their return home, they declared—I for my part do not believe them, but perhaps others may—that in sailing around Libya they had the sun upon their right hand." Herodotus couldn't even imagine what had actually happened. They had passed through the unknown Southern Hemisphere and sailed around the Cape of Good Hope.

Plato's effort in the *Timaeus* to chart the earth's location in the cosmos seems even bolder when one considers that attempts to map the known world were rudimentary. In the sixth century BC, the Greek philosopher Anaximander drew what may have been the first map of the known world. The Mediterranean was placed at the center of the world (hence its name in Latin, "middle land") and was surrounded by the three continents, Europe, Libya, and Asia. The Nile flowed south into the southern part of the outer ocean. The western ocean was named the Atlantic and was linked to the Mediterranean through the Pillars of Heracles. Anaximander believed that the earth was a cylinder with a diameter three times its height, roughly the proportions of a can of tuna. More than a century later, Herodotus agreed that the world was flat. By that time, though, the geometry-mad philosopher Pythagoras had—according to much later histories—deduced that the earth was a sphere. Contrary to the legend of Christopher Columbus, many educated Greeks agreed that the earth was round. In the *Timaeus* Plato himself fixed the earth in the center of the universe and said that the creator had "made the world in the form of a globe . . . having its extremes in every direction equidistant from the center, the most perfect and the most like itself of all figures."

The Greeks began to colonize the western Mediterranean starting around 600 BC, with the founding of Massalia, a trading outpost that has since grown into the French city of Marseilles. Herodotus credits seafaring Greeks who lived in Asia Minor with making the first trips deep into the western Mediterranean. "It was they who made Adria known, and Tyrrhenia, and Iberia and Tartessos," he writes. Adria is the northeastern coast of Italy, which shares its name with the Adriatic Sea. Tyrrhenia was the land of the Etruscans on Italy's west coast. Iberia was the Mediterranean shore of what is now the Spanish peninsula.

The fourth place that Herodotus lists, Tartessos, is something of a mystery, even today. Kolaios the Greek was not the only sailor to report back on its mind-blowing riches. While Plato is the only writer known to have written about Atlantis, many ancients mentioned Tartessos by name. Yet it has never been found, either.

The historian Rhys Carpenter explained how the first Greek

sailors would likely have made their way west over time. Rowing their state-of-the-art penteconters, fifty-oared warships, they would have sailed from the Tyrrhenian coast to the isle of Elba and on to Corsica, from whence they would have sailed south to Sardinia. Here they would likely have encountered Iberian sailors who convinced them to sail across three hundred miles of empty sea to the Balearic Islands, from whence they could reach the Iberian Peninsula.

We can only wonder what these Greeks thought as they journeyed south along the coast and passed beneath the fourteen-hundred-foot-high Rock of Gibraltar, the final checkpoint between the known world and the endless sea of the Atlantic. Here the vast water of the Mediterranean narrowed to seven miles across. Duane Roller notes that sailors who crossed through the strait noticed a sudden change in the tides and waves and "would find the water turning from blue to a less benign green." The rock and its partner across the water must have become familiar sights, however, because to pass through the Pillars of Heracles was the only way to reach Tartessos—a land perched on the lip of the infinite sea, where fortunes in silver were to be found by those brave enough to risk the journey.

CHAPTER EIGHT

As Seen on TV

Hartford, Connecticut

Long before I ever took an interest in Atlantis, I traveled to Cusco, Peru, to interview a hard-core explorer with a reputation for finding lost cities. He'd recently returned from several months in the Amazon jungle and with his sunken cheeks and long beard looked as if he'd just stepped out of an El Greco painting. We talked a bit about ancient places that now existed only as mentions in old manuscripts, and I asked him which vanished site he'd most like to find. Without hesitation he said, "Tartessos."

A few years later, when I was hit with the sudden burst of news alerts about an Atlantis discovery, I began scrolling through them skeptically until a magic word caught my eye: *Tartessos*. The reports turned out to be linked to a National Geographic documentary called *Finding Atlantis*, which claimed that Plato's lost city had been found right where he'd said it was, outside the Pillars of Heracles. The unlikely star of the show was a history professor from the University of Hartford, Richard Freund. With his round face, wire-rimmed spectacles, and neat mustache, Freund looked less like a swashbuckling international adventure hero than a middle-aged Connecticut rabbi, which was another of his identities. His lack of flash didn't dim his confidence. At the documentary's start, Freund made clear to his audience that the stakes of his quest were enormous. "This city of Atlantis is seen by many as the mother of Egypt and Mesopotamia and Israel and Europe and all the other civilizations that began in this area," he explained, echoing Ignatius Donnelly's diffusionism theory. "And if it began here, we may be looking at the single most important site for humanity." He was standing in Doñana National Park, on the southwest coast of Spain.

Freund's argument was based on a radically simple solution to the question of Atlantis's location: When writing of Atlantis, Plato related a tale that Solon had heard from the Egyptians, who had in turn learned it from earlier sources. Thus, when speaking of the kingdom he called Atlantis, Plato had really been describing a *different* lost city, Tartessos.

The historical record for Tartessos is certainly much deeper than that for Atlantis. The early Greek geographer Hecataeus is quoted in a fragment of a lost work as referring to a "Tartessian polis," or city-state. Herodotus, writing in the century before Plato, placed Tartessos "beyond the Pillars of Heracles" and wrote that the kingdom was ruled by a wealthy monarch named Arganthonios, a name that means "Silver-Locks." (This may refer either to the area's mineral riches or to the king's advanced age. Herodotus claimed that Arganthonios reigned for eighty years and died at the age of 120.) Aristotle wrote that Tartessos was the name of a river that flowed from the Pyrenees Mountains between Iberia and Gaul to a spot outside the Pillars. Roman sources referred to a River Tartessos, now the Guadalquivir River, near the city of Cádiz, which sits, still, about sixty miles northwest of the Strait of Gibraltar. Where this river met the sea, it was split into two mouths by a large island. On that island, the second-century-AD geographer Pausanias wrote in his *Description of*

Greece, was built a city, also called Tartessos. To recap: a wealthy island city, opposite the Pillars of Heracles, in the very land, Gades/Cádiz, that Plato had mentioned in the *Critias*.

Richard Freund believed that Tartessos, in addition to being Plato's source for Atlantis, was another name for the land of Tarshish, mentioned several times in the Old Testament, perhaps most famously as the distant place Jonah sails for prior to his miraculous encounter with a whale. In the tenth century BC, King Solomon of Israel (he of the famed let's-cut-this-baby-in-half wisdom), in partnership with the Phoenician king Hiram of Tyre, owned a fleet of ships that sailed for Tarshish every three years. These returned "bringing gold and silver, ivory, apes and monkeys." One group of Phoenician traders, the Greek historian Diodorus Siculus wrote, having carried olive oil and other wares to exchange in Tarshish, received so much silver in return that they cast new silver anchors to replace their lead ones—"and there still was a great quantity of the metal left over." Freund notes in his book *Digging Through History* that the book of Isaiah, from the eighth century BC, contains this passage: "Howl, ye ships of Tarshish; for your strength is laid waste." Might a maritime disaster that struck Tarshish be related to the one that demolished Atlantis?

Freund wasn't the first scholar to make a connection between Tartessos and Atlantis, nor to go hunting for Plato's lost city along the coast of southwest Spain. The German archaeologist Adolf Schulten published a theory in 1922 that proposed Tartessos and Atlantis were one and the same. Working with the Anglo-French archaeologist George Bonsor, Schulten conducted excavations for several seasons in an area that is now part of the Doñana National Park, the marshland where Freund's documentary was filmed. In 1923, the pair excavated at a site called Cerro del Trigo ("Wheat Hill"). They found old stone blocks that indicated the site had once been a Roman colony. Because the team saw no other stones nearby,

Bonsor proposed that the Romans must have used stones from an older settlement as their building materials. Further excavations to find what lay beneath the Roman ruins were impossible due to the Doñana's high water table. Any hole they dug more than a few feet deep was quickly flooded. Whatever archaeological secrets lay buried at the site would likely remain out of reach forever.

After Schulten's inconclusive digs, the Tartessos-as-Atlantis hypothesis largely lay dormant for several decades, overshadowed by the lingering influence of Ignatius Donnelly's mid-Atlantic location theory. Then in 2004, the prestigious British scholarly journal *Antiquity* published a brief article titled "A Location for 'Atlantis'?" The author, Dr. Rainer Kühne, a physicist at Dortmund University in Germany, noted that on satellite photos of the Doñana region one could see the outlines of two large rectangular structures—possibly remnants of the spectacular temples of Poseidon and Cleito that Plato had described—on what appeared to be a chunk of land roughly five stades (or three thousand feet) in diameter, the same size he had cited for the central island of Atlantis.[5]

As usually happens when someone floats a new Atlantis hypothesis, especially one with the implicit support of an eminent publication, the media went crazy. In an interview with the BBC, Kühne gave additional detail, pointing out how the faint outline of circles could be seen surrounding the rectangular shapes. "We have in the photos concentric rings just as Plato described," Kühne told a reporter. Amazingly, both the rings and one of the rectangles also more or less matched the precise dimensions that Plato had given in the *Critias*.

Freund's documentary built on Kühne's thesis, compiling a number of other compelling similarities between Plato's Atlantis and the

---

5 According to Kühne's article, the smaller of the two rectangular structures can be found by entering the coordinates 36°57'25N and 6°22'58W onto a satellite map such as Google Earth. The center of the second structure, he writes, is five hundred meters southwest of the center of the first.

Doñana Park site. Southwest Spain contains some of the world's greatest copper deposits, which have been mined since Phoenician times. The narrator of *Finding Atlantis* points out that the ancient Greek word *orichalcum*, the mysterious metal that Plato wrote "flashed with . . . red light," is often translated as "mountain copper." The region's geology shows evidence of having endured several of what scientists sometimes call "high-impact events." The famously unstable Azores-Gibraltar Transform Fault due west of the park could have caused tsunamis capable of laying waste to a coastal kingdom in a day and a night. A layer of methane found several meters below the ground at one spot in Doñana might be evidence that organic matter—flora, trash, or human remains—had decomposed after being smothered and trapped suddenly under debris carried by a tsunami. The existence of Kühne's rings appeared to have been confirmed through electrical resistivity tomography (ERT), a geophysical method that uses electrical current to identify objects under the ground.

Having assembled this impressive trove of evidence, near the end of *Finding Atlantis* Freund offered what he called his "smoking gun": two small figurines, discovered while searching inside the circular area identified by Kühne. "People wait a whole career to find just one of these little figurines, and we found two!" Freund exults in the documentary. He identified them as possible images of the ancient goddess Astarte, who was worshipped in various forms for nearly four thousand years. Freund saw a possible connection to the Phoenicians. This race of seafarers, based in the area in and around modern Lebanon, built up a massive trading empire between the second millennium BC and their conquest by Persia in 539 BC, with colonies stretching the length of the Mediterranean. One such colony was Gades/Cádiz. The Phoenicians are credited with spreading the use of the alphabet, but since almost none of their writing has survived, their history is obscure. Based on the discovery of these figurines, Freund speculated that historians may have gotten the exploration of the Mediterranean backward—the Phoenicians might have actually originated in Spain and migrated *east*. A vanished Phoenician settlement on the southwest coast of Spain might have been the inspiration for Plato's story. "That would make Atlantis the prototype for all other Phoenician outposts," he writes in *Digging Through History*. Such an idea would rewrite the chronology of western civilization.

If anything, the press response to Freund's documentary exceeded the reaction to Kühne's *Antiquity* article. The natural historian Simon Winchester, author of respected books on the Krakatoa cataclysm and the Atlantic Ocean, wrote in *Newsweek* of Freund's claim to have found Atlantis: "Beguiling new research into one of archaeology's greatest mysteries appears to have thrown up remarkably persuasive evidence that remains of the ancient city are to be found in the great Hinojos marsh on the southwestern coast of what is today's Spain." He invited readers to plug in a set of GPS coordinates and have a look at the site on Google Earth. "It is a remarkable site, and you will gasp."

I entered the coordinates. I squinted. I saw a brown smear. I did not gasp. Had Freund really solved the twenty-four-hundred-year-old mystery?

Freund's offices were located in the basement of a building that looked like an Eisenhower-era recreation center. As I waited at his assistant's desk—Freund is the director of the Maurice Greenberg Center for Judaic Studies—I admired some photographs of artifacts he'd uncovered at digs in the Middle East. The subterranean air was swampy; a dehumidifier hummed in one corner. Eventually, I was waved in to an inner office. Freund sat behind a large, messy desk covered in papers and very-old-looking books in several languages. He was obviously relishing his sudden fame as the world's most famous Atlantologist.

"I've received about five thousand e-mails!" he told me, handing over a thick folder. "Here's a selection of five hundred. From kids, from crazies. National Geographic was just overwhelmed." He read aloud from a couple of letters and then handed these to me as well. "This might be something you and I could collaborate on—*Letters to and from Atlantis*. A whole book!" Freund wanted to make sure I knew I was missing out on a potentially hot property: A writer for *The New Yorker* had contacted him about doing a book together. "Anne Rice's agent says she's working on a nonfiction book about Atlantis!" The organizer of the triennial Atlantis conferences in Greece was all but begging him to attend, but Freund had prior plans to oversee the archaeological dig of an ancient city port in Israel.

Reaction to *Finding Atlantis* may have been enthusiastic, but it had not been universally positive. In the documentary Freund appears to be the decisive leader of the expedition, shepherding a team of Spanish scholars through the dusty landscapes of Doñana in a fleet of Toyota Land Cruisers. Long after watching it I learned that Freund's role was the result of careful editing. The Spaniards worked for their country's national research council and had invited Freund primarily because he had access to expensive equipment they needed. They'd been working in Doñana Park for years. Freund had been at the location for a week. The Emmy Award–winning producer of *Finding Atlantis*, Simcha Jacobovici, was famous for making the sorts of sensational documentaries that mainstream scholars despise, including one History Channel special purporting to have found the nails from Jesus's cross. And as usual when the name *Atlantis* was raised, critics howled that Freund couldn't have found it because Plato's Atlantis was a fiction.

Freund remained convinced that he'd located the true Atlantis. "This is like finding the *Titanic* or King Tut's tomb," he said, shaking his head. "There are too many things that are accurate to discount. He ticked off the evidence on his fingers: the Astarte figurines, the ERT readings (which he compared to "MRI readings for the ground"), the satellite photos. When I asked why no stones had been found during the team's subterranean soundings, which would seem to contradict Plato's description of a red, white, and black stone wall that surrounded the innermost circle of Atlantis, Freund explained that this absence was actually a *good* thing—evidence that a tremendous tsunami had obliterated the site and swept everything out to sea. A team of marine archaeologists had found the remains of enormous stone walls in the water off of the Bay of Cádiz, near the mouth of the Guadalquivir River.

"There's debris going all the way down the coast!" he told me excitedly. "Ancient walls and pillars deposited in front of the marsh—things that are nine, eleven, fifteen, eighteen meters down!"

Carbon 14 dating of core samples taken from within Rainer Kühne's innermost circle, where the figurines had been found, uncovered a sample of local oak—possibly remains of a ship—buried under forty feet of debris. To Freund, this indicated an ancient settlement suffocated by a sudden influx of sea matter. "Only in that one area of the marsh do the cores date back four thousand years," he said. That could mean a disaster around 2000 BC.

"So how do you explain the discrepancy with Plato's figure of nine thousand years between the sinking and Solon's trip to Saïs?" I asked.

"The measurements were a mistake in translation from the Egyptian," he said. "That's a very common thing with ancient sources." Freund notes in his book that for the ancient Greeks, 9 was a very powerful and mythical number. He compares it to the use of 40 in the Hebrew Bible: Noah's ark sailed through forty days and nights of rain; Moses spent forty days atop Mount Sinai obtaining the Ten Commandments; the Israelites wandered forty years in the desert, and so on. Nine thousand years was simply Plato's symbolic way of saying "once upon a time," he said.

Having already introduced the smoking gun of the Astarte statuettes, Freund had wrapped up *Finding Atlantis* with what he later called "the most compelling evidence for the existence of Atlantis." He paid a visit to Cancho Roano, a ritual site 150 miles north of Doñana first excavated in 1978. Unlike the area within Doñana, Cancho Roano is widely acknowledged as a Tartessian site, the finest ever uncovered. It seems to have been strictly ceremonial. The building has one entrance, is surrounded by a moat, and consists of a set of identically shaped rooms that radiate out from the center. To Freund, these echoed the single entrance canal, central island, and concentric rings that Plato had written about. When Freund visited a local archaeological museum and saw its collection of Bronze Age steles—slabs of stone decorated with carvings that serve as a marker or monument— he had what he called an aha moment. Several of the steles were inscribed with similar designs—that of a warrior standing next to an image of three concentric circles bisected by a single line leading from outside to the center. "I said to the archaeologist who brought me there, 'Don't you see? It's a miniature version of Atlantis!'"

Then Freund stood abruptly and said that he had to hurry off to set up for an Atlantis presentation at a local synagogue. We walked up the stairs and into the sunshine. I asked how his Spanish colleagues from the documentary had reacted to the finished product.

"Well, the folks from Doñana weren't very happy," he said, with a shrug. "It is what it is."

We shook hands and I watched him drive off. Only then did something occur to me: If Freund had made the most important archaeological discovery in history, why wasn't he going back to Spain anytime soon?

CHAPTER NINE

A Second Opinion

Madrid, Spain

Several months later I was wandering the deserted halls of an enormous government building on the outskirts of Madrid, searching for Juan Villarias-Robles. Villarias is a historian and anthropologist who works at the Consejo Superior de Investigaciones Científicas, or CSIC, Spain's multidisciplinary research council that is similar to the Smithsonian Institution. He had helped organize the research project in Doñana Park. His takeaway from the findings had been, to say the least, a little different from Freund's.

I rapped on the door matching the number I'd written down and was greeted by a man in his midfifties with eyeglasses and a neat mustache, wearing a necktie. Villarias had a tidy, spacious office, one wall of which was lined with books organized by subject. Large windows looked onto a hideous mirrored-glass building across the street. With a "please, sit down," Villarias motioned to a pair of low-slung chairs facing each other, like those on a highbrow 1970s talk show. I felt like a patient who was about to receive bad news from his doctor.

Almost no one who had appeared alongside Freund in the *Finding Atlantis* documentary was pleased with it. Part of the displeasure was the distinct impression left that Freund, with his one week of filming in Doñana, was a modern-day Schliemann who'd orchestrated a major archaeological discovery.[6] Villarias and other members of the team had been working on what they called the Hinojos Project for six years. In the wake of the initial broadcast of *Finding Atlantis*, Villarias had posted a scathing fourteen-hundred-word rebuttal on the website of the *Hartford Courant*, in which he pointed out that Freund had piggybacked onto their research project and then had run off to tell the world he'd discovered Atlantis.

"We were interested in Tartessos, not Atlantis," Villarias explained. "When Freund came to us, he had no interest in Atlantis at all: His interest was King Solomon. When he learned about our project, he thought—with justification—that we could get data that would date to the tenth century BC. That would be a way of confirming that those expeditions in the Bible to the mysterious land of Tarshish corresponded to the land of Tartessos."

This made sense. After all, Freund was a historian who specialized in biblical history. I had expected Villarias to be what Spaniards call an *aguafiestas*, or a wet blanket, on the subject of Tartessos and Atlantis, and he certainly had the right to be cranky. Having made his point about Freund, though, Villarias was more interested in talking about the possibility of finding lost cities.

"Tartessos was probably . . . I say 'probably'"—he made air quotes with his fingers—"because we don't know very much about it. It was *probably* a Bronze Age society, materially not as advanced as Greece and Rome. *Probably* the oldest organized society in the western Mediterranean, going back to about 1000 BC. There is some argument but I do believe that Tartessos and Tarshish are basically the same."

---

6 From Reuters, March 12, 2011: "A U.S.-led research team may have finally located the lost city of Atlantis . . ."

"How could you prove that?" I asked. "What sort of evidence would you need?"

"Basically, goods—material remains from tenth-century Israel or Tyre. Pottery or other artifacts that date to the tenth century would be good evidence. Perhaps King Solomon would have said, 'I'll give you some nice clothes and crafts and you give me gold and silver from Tarshish.'" No evidence had yet surfaced that would prove the exchange of precious metals for luxury goods, but Villarias was optimistic that something might turn up in the future.

Villarias's Hinojos Project was a major undertaking, a team of nine Spanish specialists in fields ranging from geology to cartography to archaeology assembled to explore the Tartessos-Atlantis hypothesis put forth in Rainer Kühne's *Antiquity* article and its accompanying satellite photos. A friend of Villarias had seen a Spanish news story about Kühne's hypothesis and remembered that Villarias had written his BA thesis on Tartessos.

"Actually, there were two German scholars," Villarias clarified, raising two fingers. "Kühne, and also Werner Wickboldt, who originally identified the two rings and two rectangles."

Villarias recalled having been intrigued by 1990s satellite photos Wickboldt produced, but also confused. As far as he could recall, the area in the photos that contained the temples had been a lake in Roman times. Prior to that, it was a large estuary that formed where the Guadalquivir River met the Atlantic Ocean. One of Spain's most celebrated geologists had established in the 1930s that the marsh had once extended all the way to the present city of Seville, which is sixty miles inland. It seemed unlikely that a majestic port city trading gold and monkeys would have been built in a gigantic swamp.

When Villarias collected a bunch of geological reports to review, though, he came across a reference to a fourth-century-AD poem by a Roman named Rufus Festus Avienus, titled "Ora Maritima" ("Sea Coasts"). The parallels between the transmission of the Atlantis story from Egypt to Plato and Avienus's reliance on ancient sources are interesting.

Avienus drew heavily on a document known as the *Massaliote Periplus*, a long-lost guide for merchant sailors, written around the sixth century BC. (The historian Rhys Carpenter defined a periplus as "a Greek literary tradition of versified marine handbooks for navigators, notably headlands, rivers, harbors, and towns along a given route." Basically, a poetic set of point-to-point directions using landmarks.) The *Massaliote Periplus*, as transmitted through "Ora Maritima," describes a sea voyage starting in Brittany near the English Channel, then tracing the perimeter of the Iberian Peninsula counterclockwise en route to Massalia, modern Marseille. Along the way, the poem provides a wealth of information about the location of the city of Tartessos.

"It's just a fragment of the poem, maybe twenty pages," Villarias said. We stood up and walked over to a map of ancient Spain that he had tacked to his wall. "Adolf Schulten"—the German archaeologist who with George Bonsor excavated in Doñana Park in the 1920s, trying to find evidence of Tartessos and Atlantis—"made the argument that because Avienus mentions names, he is copying old texts. Some of them, such as Hecataeus of Miletus's *Journey Round the World*, may have been written at the time Tartessos existed. Others, like Bakoris of Rhodes, we don't even know who that guy is."

Historian Rhys Carpenter made a convincing argument that Avienus's primary source, unmentioned in the poem, was the pioneering Greek geographer Pytheas, who had made the long sea voyage to the frozen north somewhere between the years 325 BC and 300 BC, a few decades after Plato wrote the *Timaeus*. Two short sections of "Ora Maritima" give the location of Tartessos and convey the fact that it had been destroyed sometime between Hecataeus's *Journey*, written in the fifth century BC and probably based on earlier information, and Pytheas's eyewitness account of the late fourth century BC.

> . . . This is the Atlantic Gulf
> And here is Gadir, once Tartessos called,
> Here too the Pillars of persistent Heracles . . .

> Tartessos—prosperous and peopled state
> In ancient periods, but now forlorn,
> Tiny, deserted, heap of ruined mounds!

Villarias traced his finger on the map, from Cádiz/Gades (a name derived from the Phoenician *Gadir*, meaning "walled city") past the marshes of Doñana Park and through the Pillars of Heracles at Gibraltar. "Avienus must be interpreted, though," he said. "Ora Maritima" can't be read as a Rand McNally map any more than the Atlantis story can be read as pure history. Adolf Schulten's interpretation of Avienus had led him to the Roman ruins at Cerro del Trigo, where the high water table had prevented him from searching for older ruins. No one followed up, and by the 1960s, Villarias explained, the use of ancient texts as archaeological sources had fallen out of fashion as scientific methods such as carbon dating, stratigraphy probes, and aerial photography took precedence. "Ora Maritima" was largely forgotten.

In 2005, Villarias helped assemble a multidisciplinary team. The Hinojos Project had two simple objectives: to see if the shapes that the Germans Wickboldt and Kühne had seen in satellite photos were man-made (assuming they existed at all). Second, if these shapes were man-made, was it possible to determine how old they were? The team looked at detailed aerial photos taken in 1956, after dictator Francisco Franco agreed to allow the United States to build military bases in Spain. They gathered the oldest known maps, going back to Catalan and Italian sea charts of the fourteenth century, centuries before longitude had been discovered. They recruited a biologist to analyze prehistoric pollen samples. They arranged for a new set of aerial photographs. The initial results were intriguing. Where Wickboldt and Kühne had seen two rings and two rectangles hiding under the marshes, the Hinojos team found *fifteen* forms. "Because of their geometrical and well-proportioned outlines," Villarias-Robles wrote in a follow-up report, ten of the shapes "look especially suggestive of man-made structures." This wealth of promising evidence was enough to merit further investigation.

In 2009, the team conducted an ERT test of what Freund describes in *Digging Through History* as "a distinctive marking in the ground in the places where the concentric circles of the inner city of Atlantis would have been located." Such gaps often indicate a chemical "shadow" of old building materials that have since disintegrated. The ERT results showed that the rings seen on the satellite photos were real. "It took us all by surprise," Freund recounts in his book. "The intermittent breaks in the ERT layer were the remnants of the ancient walls of a Bronze Age city that had been there thousands of years before."

"We got very excited," Villarias told me as we sat down again. He didn't sound especially excited. "The trouble is, when we finally obtained all the carbon 14 dates, from even deeper samples, the age of those anomalies cannot be more than two thousand years old." In other words, at least four hundred years younger than Plato himself. Villarias's best guess was that the shapes were caused by animal enclosures made of degradable materials like wood or mud brick, that had held horses or cattle belonging to the caliph of Córdoba. "When the Christian reconquest took place in the thirteenth century, we know there was a very dramatic depopulation of the area," he said.

"But what about the ancient figurines?" I asked of the Astarte statues whose discovery might rewrite ancient history.

"That's a funny story," Villarias said. The corners of his mouth turned slightly upward beneath his mustache. The figurines were found while the documentary was filming, one by historian Ángel León and one by Sebastián Celestino, one of Spain's leading archaeologists and an authority on Tartessian culture. "Richard Freund and the camera people got very excited. Freund came up with this interpretation that these figurines were representations of the Phoenician goddess Astarte, who is the Roman goddess Venus more or less. Astarte was probably very important in the time of Tartessos. So while you saw Freund making the point that these were representations of Astarte, Sebastián, who is an expert and knows much more than Freund, was touching the figurines and telling me in Spanish, 'I don't think so. These figures are too round.' Whereas Phoenician statuettes have more straight lines. The figures are broken, so we don't have the complete features, but similar statuettes have been found in Andalusia. These could be late Roman or even later, from the baroque." That would mean they had been created about two thousand years after Plato died.

"Did you mention this to Freund?"

"We couldn't reach the producers before the documentary was released to warn them. And he didn't bother to check with us."

"Let me guess—the Cancho Roano stuff doesn't hold up, either," I said. This was Freund's "most compelling evidence" that Tartessos had been Atlantis.

"Cancho Roano is a Tartessian site—no question about it. Sebastián has been working there for like twenty years. It was begun in about 600 BC, which is late in the history of Tartessos. We know from Avienus and from Greek sources that Tartessos was on an island, and so of course surrounded by water. Freund came up with the idea—which I think is bright—that Cancho Roano is a replica or a microcosmic representation of a city surrounded by water. But it's very, very, very far-fetched to bring Atlantis there." The three concentric rings bisected by a line weren't a symbol for Plato's lost city but for a warrior's shield. Similar symbols had been found throughout Europe.

One thing that the Hinojos Project had been able to confirm is that some sort of cataclysm struck the southwest coast of the Iberian Peninsula around 2000 BC and repeatedly over the years. The model is the catastrophic Lisbon earthquake and tsunami of 1755: earthquakes followed by floods. "Our geologist doesn't like to call it a tsunami because he might be labeled a sensationalist, but to me it's a tsunami," Villarias said.

"We checked the records and it so happens that a big disaster like the Lisbon one took place exactly 400 years earlier in 1356. The previous one was in 881. And before that in the fourth century. So every 350 to 450 years there is a big one. People forget until it happens to them. If that rule is accurate, and I think it is, the next one will be around the year 2150."

As for Freund's hiring divers to search for stones in the Bay of Cádiz outside the mouth of the Guadalquivir River, Villarias agreed that it was a great idea. But the CSIC team had determined that after a series of seismic events, the loose, wet ground in the Hinojos Marsh had subsided, dropping like a failed soufflé. Water, as well as any debris such as stones and dead bodies, would have been trapped in the estuary rather than being flushed into the ocean. This entombment of organic material might have caused the methane they found, but they couldn't be certain. Each year during the rainy season, the Guadalquivir floods the plain and leaves behind a layer of sediment. Any traces of Tartessos—or, why not? Atlantis—were likely buried under many meters of silt and clay, probably forever. Schulten and Bonsor had given up when they hit the water table in the 1920s. Nowadays, no sane bureaucrat was going to authorize massive excavations in the middle of a nature sanctuary.

After crushing my hopes of having found Atlantis, Villarias suggested we grab a bite to eat. We walked over to Madrid's busy Calle de Alcalá and sat down in the empty dining room of the sort of classic Castilian restaurant that hasn't changed its menu since the Spanish Civil War. (It was two fifteen, extremely early to be lunching in Madrid.) We each had a glass of wine and ordered paella. I asked Villarias why he thought it was that only amateurs seemed to be interested in searching for Atlantis.

"That wasn't always the case. Going backward from the '60s you have a long line of serious scholars going back to the Renaissance, people like Schulten." He cracked a piece of bread in two. "I'm curious. I may do it on my own."

"Really?" I hadn't gotten the impression that he took Atlantis seriously.

"Plato deserves an anthropological analysis. Is it a myth? It's intriguing that he names his sources. Why mention Solon? Stuff like the nine thousand years, you can't take that literally." He dismissed the notion with a wave of his butter knife. "Anthropologists have a long history of being able to pull out the contaminants like that. They have used the same approach with some of the Genesis Bible stories, with Sodom and Gomorrah, with the Great Flood."

A recent interpretation of an ancient cuneiform tablet posits that the fire and brimstone that an angry god hurled down on the Sodomites was actually deadly debris from a comet that hit the earth in 3123 BC. The hunt for Noah's ark has almost certainly consumed more money and hours than the search for Atlantis, with one team after another picking the faint clues out of Genesis and ascending the slopes of Mount Ararat in hopes of finding proof that the biblical deluge was real. The astronaut James Irwin, whose Christian faith was bolstered by his walk on the moon, led two well-publicized but unsuccessful expeditions in the 1980s. Certainly, there was no shortage of ancient flood myths.

Villarias explained how an anthropological approach would work: "Analyze Plato's narrative in order to see if that narrative actually has a nucleus, an original core of historical information."

To search for that nucleus, Villarias said, you'd first look for the elements in the Atlantis tale that are consistent with Plato's other writings, and those of his predecessors, such as Herodotus. If anything remained that couldn't be explained by either of those sources, "one could safely assume that the story echoes, or encodes, some historical truth." That core remnant would then be compared to the other literatures and philosophies of the ancient world, starting with Egypt. "Supposing a consistency is then found, the results of the quest would be that at least the information in the narrative regarding Egypt is true." Assuming that Plato was telling the truth and that Solon didn't mistake Egyptian mythology for history, we'd be a long way toward "supposing that the land of Atlantis really existed after all."

CHAPTER TEN

Washed Away

Doñana National Park, Andalusia, Spain

Eighteen hours later, having caught the high-speed train to Se-ville; having driven my rented Fiat Panda nose-first against a wall before realizing that I did not know how to shift its manual trans-mission into reverse; having found a kind stranger to show me how to back up my car and locate the highway; having driven through the departures area of the Seville airport three times while trying to find my hotel; and having slept fitfully for a few hours before rising in the dark to drive seventy miles southwest, I found myself sitting in the passenger seat of a Toyota Land Cruiser and plowing through the Atlantic surf as if I were headed to a clambake in a light beer commercial. At the wheel was naturalist José María Galán. His short-sleeve PARQUE NACIONAL DE DOÑANA shirt was nattily acces-sorized with a scarf and a Yellowstone baseball cap. He was compar-ing the regularity of the Old Faithful geyser (or *high-zer*, as he pronounced it), which he had recently visited, to the predictability of earthquakes and tsunamis on the Spanish coast. "Look at those waves coming in," he said, pointing at the incoming whitecaps. "Now imagine one of them sixty meters tall."

Though it's not usually associated with seismic activity today, the

Iberian Peninsula has a history of geological instability of the sort that might destroy an island empire in a matter of hours. At 9:40 A.M. on November 1, 1755, two tectonic plates 120 miles west of Doñana Park faulted, resulting in an earthquake whose magnitude has been estimated at between 8.5 and 9.0 on the Richter scale. (The 2010 Haiti earthquake, which leveled Port-au-Prince and left more than two hundred thousand dead, registered a 7.0. A 9.0 quake would be a hundred times as powerful.) In Portugal, much of Lisbon, including thirty churches celebrating All Saints' Day, collapsed from the shock. Fire swept through the city. Two-yard-wide cracks split the ground. Thousands of terrified citizens flocked to the port city's newly built marble quay to escape the inferno; some boarded ships in hope of escaping. Thirty minutes after the first shock, the mob that had swarmed the harbor witnessed an amazing sight: The sea withdrew, leaving the bed of the Tejo River exposed, strewn with lopsided boats and flopping fish stuck in the muck.

The Reverend Charles Davy recorded what happened next: "In an instant there appeared, at some small distance, a large body of water, rising as it were like a mountain. It came on foaming and roaring, and rushed towards the shore with such impetuosity, that we all immediately ran for our lives as fast as possible." Thousands were dragged into the sea, and boats loaded with refugees "were all swallowed up, as in a whirlpool, and nevermore appeared." Candles lighted for All Saints' Day celebrations started fires that burned through most of Lisbon's remaining structures. As has so often happened with floods throughout history, the catastrophe was explained as the vengeful act of a god angered by the impiety of mortals.

Doñana today is a peaceful oasis on Spain's heavily developed coast. For nature lovers, there's a lot to see. Galán pointed out deer and foxes (Doñana had once been a royal hunting ground) and the subtle switchbacking sand trail of a viper. For seekers of lost cities, a little more imagination is necessary. A lot of trade had obviously come through here long ago. "The only rocks we have here are small piles that ships dumped after using them for ballast," Galán told me. Pieces of broken pottery in all shapes and sizes were visible everywhere. Avienus's description of "tiny, deserted heaps of ruined mounds" was still accurate. Small, identical hills of sand turned out to be the remains of ovens used to make ceramics. Buried in each mound was a cornucopia of pottery shards: Phoenician, Roman, Muslim, all mixed together. Only when we were driving away did I notice that the mounds were evenly spaced apart. "Archaeology is very subtle," Galán said. "You have to be very close to something or very far away."

We drove a few miles inland to the Cerro del Trigo, the spot where Adolf Schulten had hoped to find Atlantis. A few ancient Roman walls remained exposed in half-filled trenches. "It looks like you should be able to excavate here easily, but there's water half a meter down," Galán said, anticipating my next question. There's also the aboveground water problem. We got back in the Land Cruiser and drove through a bone-dry stretch of sand and scrub. When the autumn rains arrive in October, the Guadalquivir River floods the lowest areas of the park, bringing the tons of sediment that Juan Villarias-Robles described and creating a massive bog that lasts until May. This desertlike area would be transformed in a few weeks by rains into an inland sea. I asked Galán how deep the water would get here once the rains began. "By February, up to here," he said, holding his hand out the window. Almost five feet high.

We stopped at the Marisma de Hinojos, where Wickboldt and Kühne's circles and rectangles had appeared on satellite photos. It looked like nothing more than a dry floodplain. I felt an odd sensation, knowing that Atlantis might be a hundred feet below me, packed under layers of sand and clay. My doubts that this habitat would ever be disturbed in the name of Atlantology were confirmed when we met two of Galán's colleagues crawling up dunes on their hands and knees picking century-old shotgun pellets out of the sand so that endangered birds wouldn't eat them.

On the way back to the park's headquarters, Galán stopped to examine some tiny scorpion tracks in the sand. A gust blew up, and the trail vanished in the cloud. "See, in the end nature erases everything," Galán said, holding his scarf over his mouth. "I think that's the real story of Atlantis. No matter how big and powerful you get, you can disappear like *that*."

CHAPTER ELEVEN

The Truth Is out There

All over the Map

At this point in the story I should confess something. Atlantis has already been found. Right off the coast of Cadíz, in fact, almost exactly where I'd been driving with José María Galán. I know this because I read a brief 1973 news item about it in *The Boston Globe*. An instructor at Pepperdine University, Maxine Asher, had used her psychic powers to zero in on signals that told her where the island empire had sunk. Incredibly, divers from her expedition (which also included students who'd paid their own way, expecting to earn college credit) were able to locate compelling evidence of the lost city on the very first day out—roads and columns decorated with concentric-circle designs. Asher was careful not to overstate the importance of her findings. "This is probably the greatest discovery in world history," she told a reporter, "and will begin a new era of research in anthropology, archaeology, and underwater sciences."

Asher was chased out of the country by Spanish officials shortly thereafter—one of her students, Tony O'Connell informed me, claimed to have seen a draft of her triumphant press release two days prior to the actual discovery, and the alleged roads and columns were never seen again. But she was by no means the first person—or the

last—to put forth an Atlantis discovery divined solely by extrasensory means. Perhaps the most famous of these was the Kentucky-
born psychic Edgar Cayce, known as "the sleeping prophet." Cayce
believed that he could lie down and enter a "superconscious" medita-
tive state. Once plugged into the collective wisdom of the universe,
he could answer questions both personal and profound. From 1901 to
1945 Cayce gave more than fourteen thousand of these readings, as he
called them. Though he considered himself to be primarily an alternative healer, about seven hundred of his psychic bulletins dealt with
Atlantis in some way. According to his supporters, Cayce never read
Plato or Ignatius Donnelly, so any similarities on the subject must be
either coincidental or evidence of great minds thinking alike.

Today the impressive headquarters for Cayce's Association for Research and Enlightenment (ARE), located in Virginia Beach, houses a
sort of extrasensory institute, complete with museum, day spa, and
holistic healing school. Yoga classes and tai chi are offered. There is
also a library that holds typescripts of Cayce's original readings and a
separate room for Atlantis-related materials, including maps.

"A lot of people had readings done, and they had past lives in Atlantis," a helpful research librarian named Laura explained cheerily
when I called to ask about Cayce's insights on Atlantis. "There were
three destructions. The Atlanteans had the Tuaoi Stone"—a massive
crystal that Cayce said provided them with healing powers as well as
energy to operate sophisticated aircraft and submarines—"but they
powered the stone too high." This act of arrogance set off geological
turbulence worldwide. Prior to the final destruction of Atlantis,
which Cayce dated to 10,500 BC, important artifacts and stone tablets containing the recorded history of humanity were secreted away
to three Halls of Record located in the Yucatán, Egypt ("under the
Sphinx's paw," Laura the librarian specified), and, per a 1933 Cayce
reading, "under the slime of ages of sea water—near what is known
as Bimini, off the coast of Florida."

Cayce claimed to be able to see the future as well as the past. "Poseidia will be among the first portions of Atlantis to rise again," he exclaimed during one reading. "Expect it in '68 and '69; not so far away!"

A large binder of psychic readings given while diagnosing cases of asthma and kidney stones might not be enough evidence for conventional archaeologists to start writing grant proposals, but Cayce's predictions about Bimini—an island chain that's part of the Bahamas—have resulted in what is probably the most concentrated effort to find Atlantis. Starting in the late 1960s, several large-scale underwater explorations have been undertaken in the area of the islands, many of them sponsored by the ARE. The most famous discovery was the so-called Bimini Road, located in 1968, conveniently confirming the prophet's predicted date. Initially believed to be a J-shaped, man-made limestone path about a third of a mile long, it turned out to be a natural formation. This evidence has not diminished the zeal of ARE-supported projects, and searches for Cayce's three Halls of Record are ongoing. In 2011, the group announced that it had carbon-dated a rock from an underwater foundation wall near Bimini to 20,000 BC. Cayce's channeling also provided information regarding Atlantis's fellow mythical sunken continent of Mu, a name that he used interchangeably with Lemuria.[7] The ARE website posits that recent gene research may prove a mass diaspora from Mu between 50,000 BC and 28,000 BC. This opinion is not widely shared.

Another writer famous for her supernatural insights into Atlantis

---

7 Mu is a hypothetical lost continent invented by the nineteenth-century antiquarian Augustus Le Plongeon, who equated it with Atlantis. He also believed, among other things, that inscriptions on Mayan pyramids showed the influence of Freemasonry and told the story of Atlantis's destruction. Lemuria was originally a continent invented by a zoologist to explain the presence of lemur fossils in both Madagascar and India. The theory has long since been discredited, but the concept of Lemuria lives on in pseudoscientific works such as Cayce's.

was the late nineteenth-century Russian-born occultist Madame Blavatsky, whose head would surely be carved alongside Cayce's on the Mount Rushmore of psychics. Famous for her séances and for founding the grab-bag spiritual movement known as Theosophy, Blavatsky popularized the idea of Atlantis as the ancient home of a race of supermen. She claimed that her book *The Secret Doctrine* was based on a manuscript written in Atlantis (translated from the original language, Senzar), which was at its height in the years prior to 850,000 BC, at least half a million years before the first *Homo sapiens* is believed to have emigrated from the African continent. The populace of Blavatsky's Atlantis enjoyed such modern conveniences as electricity and airships powered by psychic energy called *vril*. The causes she attributes to its downfall seem obvious in retrospect: a group practicing black magic spoiled everything by breeding human-animal hybrids akin to centaurs, which were exploited as warriors and sex slaves.

Had Blavatsky's thoughts on "cosmic evolution" merely served as fodder for future New Age fantasies about Atlantis—you can still browse a nice selection of tarot cards at the Theosophical Society bookstore on East Fifty-Third Street in Manhattan—she could be written off as a harmless crank. But her ideas about "root races"—a division of humanity into higher and lower species—were adopted by German mystics with a passionate interest in demonstrating that the superior Nordic race could trace its lineage back to a mythical island. Blavatsky had written of the Aryans as the most developed of the root races of Atlantis. The term *Aryan* (from the Sanskrit word for "noble") had originally been used by linguists to describe peoples stretching from northern Europe to India whose languages had shared origins. With the rise of National Socialism in the 1930s, any theory supporting the notion that a master Aryan race was responsible for laying the foundations of culture found a warm welcome in Berlin. A special Nazi research institute, named the Ahnenerbe, was created for the purpose of finding and disseminating scientific evidence of Germany's glorious past.

The leader of the Ahnenerbe was Heinrich Himmler, who also led the Gestapo and the Schutzstaffel, or SS, the paramilitary force responsible for carrying out the Final Solution outlined by Adolf Hitler. Himmler's top adviser in the Ahnenerbe believed that the German peoples could be traced to Plato's Atlantis, which he theorized had sunk in the Atlantic Ocean. In the late 1930s, as Heather Pringle describes in The Master Plan, Himmler sponsored expeditions around the globe to search for evidence of this lost utopia. One trip was to the Canary Islands. Early reports sounded promising, but a major follow-up expedition scheduled for late 1939 was canceled after the German invasion of Poland in September of that year.

The Nazis' favorite work of Atlantean speculation was the World Ice Theory, an idea based on an epiphany by its originator, the Austrian engineer Hans Hörbiger. He had imagined that the cosmos was filled with small ice planets that Earth sometimes captured in its orbit as moons. When these satellites eventually began their descent through the atmosphere, their spinning mass created its own gravitational pull. This pulled the oceans toward the equator, causing waves thousands of feet high. The capture of our current moon had been violent enough to produce earthquakes, cracks in the crust layer, and enormous volcanic explosions as the Earth's molten core escaped. When the oceans coalesced around the planet's girdle like a gigantic spin cycle, Atlantis was among the civilizations washed out.

Juan Villarias-Robles's description of using anthropological analysis to pull the contaminants out of the ancient world's most famous stories seemed sensible, but the World Ice Theory was a mythological Superfund site. Part of its appeal to the Nazis was that it contained very little science or math—and therefore served as a counterweight to Albert Einstein's "Jewish" theory of relativity.

Hörbiger's famous defense of his unscientific methods—"Calculation can only lead you astray"—may be the least Platonic sentence ever uttered.

Reading about the World Ice Theory I couldn't help but think of two people. One was Tony O'Connell. The only time I'd seen him angry was when I'd asked at the coffee shop one day about Cayce and Blavatsky and their unconventional methods. "These people who just make things up without evidence get my blood pressure pumping," he said, turning red. Tony was not a big fan of Mu, either.

The other person I thought of was Rand Flem-Ath, whom I telephoned at his home on Vancouver Island. I should state for the record that Flem-Ath is one of the least Nazi-like people I've had the pleasure of speaking to. A librarian on Canada's laid-back west coast, he created his intriguing last name by combining his surname with that of his wife and sometime coauthor, Rose, also a librarian. The photos I'd seen of him online made him look like a friendly, furry creature from an enchanted forest.

Flem-Ath is the leading proponent of what's called the Earth Crust Displacement Theory, which is sort of like Plate Tectonic Theory on fast-forward. He also believes that Atlantis was located in Antarctica and is now buried under ice and snow. Flem-Ath's theory, which he has expounded on in several similar books, is brilliant in its simplicity and its irrefutability. This winning combination has made him both an A-list guest on the Atlantis documentary and talk-radio circuit and a case study for debunkers of pseudoscience. Antarctica wasn't always cold, Flem-Ath posits. Around 9600 BC, when it was still known as Atlantis, the continent was situated in the tropics. Then it migrated south very rapidly and froze over.

Where the World Ice Theory crowd disdained Einstein's genius, however, Flem-Ath eagerly drops Einstein's name to support his own hypothesis that Antarctica had changed latitude. In a letter to the originator of the Earth Crust Theory, Charles Hapgood, in 1953, Einstein wrote, "I find your arguments very impressive and have the impression that your hypothesis is correct." The following year the twentieth century's greatest scientist wrote the foreword to Hapgood's book *Earth's Shifting Crust*.

Hapgood was a New Hampshire history professor who hypothesized that the earth's outer skin occasionally shifts violently in a relatively short period of time. The two inner layers, the core and mantle, remain unchanged. (The writer Paul Jordan, who calls Flem-Ath's theory "perhaps the ultimate catastrophist vision of Atlantis," compares the effect to an orange whose skin rotates while the fruit wedges inside remain immobile.) Flem-Ath applied Hapgood's theory to a literal reading of Plato's Atlantis story, with the sudden shift causing not only Plato's earthquakes and floods but also rapid climate changes. These shocks, Flem-Ath speculated, had been passed down as myths.

"One thing that seems certain is that a tremendous amount of things were happening around 9600 BC," Flem-Ath told me. "Melting ice caps. Mass extinctions in North and South America. Suddenly, virtually simultaneously, agriculture appears on several continents but with different crops. I believe a single idea, mobile crust, solves these problems on a global scale."

Hapgood's 1966 book, *Maps of the Ancient Sea Kings*, used late Renaissance-era maps to try to prove that Antarctica had been ice-free prior to a shift in the position of the poles around 9600 BC. The most famous of these maps is probably the Piri Reis map, a large fragment of a hand-drawn world map assembled in 1513 by the Ottoman admiral after whom it is named. The map was mislaid until 1929, when it was rediscovered during renovations of the former Ottoman sultan's palace in Istanbul. Geographers generally agree that the Piri Reis map is genuine and was based on portolan charts, ancient maps by Ptolemy, modern maps by Portuguese sailors, and the New World discoveries of Christopher Columbus. Indeed, the map has been celebrated as a rare copy of Columbus's own maps, all of which have been lost.

The map's southernmost section is what has attracted the most interest from Atlantologists. Three hundred years before mainland Antarctica was first sighted in 1820, Piri Reis drew a large continent on the bottom of the world. Thinkers as far back as Aristotle had hypothesized the existence of a landmass at the bottom of the globe, acting as a counterweight to the lands of the Northern Hemisphere. But Hapgood believed Piri Reis's mystery continent at the bottom of the world was in fact an ice-free Antarctica, because its general shape matched up with maps of subglacial Antarctica that were being assembled in the 1950s. Piri Reis, Hapgood surmised, had based his depiction on ancient maps, which subsequently vanished.

Flem-Ath explained that his eureka moment came when he compared Hapgood's seismological map of subglacial Antarctica with one of Atlantis published in 1664 by the German Jesuit scholar Athanasius Kircher. On Kircher's map, Atlantis is a continent that sits in the middle of the Atlantic Ocean, between Europe and South America. Flem-Ath speculated that Kircher had based his own map on an ancient Egyptian one that might have been stolen by the Romans. "It was a near-perfect match" with the modern Antarctic one, he told me.

I wasn't so sure about that. For starters, even the illustrations in Flem-Ath's book didn't look that much alike. Also, the cartographic resemblance Flem-Ath sees applies only if Kircher knew exactly where Atlantis was located but had somehow mixed up the locations of Spain and Africa. Seemingly Flem-Ath shared Ignatius Donnelly's tendency to equate coincidence with evidence. Just because my kids' snow days always seem to occur on my babysitter's day off doesn't mean she controls the weather.

Still, I was trying to keep an open mind. I asked where the Egyptians would have gotten the maps.

"I think the survivors of Atlantis are those that got the boats," Flem-Ath told me. "On boats you have two things that are portable: astronomy and maps."

He had a point. "Is there any way you could ever prove this?" I asked.

"Well, the easiest thing would be if a large part of ice fell off Antarctica and there were human structures underneath."

The biggest problem I had with Flem-Ath's theory wasn't its audacity, nor was it his unshakable faith in diffusionism and catastrophism. It was that his forward-looking ideas were largely based on scientific information from the era of "Our Friend the Atom." Hapgood's original theory and Einstein's noncommittal affirmation of it were proposed in the 1950s when the theory of continental drift was in its infancy, but Flem-Ath hasn't updated his evidence much past that time. As we chatted, he kept citing data that was fifty years old and sometimes older. I started tapping my fingers when he began talking about how some ancient ruins near Lake Titicaca—very important to the World Ice Theory—had been built more than ten thousand years ago, an idea that has been disproven many times over. (The site's structures seem to have been built several centuries after Plato died.) When he mentioned that ancient myths indicated Machu Picchu in Peru had been built by the Incas as a refuge from floods, I got impatient.

"Rand, all of this stuff you're telling me is considered beyond the fringe. It's been discredited."

"Well, maybe, but that's not a very important part of my theory," he said. He admitted that some of his sources were old but insisted that the Earth Crust Displacement Theory was still ahead of its time. "I'm better off bypassing scientists and reaching for a general audience, maybe two or three generations down the road," he said.

In the last line of his book *Atlantis Beneath the Ice*, Flem-Ath proposes what might happen at that future point: "Science and myth might merge." It's an idea that went out of style not long after Plato ended the *Critias* midsentence. It didn't require the powers of an Einstein—or the foresight of an Edgar Cayce—to see that such a partnership was unlikely to make a comeback anytime soon.

CHAPTER TWELVE

Dr. Kühne, I Presume

Braunschweig, Germany

Having heard two very different versions of the Tartessos hypothesis from Richard Freund and Juan Villarias-Robles, I decided it seemed like a good idea to dig a little deeper by meeting Rainer Kühne and Werner Wickboldt, the German researchers who had reignited the search for Atlantis with their analysis of the Doñana satellite photos. Conveniently, both men lived in the same midsize city near Germany's old east-west border. Inconveniently, they disliked each other intensely. I booked a flight to Düsseldorf and rode the train four hours to Braunschweig.

The week before my arrival in Germany I had reread Kühne's *Antiquity* article and e-mailed to remind him of our appointment. I promised to send a confirmation note the day before I got there. "Hi Mark," he replied, two days later. "I use a public PC only and cannot check my email every day." This struck me as a little odd for a professor of physics. I agreed to telephone him at home when I arrived at the Braunschweig train station. It was an autumn Tuesday, but Kühne said he'd be home all day.

My taxi dropped me off in front of an apartment block. I pressed the buzzer, and Kühne met me at the door. He was in his early forties, frightfully thin, with sunken freckled cheeks and thinning reddish hair with flecks of white in it. His old striped sweater hung loose on him. I thought of something the organizer of the Atlantis conferences had told me: "We invite Kühne every time, but he says he has no money." We shook hands and he led me into his one-bedroom apartment. I'd been up late the night before and had caught a train at dawn, so I was hoping he'd offer me a cup of coffee and warm up with a little get-to-know-you chitchat. Instead, he motioned for me to take a seat and sat down across from me as if ready to play chess.

Between us was a coffee table covered with books, maps, and papers. The piles were so precisely lined up that they might have been laid out with surveying tools. A pen and paper had been attached to a clipboard for my use. Kühne sat up very straight on the edge of the sofa and folded his hands in his lap, then pushed the clipboard slightly in my direction.

"So, you have questions about my Atlantis theory," he said.

"Um, yes. How did you become interested in Atlantis?"

"That was when I was a child, about ten years old. I read a cartoon book, a duck story where he had discovered Atlantis in the deep sea. This was the book here, just a moment." He stood up and took two steps to his bookcase. One entire shelf appeared to be taken up by a row of identical bound volumes, presumably physics journals of some sort. Did he just say *duck* story? Maybe *düch* was a German word I could look up later, some category of Bavarian folklore. "It was this one here. You know it, perhaps?"

He opened the book, *The Secret of Atlantis*, and pointed out a cartoon of Scrooge McDuck, Donald's wealthy uncle, encountering a vast undersea city inhabited by men-fish. I was indeed familiar with this work, having read it in the third grade. It had not, to the best of my recollection, been footnoted in his *Antiquity* article.

"I bet that's just what Plato had in mind," I said, an uncaffeinated man's sad attempt at a joke. Kühne stared at me blankly for two seconds.

"They are looking for a coin they have lost," he said. "This is the story." He placed the book back in its assigned spot on the shelf. "Then I looked up in the encyclopedia that Atlantis exists outside of the cartoon book. We know this because Plato reported on it." Kühne began his boyhood research reading books from his local library that placed Atlantis in unlikely spots such as the Bahamas and England, before finding Jürgen Spanuth's *Atlantis of the North*. Spanuth's theory posited that Atlantis had existed on the island Helgoland, in the North Sea off of Germany.

Kühne told me he wasn't convinced by Spanuth's book, but he was impressed by two of his arguments. "First, Plato does not write only of Atlantis but also of its opponent, Athens. Spanuth thinks the Athens Plato describes is of the Mycenaean time"—that is, of the Greek Bronze Age between 1600 and 1100 BC. Plato's story is really a tale of two cities, but this fact rarely comes up in discussions about Atlantis.

"Also," Kühne continued, "Spanuth says the war Plato describes is a war between the Sea Peoples and Egypt."

Like Atlantis, the Sea Peoples are one of the great unsolved mysteries of antiquity. Hieroglyphs on the walls of an ancient Nile temple tell the story of two invasions of Egypt during the thirteenth and twelfth centuries BC. The attacks were launched by a fearsome confederation of armies who arrived in boats from the Mediterranean. Kühne's *Antiquity* article had carried forward Spanuth's idea that the Sea Peoples were transformed into the Atlanteans sometime between their defeat and Plato's writing of the *Timaeus*.

Intrigued by Spanuth's new interpretation, Kühne tried to locate Atlantis. "Plato said exactly where Atlantis was," he told me. "In the Atlantic Sea, beyond the Strait of Gibraltar, facing the Gaderian country. This is pretty clearly west of Gibraltar, south of Spain, or north of Morocco. Of course it cannot be in the center of the Atlantic Ocean because it is impossible, geologically. Plato described a great rectangular plain surrounded by mountains, but the capital of Atlantis was situated on the south coast, which later sank and became a mud sea. Where is the south coast in front of Gibraltar? What about Spain or Portugal?"

I assumed Kühne's questions were rhetorical, since we were not actually having a conversation. He was delivering a monologue that sounded like a very technical PowerPoint presentation without the diversion of the visual aids. He had been speaking nonstop for about forty-five minutes. His body language was pure FORTRAN.

"The great plain that Plato described should be in Spain, between Cádiz and the border with Portugal, southwest of Seville. Plato also described the capital of Atlantis within the plain as fifty stades from the coast." About nine kilometers, or six miles. "So you look nine kilometers from the southwest coast and you are directly in the marshes of the Doñana Park."

Kühne removed a map from one of his piles and unfolded it on the table. He began to describe in detail the various features of the landscape in Doñana—marshes, rivers, dunes. I thought to interject and mention that I'd seen all these things in person, but Kühne seemed to be building momentum toward something. I wasn't sure if I could stop him anyway. Finally, pointing to a spot I recognized from Werner Wickboldt's satellite photos, he said, "And this is what I thought was the Temple of Poseidon. This was my hypothesis ten years ago, yes. I'm not certain now if this idea was right."

The scientist whose article in *Antiquity* had launched two major projects in Doñana was having second thoughts about his theory! This detail had been left out of the *Finding Atlantis* documentary. Kühne's thinking had evolved. He still thought Tartessos had been real. Atlantis was proving to be a little more complicated.

"What changed your mind?" I asked.

"Okay, first I say why I believe that Atlantis was not *only* fiction," he said. Kühne explained that several of the details Plato gives about ancient Athens matched up with the Bronze Age city. For example, a long-lost spring that he locates on the Acropolis was rediscovered in the twentieth century. It had been smothered by an earthquake around 1200 BC. "Plato said that because of this earthquake, people who know the art of writing disappeared." Scholars of ancient history agree that after an unexplained societal upheaval, Greece fell into a long period of illiteracy that also began around 1200 BC. Plato writes that before this cataclysm, the Acropolis had been many times its current size, stretching from the River Ilisos to its tributary the Eridanos, a distance of nearly a mile. "Of course, Plato cannot be entirely right because the Acropolis should be as large as Athens of his time. An impossibility, much too large. So Plato had a bit of fantasy. But it is clear he wrote about Athens and no city elsewhere."

As for the Atlanteans, Kühne said, the priests of Saïs in Egypt had told Solon the story of "the war against the Sea Peoples, also about 1200 BC. These descriptions exist today in Medinet Habu in a temple." This temple is part of the vast Theban necropolis built along the Nile. Its hieroglyphs have been a primary source of Egyptian history since the decoding of the Rosetta stone in the nineteenth century. "The similarities are that both the Atlanteans and the Sea Peoples came from islands; that they ruled over Libya; that they had armies, a strong navy, and a large number of troops; that they fought against all eastern Mediterranean countries; that they finally lost the war; and after the war there occurred floods and earthquakes." Or at least the hieroglyphs could be interpreted that way.

"But it is not exactly the same because Plato wrote that the Atlanteans had triremes"—Greek warships with oars—"but the Sea Peoples had sailing boats. The Atlanteans had chariots that could not move without horses. The Sea Peoples had carts and no horses, but oxen. And of course the Sea Peoples were beaten by the Egyptians, but the Atlanteans were beaten by Athens. So I don't think that Plato has written about historical truths but has either taken historical truth and heavily distorted it or he made a fiction out of it."

Kühne spoke excellent English—all Germans I met seemed to speak excellent English—but he pronounced the names of ancient peoples and places in his native accent. He rattled off long, comprehensive lists from memory. When he started rapidly naming the many tribes that had lived in the Middle East at the time of the Sea Peoples invasion, I couldn't understand anything he said (not even weeks later when I repeatedly listened to a recording of it while simultaneously reviewing my interview notes and scanning websites about ancient history). It was a lot more detail than my tired brain could process. I thought about the three flights I had the next day, a twelve-hour journey to the Greek islands via Munich and Athens. I wondered if they served good coffee in Greece. It occurred to me that I needed to use the facilities.

"Rainer, may I use your bathroom?"

"And now we see an interesting thing!" he said, taking out a new stack of photographs.

Maybe I could wait. "What's that?"

"When you look here, the cities have no similarity to Atlantis. No large concentric circles. No harbor. No triremes. Chariots, yes, perhaps. But everything else is completely different. No large plain. No channels. So something must be wrong."

"So what you're saying is it's not really possible to search for Atlantis."

"It depends. Can you search for Gotham City in the Batman comic? Of course, if you have only the Batman comic, you will say no. But if you dig it out, you can find New York. So is it Gotham City or not? If you know nothing of Gotham City you say, New York found. If you know New York first, and not Gotham City, you would say this is New York but not Gotham City. It depends on your point of view. If you know about Atlantis but not the historical facts, some people would say it is Atlantis."

I wasn't so sure about Kühne's either/or distinction; he seemed to be saying the Atlantis tale had to be either completely true or false. At the very least the Sea Peoples deserved a closer look. Instead of expressing my concerns, I asked again if I could use the bathroom. Kühne ignored the question and removed a satellite photo of Doñana from his pile and started to point out microscopic things he saw in it.

"Where did you find this picture?" I asked, crossing my legs.

He raised his head, startled by the interruption. "It is from the Internet. I don't know where. I lost it." He returned to pointing out features on the satellite photo. I couldn't sit through another laundry list.

"How did you happen to publish that first article in *Antiquity*?"

Kühne looked up and smiled. "It was luck! Hee hee! I tried to publish something in *Antiquity* when I was twenty-two years old. I had not much success. It was rejected. Then in 2003 I restarted it with the idea that Atlantis maybe was referred to as Tartessos. I was rather certain then that they were the same."

"And now?" I asked.

"Now? Mmmm, maybe it really was only Tartessos." He pulled a new satellite photo from his stack. "Where are the circular harbors, the inner rings?"

"Hmm, good point. Rainer, I really need to use the bathroom."

"This is only a cross section . . ."

"RAINER, I NEED TO USE THE BATHROOM," I said, standing up.

Kühne stood up, too. "The bathroom, yes, it is in the hallway."

As I was returning to my seat, I noticed that Kühne's neatly made bed was covered with stuffed animals, lined up in a neat row. Kühne was still standing, like an android in sleep mode while awaiting my return.

"Rainer, what do your friends and family think about your interest in Atlantis?" I asked, sitting down.

"They don't know much about it. My parents are not scholars and friends are few. Of course I had students when I was doing physics. But they were talking about physics and not about Atlantis. I'm also staying alone for twenty years. My personality is a loner. Other people cannot be alone but I can. I have a great theory about magnetic monopoles. This is a generalization of quantum electrodynamics and also of general relativity. My paper was published in a scientific journal, but the prestige is nearly zero. It does not help to find a job. But I have the physics theory and maybe in one hundred years someone will prove it. Why not! Ha ha!"

"Maybe."

"Other people also publish their theories not in the best journals but they are confirmed now." He mentioned Alfred Wegener and Gregor Mendel, respectively the discoverers of continental drift and genetics. If Galileo and Copernicus are the icons of heretical Renaissance thinking, then Wegener and Mendel, whose ideas were rejected as too radical by scientists with more prestigious credentials, are their modern heirs. They were the patron saints of all amateur researchers whose work isn't taken seriously, which would include almost anyone interested in Atlantis. "So maybe not during my lifetime but maybe after I am gone."

"What about teaching physics?"

"I have given up on finding work. Two years ago, I learned I have Asperger's syndrome. It is a mild form of autism."

Ah, okay. That explained Kühne's ability to examine near-identical satellite photos for hours on end and pick out tiny bits of data. The memorized lists of names. The missed social cues. I thought of my own autistic son and his habits that seemed odd to those who didn't live with him. The last three hours were starting to make a lot more sense. The exasperation that had been building inside me gave way to embarrassment.

"That is why I can give a monologue on Atlantis for two hours but I can't talk about the weather," he continued. "I can't make small talk. I can't work with others in a group. When I was a boy I could focus on my exam for two hours like I was somewhere else. Then I would give it to my teacher and not remember what I had written."

Kühne didn't seem sad when he told me these things; he was just sharing some interesting facts. I asked what his reaction had been to the Freund documentary.

"The producer, Simcha Jacobovici, he is not a scientist. He does some speculations about a tomb of Jesus and so on." That was another of Jacobovici's documentaries, *The Lost Tomb of Jesus*, which sounded like the kind of film I would have loved in grade school. "First he asked Richard Freund, have you found Atlantis? And Freund said yes. 'The circle here is Atlantis and this cross section here is the harbors,' so he had the confirmation that this is Atlantis.

"Then he asked me: 'Is this Atlantis?' And I said, well, no. Maybe it was Tartessos and Tartessos was a model of Atlantis. Then, Jacobovici asked Juan Villarias-Robles and Sebastián Celestino: 'Have you found Atlantis?' They said, 'NO! We have found something of the Middle Ages. Of the Muslim period.'

"Of course Jacobovici must have money to pay his film team. He cannot make a film about 'We have found here some rectangles and a circle, maybe it is something of the Middle Ages.' No one will see that film. So the film is made and they have to sell it somehow; they call it *Finding Atlantis*. Richard Freund says that it is Atlantis, so he is shown in front. I said Atlantis, no, but maybe Tartessos, so I am shown a bit smaller."

"I think you were on for three seconds," I said. Kühne makes one brief appearance in the documentary, standing uncomfortably in the Andalusian sun wearing a dark baggy suit amid the empty dry-season marshes.

"I counted it, fifteen seconds. Yes. You see me walking for twelve seconds and for three seconds I say the sentence 'I am standing here in Doñana.' It sounds like the first sentence I ever spoke, when I was two and a half years old: 'Rainer has fallen out of the bed.' That is what 'I am standing here in Doñana' sounds like. It is so stupid! I have a theory about Tartessos and instead I say 'I am standing here in Doñana.'"

Much of the appeal of Kühne's original *Antiquity* article had been his demonstration that the shapes of Wickboldt's satellite photos matched closely with Plato's oddly specific measurements. It occurred to me that someone with Kühne's brilliant mathematical mind and powers of concentration might have insight into Plato's use of numbers. I asked what he saw in them.

"See this large plain?" he asked, sketching a rectangle with the numbers 3,000 and 2,000 along the sides. He traced the perimeter with his finger. "Ten thousand stades. The Greek word for 10,000 is *myriad*, which also means 'largest possible number.'"

"And?" I leaned forward expectantly.

"I think Plato maybe made a joke."

CHAPTER THIRTEEN

The Fundamentalist

Elsewhere in Braunschweig

Shortly after Critias concludes the first part of the Atlantis tale in the *Timaeus*, Timaeus warns Socrates that he should not be surprised if certain topics—such as the gods or the creation of the universe—cannot be explained precisely. Humans are flawed. Unlike the tale of Atlantis, the account of the cosmos he's about to give should be seen not as the truth but as "a likely story." Only after my meeting with Kühne, as I rode a crosstown tram through central Braunschweig, did it occur to me that "a likely story" was the catchphrase of another famous cartoon waterfowl, Daffy Duck. The man I was meeting, Werner Wickboldt, had formulated a hypothesis that differed from Kühne's in only one major respect—Wickboldt considered Tartessos-as-Atlantis to be an extremely likely story.

As with Kühne, Wickboldt was not quite what I had expected. I knew him only as a semiretired teacher of dental technology who had initially been reluctant to speak with me and was prone to leaving crabby rebuttals to the comprehensive comments Kühne posted whenever his *Antiquity* article was cited on Atlantis-related web pages. "Kühne adopted my hypothesis and made it for his own" was the typical response to one encyclopedic Kühne post. "Inside his article he refers to me in an irritating manner."

My fears of spending an afternoon with some crotchety *Burgomeister* evaporated when Wickboldt rode up, smiling, on his bike. He insisted on taking me for a tour of downtown Braunschweig before talking about Atlantis. The city had suffered a day and night of Atlantis-caliber destruction courtesy of the Royal Air Force late in World War II, after which its charming medieval center had burned for almost three days. One building, easily identifiable from a photo in which Hitler attends an early Nazi rally, was actually a perfect replica completed in 2004, with a shopping mall inside. (This seemed like a nice reminder of Plato's concerns about confusing perception with reality.) The rest of the modern city center built in its place looked like a case study of the sort of urban planning cautionary tale that keeps Jane Jacobs books in print. "They say that this part of the city was destroyed *after* the war," Wickboldt told me with a snort.

As it turned out, the past decade's Atlantology renaissance could be traced back to a single meeting—a play date held at Wickboldt's home in 1988. "My son went to the same school as Kühne," Wickboldt told me as we strolled past some buildings that someone, presumably under the influence of hallucinogens, had decided would look nice covered entirely with colorful pop art illustrations. "He visited my home once in the afternoon, and we began to talk about Atlantis. We talked from four to ten." Wickboldt developed his ideas over the following years, and a local newspaper wrote about his theory in 2003. Kühne published his *Antiquity* article, based on very similar ideas, in 2004.

Where the two men had once shared virtually identical hypotheses, they now differed on one key point. Wickboldt had not lost faith.

"I believe in the original text, even the part that someone got it from the priest of Egypt," Wickboldt told me when I asked which parts of the story he doubted. "I'm convinced that Plato reported true European history." Wickboldt saw no reason to think Plato's numbers shouldn't be taken literally. The shapes he'd identified on the satellite photos were probably vanished temples, no matter what Juan Villarias-Robles and his team had found there.

Wickboldt's literal rendering of the *Timaeus* and *Critias* reminded me of strict constructionist judges who believe the US Constitution is a sacred document that should be interpreted only as its writers intended. This isn't to say he, like certain Supreme Court justices, didn't have his own esoteric explications of key passages. He believed that Plato used the word *island* to describe a river delta, such as the one at the mouth of the Guadalquivir where ancient sources had located Tartessos. When the standard Greek stade didn't quite match up with the measurements of Doñana Park, he found an old Portuguese stade that did fit. One of the more interesting of Wickboldt's adjustments was the idea that Plato's nine thousand years was correct, but that "the Egyptians used a calendar of twelve thirty-day periods plus five separate days," he explained to me in a loud second-story café. "Out of ancient texts referring to Manetho we learn that the Egyptians call thirty days a year."

Manetho was a great third-century-BC Egyptian historian. If one divides 9,000 by 12 and counts back from the date Solon probably visited Egypt, the result falls within the thirteenth century BC— roughly the same time period as the invasion of the Sea Peoples and the earthquake at the Acropolis. "It's possible that this was the time of Atlantis's collapse and that Tartessos was built on top of it," Wickboldt said.

Wickboldt invited me to his home for dinner, but I was fading fast after a long day. I still needed to find my way to Hanover for my morning flight. He listed a bunch of obscure German sources that I might want to investigate, then mentioned one that sounded familiar. "You should really take a look at the Parian Marble," he said

as I paid the check. Wickboldt was an enthusiastic talker, but he became even more excited by this new topic. "Part of it is at Oxford
University, and the oldest part is now lost, but they have a drawing
of it. There's an English translation."

Tony O'Connell had told me about the Parian Marble, or Parian
Chronicle, with much less skepticism than he had for most such evidence. The stele was a chronology of important events that had been
carved on the Greek island of Paros, probably in the year 263 BC.
(The two oldest chunks had been sold to a British earl in the early
seventeenth century. The older of these was subsequently lost, a fact
that never seemed to be raised by British politicians who insisted
that the Elgin Marbles taken from the Parthenon in Athens couldn't
possibly be returned because the Greeks didn't know how to properly care for them.) Its timeline goes all the way back to Cecrops, the
mythical first king of Athens, dating his accession to approximately
1581 BC. Like most things regarding Cecrops, though, that date
probably was not meant to be taken as truth. According to legend he
had been born from the earth rather than human parents and had a
tail like a snake.

The reason the Parian Chronicle was so interesting to Wickboldt
was that its chronology seems to match several names and events
that Plato mentions in the *Timaeus* and *Critias*. The priest at Saïs also
names Cecrops as the oldest of Athenian kings and reports that Athens had been drowned three times since the sinking of Atlantis. The
second of these floods was that of Deucalion, which the Parian
Marble dates to 1478 BC. Even if the Parian dates aren't precisely
correct—as seems extremely likely—one of these deluges might be
linked to the inundations of Athens and Atlantis. And if that were
the case, other important details might be found outside of Plato's
work. But first one had to know where to look.

CHAPTER FOURTEEN

The Pillars of Heracles

Gibraltar

If the concentric circles are Atlantis's defining geological character-istic, then Plato's careful placement of the lost kingdom opposite (or outside, or *pro*—Tony O'Connell had been correct when he warned me the translation of ancient Greek is not an exact science) the Pillars of Heracles is the number one geographic clue. Hard evidence of At-lantis was proving so difficult to come by—even evidence which, like the location of the Pillars, is debated by Atlantologists—that when I'd found myself with an extra day before departing Spain I couldn't re-sist a sudden compulsion to see them.

The trip south from Seville was strangely dreamlike, as long drives sometimes are when one travels alone. After an hour on a brand-new, empty toll road, I had passed fewer cars than I had gi-gantic windmills that looked like upturned boat propellers. I stopped for a coffee at a roadside cafe where at 9:00 A.M. a dozen men were drinking large brandies over ice and the proprietor's wife was doing a brisk business selling bunches of fresh-picked asparagus as thick as my thigh.

I followed the road signs toward Cádiz[8] until the highway forked east, away from the Atlantic coast. Eventually, the hills of Andalusia flattened out into a road that wound through a series of southern Spanish towns: Los Barrios, San Roque, La Línea. And then suddenly, through the windshield, appeared one of the strangest sights on Earth: a fourteen-hundred-foot-high chunk of shale towering over the flat sea. I parallel-parked my car in Spain, dropped a few euros in the parking meter, and walked across the border into the United Kingdom.

Gibraltar's three square miles of overseas British territory are occupied primarily by the giant rock, with the remaining space essentially a 1950s London theme park. Double-decker buses carry British retirees around in circles, past red telephone booths and baton-twirling bobbies. Restaurants advertise fish and chips and full English breakfasts. On the day I arrived, banners everywhere saluted Queen Elizabeth II on her Diamond Jubilee. The British had been here for three hundred years; it was hard to imagine Gibraltar occupied by anyone else. But this coveted spot had been taken from the Spanish, who had in turn pushed out the Moors, the Islamic invaders who'd swept across the strait from Morocco and named the rock Jebel Tariq, or Mount of Tariq. Over time that name was corrupted into Gibraltar. The Vandals and Visigoths had taken the rock from

8 In addition to being another geographic clue to the location of Atlantis, Cádiz was the birthplace of one of its many ironies. Professional and amateur historians agree that the Library of Alexandria in Egypt was once the world's greatest repository of ancient knowledge and that among its many thousands of scrolls was information that today could confirm or refute the truth of Plato's Atlantis. (Part of its original collection was probably purchased from the library of Aristotle's school in Athens, the Lyceum.) According to one account, Rome's ambitious quaestor in Cádiz, Julius Caesar, one day stood inside a temple gazing at a statue of Alexander the Great. Looking upon the image of the man who'd conquered half the known world, Caesar vowed to equal his achievements. A little more than a decade later, having crossed the Rubicon with his army, Caesar laid siege to Alexandria, the city founded by Alexander as a center of Hellenistic learning and culture. During Caesar's attack he set fire to ships in Alexandria's harbor. The flames are believed to have spread all the way to the great library, destroying a large part of its collection.

the Romans, who'd taken it from the Carthaginians; Hannibal crossed his elephants near here on his way to attacking Rome.

The first recorded occupiers of Gibraltar were the mysterious Phoenicians, who built nearby a temple to the legendary Melqart, a hero associated with voyages to distant lands. The Greeks adopted Melqart as the god they called Heracles for their own worship before passing him on to the Romans. To the Greeks, Heracles was not just a traveler but also a strong man, a son of Zeus who was required to fulfill twelve labors as penance for a horrible crime. Among these labors was one with possible links to Atlantis: a journey to an island in the far west called Erytheia—a land that several pre-Platonic writers had equated with Tartessos and the lands beyond the Pillars. Here Heracles defeated the three-bodied giant Geryon and stole his cattle. In one Greek version of the Geryon myth, the Pillars mark the farthest and westernmost point of all Heracles's travels.

In the spirit of Herculean tasks, I decided to walk up to the top of the Rock rather than take the cable car. Halfway up, I was greeted by a group of small Gibraltar apes, the only such primates on the European continent and, some have suggested, possible descendants of those that King Arganthonios once sent from Tartessos back to Hiram of Tyre. Seeing that I had no food to share, they turned heel and abandoned me for a minivan discharging a load of sunburned Brits. At the very top of the Rock I paid five euros to enter the special Pillars of Hercules viewing area, marked by the ugliest piece of public statuary I'd ever seen. It appeared to be a gigantic two-columned Soviet bowling trophy.

The view across, however, was astounding. Through a light haze I could see Jebel Musa, the twin pillar of rock on the coast of Morocco. (Some believe that Gibraltar's less famous African partner was Monte Hacho, a similar rock farther east.) It wasn't hard to imagine that this spot would have marked the end of the known world, or that whoever held it would have possessed a huge strategic advantage at a time when most great Mediterranean powers were built on strong navies. Greek knowledge of what lay beyond the Straits was certainly limited in Plato's time. Herodotus wrote, "I have never seen nor, despite my efforts, been able to learn from anyone whether there is an ocean beyond Europe." This ignorance was due at least in part to the Carthaginians severely restricting their access to passage through the Pillars starting around 500 BC. It's possible that Plato heard false information that the Carthaginians, who ruled the western Mediterranean during his lifetime, had spread about what lay in the unknown ocean. Plato could have heard these tales while visiting Syracuse, since Carthage also controlled half of Sicily.

There was another possibility that I knew I had to face. Perhaps Plato was talking about another of the many sets of Pillars that Tony O'Connell had mentioned. If Plato had been referring to, say, the Bosphorus connecting the Black Sea and the Mediterranean, or the Strait of Messina between Sicily and the toe of Italy's boot (which Tony thought was likely), then Atlantis could have existed much farther east. If that were true, it would be hard to find a stronger candidate than one particular group of islands just south of Sicily, rich in myth and history, that had been well-known to the ancient Greeks centuries before Plato's time.

CHAPTER FIFTEEN

The Mysterious Island

Malta

A question occurred to me staring down at the blue Mediterranean from my window seat on Air Malta. Even if someone proved tomorrow that the Maltese archipelago *had* been Plato's Atlantis, would that discovery squeeze onto a list of the top five strange-but-true facts about Malta? Perhaps not. The oldest known structures in Europe can be found on Malta's two main islands, although geologically the islands are actually part of Africa (and sit farther south than Tunis). Malta's thriving population vanished around 2500 BC for unexplained reasons. The apostle Saint Paul, who'd been blinded by a vision of Jesus on the road to Damascus, shipwrecked in Malta in AD 60, on his way to what would be his martyrdom in Rome. The Knights of Saint John, a still-extant religious order that dates back to the eleventh-century Crusades, were granted Malta as their private headquarters in 1530 by the Holy Roman emperor Charles V, to whom they paid an annual tribute of one Maltese falcon. The knights' presence did not dissuade Turkish invaders from attacking the Maltese island of Gozo in 1551 and dragging all five thousand of its residents off into slavery. Even today, Malta is home to unsolved mysteries. Judging from my nonscientific observations, it has the world's highest per capita rates of fat men and beautiful women.

I was welcomed to Malta by a familiar face. Since the mental image I'd kept of Tony O'Connell was of him bundled up in a sweater against the chilly Irish spring, it was a little hard to recognize the man who greeted me in the blinding sunshine outside the baggage terminal in sandals and shorts. He seemed to be in an excellent mood. "I don't suppose you've found Atlantis already," he said. "If you have, Anton certainly won't be too pleased."

Anton was Dr. Anton Mifsud, full-time pediatrician and part-time Atlantologist. Mifsud was the preeminent proponent of the theory that Malta was the original site of Atlantis and had published a well-argued book to support it. Tony kept a small apartment in the Saint Julian's Bay neighborhood (Malta's climate was beloved by northern Europeans) and had become friends with Mifsud through their shared interest. Tony had sent me a copy of Mifsud's book, *Malta: Echoes of Plato's Island*. He had arranged for the three of us to have dinner once Mifsud returned from his rounds.

At Tony's apartment he and I looked through photos of his and Paul's civil partnership ceremony. Tony pointed out the new $100 suit he'd purchased for the occasion. "Ah, look at that old potato-head," he said, pointing to himself. "We went out to the pub that night and everyone was lovely. Even the village homophobe wished us well."

Mifsud, I learned that evening, was the sort of pediatrician who got up each day at 4:00 A.M. to ride his bike for two hours (he was an exception to my fat Maltese men theory), then made house calls for twelve hours, driving all over the main island. He was in his early sixties, bald with a neatly trimmed goatee, and wore small rimless eyeglasses. Even after a full day of battling Malta's awful traffic and inoculating screaming toddlers, he vibrated with the energy of a teenage boy. Mifsud cackled at his own jokes and had the infectious habit of affirming his own statements. A single "yes?" at the end of a sentence meant "Do you follow me?" The declarative "yes" served as an exclamation point. The double "Yes? Yes!" conveyed the feeling of "I know—I couldn't believe it either!"

The evening was warm. We sat at a table near an open window and ordered drinks. I asked Mifsud how a busy physician had become attracted to Atlantis.

"There was a friend of mine; he told me he was investigating the angle that Malta was Atlantis. It had been ingrained in me the idea that Atlantis was a myth, yes? Of course I laughed in his face. I wasn't expecting him to be such a nerd. He said, 'I thought you were a scientist. Scientists are not biased.' So I said, 'In three weeks I will prove to you that Malta could never have been Atlantis.' That was in 1999 and I have been investigating since!"

In 2000, Mifsud published *Echoes* with the help of his son and two friends. Its preface offers a sort of manifesto for serious, but uncredentialed, Atlantologists. The best type of archaeologist to search for Atlantis, he explains, is neither the quack nor the professional but the amateur whose "principal motivation is to search for the truth" rather than perpetuating the "preconceived notions" of the Establishment.

The truth as Mifsud had deduced it was this: Thousands of years ago, Malta had been a much larger landmass but had shrunk due to rising sea levels. Between 3500 BC and 2500 BC, the Mediterranean's oldest known temple-building civilization lived in the Maltese archipelago. After this society's sudden demise due to a probable natural disaster around 2200 BC according to Mifsud, the Egyptians recorded in their temples memories of the lost culture of Malta. These stories were then passed along to Solon as the accounts that became Plato's Atlantis tale.

Part of what made Mifsud's theory intriguing was the extraordinary amount of original research he'd done. If he had a native

Maltese's tendency to root for the home team, he also had a philologist's passion for finding the earliest possible sources. "No one ever looks at the original Greek," Mifsud said. "Unfortunately, every time a manuscript is copied, the editor puts his own interpretation on it. Plato wrote in 360 BC. His manuscript probably ended up in the library at Alexandria. In 400 AD, it was transferred to Constantinople"—the new capital of Western thought after the fall of Rome and banning of pagan temples in Alexandria—"and stayed there until about 1450, when Constantinople was taken and the manuscripts returned to Europe. Most of them were taken by the Medicis and they commissioned this guy, Marsilio Ficino, to translate the Greek into Latin." The Medicis had sponsored a school in Florence, based on Plato's Academy, that was one of the primary catalysts of the Italian Renaissance. Its members, led by Ficino, produced new Latin translations of all Plato's works. "And I have that one now, the earliest version. Yes? Yes! I saw it at an exhibition in Florence."

The most obvious problem with the Malta-as-Atlantis theory is the location of the Pillars of Heracles. Malta sits much closer to Athens than to the Strait of Gibraltar. Mifsud asked a classics professor at the University of Malta for his interpretation of Plato's description and was very pleased with the result. "The words Plato uses are *Steles of Hercules*," Mifsud told me. A stele is a stone slab, inscribed or decorated, like the warrior stele Richard Freund had gotten excited about in Spain. "The proper word for *pillars* is something else. So the Steles of Hercules are not the Pillars of Hercules. Even if they were the Pillars of Hercules, the Pillars are only recently situated at the Strait of Gibraltar."

"How do you know that?" I asked.

"I'll tell you where I got it from—I went to Herculaneum!" Because even the most durable papyrus becomes brittle and disintegrates after a few centuries, the Herculaneum papyri are some of the few premedieval manuscripts that exist. Hundreds of blackened cylinders were found during the excavation of a wealthy Roman's villa that was buried under a hundred feet of ash when Mount Vesuvius erupted in AD 79. (The same eruption smothered Pompeii.) These rolls turned out to be a vast library of Greek and Roman literature. Since the villa was excavated in the 1750s, hundreds of these delicate manuscripts have been deciphered. "Three of the papyri"—by authors other than Plato—"show that the Pillars of Hercules were situated in the central Mediterranean," Mifsud said.

Appetizers arrived. "Dig in, lads, and grab something," Tony said, pushing the plate in our direction. "Whoever wants the prawn can have it."

Mifsud continued. "There is another manuscript that confirms Plato, yes? Yes! Eumalos of Cyrene."

"It's true; he did," Tony said, nodding in agreement. Eumalos of Cyrene was an obscure source who aside from a few brief mentions in nineteenth-century literature, only Mifsud, of all the Atlantologists, seemed to know about. (Mifsud had discovered him in an appendix to an 1830 guide to Malta, written in Italian.) Eumalos was a Greek copyist living in North Africa two or three generations after Plato's lifetime. According to the 1830 appendix, Eumalos once transcribed a text stating that "the famous . . . Ogyge was the king of Atlantis, the island that once existed between Libya and Sicily and was submerged. This large island was known as Decapolis, Atlantika, by our forefathers of Cyrene as well as by the ancient Greeks." Ogyge (usually called Ogyges) lent his name to Ogygia, the island where Odysseus is kept by the nymph Calypso in the *Odyssey*. Several ancient writers hypothesized that Ogygia was actually Malta, which the guidebook's translation of Eumalos notes "is nothing more than the summit of the Mount of Atlantika."

If the translation of the Eumalos manuscript was real, it was an incredible piece of evidence—a contemporary of Plato sending a certified letter from twenty-four hundred years ago saying, essentially,

"Atlantis was real, and it was Malta. Best regards, Eumalos of Cyrene." Unfortunately, there was no way to confirm the credibility of Eumalos any more than one could confirm Solon's notes from Saïs, regardless of how enthusiastic Mifsud was about him. The good doctor may have been a man of science, but he did gravitate toward interpretations that favored Malta. I later called a retired classics professor who'd written a book about the Pillars of Heracles. He'd never heard of Eumalos, he insisted *stele* and *pillar* meant the same thing for the purposes of Atlantis, and he saw only two logical reasons for Plato to refer to the Pillars of Heracles: Either he literally meant the Strait of Gibraltar or he metaphorically meant a spot beyond the edge of the known world.

"Anyway, I know that Tony favors the Michael Hübner hypothesis," Mifsud said, and winked at me. Hübner was the German Atlantologist who had used data analysis of Plato's descriptions to narrow down the possible locations for Atlantis. I'd seen his presentation online, and it was impressive. Hübner believed Atlantis had existed along Morocco's Atlantic coast.

Tony sighed and tilted his head toward Mifsud. "What I *said* was that Hübner presented his case very well. There is one thing in there that really annoys me. Well, a number of things."

One of the things Hübner's theory lacked—that virtually all Atlantis theories lacked—was a reasonable explanation for the checkerboard canals that Plato describes. For Mifsud, this was an ace to play. One of Malta's chief mysteries is an enormous network of crisscrossing tracks, known as cart ruts, etched deep into its soft limestone. They are believed to be at least four thousand years old and are found all over the main island and its satellite, Gozo. Some cart ruts appear to run between temples; others disappear into the sea. They have defied explanation for centuries. (*Chariots of the Gods* author Erich von Däniken suggested they are evidence of alien takeoffs and landings. Perhaps Malta was a hub for extraterrestrials making connecting flights to Mu.) Mifsud was convinced that these were the remnants of the incredible irrigation system that brought water from the mountains to Atlantis's fertile plain, as Plato described it.

"In Malta there are two archaeologists who give a function to the cart ruts," Mifsud said. "One says they were used for the transport of agricultural produce. The other says they were also used for the transport of water, exactly as Plato said. Yes!"

"I don't care what she said," said Tony. "We've been over this. She's wrong."

"If archaeologists are stating something that fits into the theory, why fight with the archaeologists?" Mifsud said.

"How can water flow *uphill*?" Tony asked.

"An uphill is also a downhill!"

"Here's a question for both of you," I said. "Did the dates we got from Plato arrive to us uncorrupted, or did someone screw them up a little along the way?"

"No, no, no," said Mifsud. "I think Plato meant what he said about the nine thousand years, and this I say on the strength of a manuscript I found in the Vatican Secret Archives. I can't talk about it but it was *really* trustworthy." The Vatican Secret Archives, while not actually as secret as their cloak-and-dagger name implies (researchers can petition for access), are said to contain more than fifty miles of shelving containing items going back to the early Middle Ages.

"You also have the fact that Plato mentions nine thousand or eight thousand years, two or three times," Tony said. "So it would have had to be corrupted or interfered with on a number of occasions rather than just a slip of a pen."

"What if Solon or the priest at Saïs just got it wrong?" I asked. "Maybe one of them hadn't slept well or had whatever awful food poisoning you could get in 600 BC. The ancient Egyptians drank beer, right? Maybe they were hungover."

"Basically, we have to work with what we've got: Plato's writings,"

Tony said. "You can speculate all you like and still it's only speculation. Obviously some degree of reinterpretation is required, and that's it. There's nothing else you can do. Anton is bringing in corroboration from other sources that enhances his interpretation."

"There are people who say, 'Plato didn't mean this; he meant something else,'" Mifsud said. "And if we do that we can make a dog into a cat. So I wouldn't want to tinker with anything that Plato said."

This wasn't *entirely* accurate. As with his reinterpretations of Plato's words *Pillars of Heracles* and their location, Mifsud was willing to correct information that he felt others had gotten wrong. His explanation for the nine thousand years was that Plato had actually used the Greek word for seasons.

"Plato says Egyptian art started ten thousand years ago, but it didn't. It started at the beginning of the dynasties, 2900 BC, yes?" The start of the Second Dynasty, which most people would recognize as "classical" Egypt, has been dated to approximately 2890 BC. (Mifsud had spent several weeks traveling in western Egypt and co-authored an engrossing book about a mysterious Egyptian statuette found in Malta in 1713. His output as a part-time writer was enviable, and I half hoped his productivity was pharmaceutically induced, and that he might have some extra samples of whatever he was taking.) Mifsud had also sponsored three carbon datings on Malta that showed some sort of cataclysm, possibly a tsunami, had hit the islands in 2200 BC.

The year 2200 BC is another big question mark in ancient history. Around that time, for unknown reasons, societies collapsed more or less simultaneously in Mesopotamia, Egypt, Crete, Palestine, the Indus Valley, and possibly China. A gap appears in Malta's archaeological record as well. Mifsud used information from the writings of the second-century-BC Roman historian Aemilius Sura to date precisely the fall of Atlantis in Malta. "If you use his dates, you get 2198 BC. Yes! I'm proposing 2200 BC. Is that too good? Just two years!"

Mifsud had recently returned from his trip to the Vatican archives, searching for definitive proof of the Eumalos manuscript.

"Did you find anything?" I asked.

"No. I did find other interesting things. Like the death of one of the popes. There was an autopsy and I found it."

"You found an autopsy?" Pope John Paul I's sudden death in 1978 had inspired some Atlantis-quality speculation of its own at my Catholic school, largely based on the church's insistence that Vatican protocol prohibited papal autopsies. Perhaps Mifsud had stumbled onto an older, equally juicy mystery. "Was there foul play?" I asked.

"No. This pope, they found a perforated duodenal ulcer. Because he was a man who liked to eat and drink." Mifsud held his hands out to indicate a full papal belly. "Hee hee! I asked for photocopies and they did it, two pages."

"Another conspiracy theory disproven," Tony said.

"Are there things about the original Atlantis story that ring true to you?" I asked. I was thinking of Juan Villarias-Robles's notion of stripping away the contaminants to reach the original core of information. "To me, what sounds right are the mountains, the muddy shoals, the circular harbor, and the location outside the Pillars."

"Why do you say 'mountains'?" Mifsud asked, sounding a little defensive. "Plato said *montes*, which can mean either a mountain or a hill. He said there were settlements on top of them—far more likely on a hill. You don't need a mountain to shield a plain." He looked at Tony, who was shaking his head dubiously. "He's still not convinced."

I wasn't convinced, either. Plato had obviously described a range of majestic peaks, and the highest mountain anywhere near Malta was Etna in Sicily, sixty miles away. When I asked about the concentric rings, Mifsud gave a somewhat evasive answer about how they had "fragmented."

But here we came to a point that is rarely raised among Atlantologists, even if the general public takes it as a given: Any remnants of

Atlantis are likely to be found underwater. Malta had probably been connected to Sicily ten thousand years ago when the Ice Age ended. The relatively few miles of Mediterranean that now separate the islands are quite shallow. According to one recent geological survey, the site of Malta's coastal capital, Valletta, had been six miles inland twenty thousand years ago. Mifsud argued that the muddy shoals of Atlantis that Plato described are the same as the Sands of Syrtis, the shallow seas near the coast of North Africa. If you look at a map of the Mediterranean, you can see it is essentially two seas, with the western half much farther north than the eastern. According to Greek mythology, the Pillars with which Heracles had marked the limit of the known world bore the words NEC PLUS ULTRA—nothing further beyond. Because Malta sits almost exactly at the midpoint, it's possible that in 2200 BC it had marked a dangerous point past which little was known.

I wanted to see Malta's temples, and Mifsud, after a brief consultation of his calendar, agreed to schedule me into his Saturday afternoon, between individual visits to his four daughters, barring any pediatric emergencies. After dinner Tony and I stopped for a beer. Tony urged me to push Mifsud on the cart ruts. "Those ruts are his blind spot."

Tony was heading back to Ireland, so after I spent a night on his couch he helped me move my things over to a bed-and-breakfast that he informed me, with some delight, was a former brothel. That afternoon I caught the bus to the capital city of Valletta, named after Jean Parisot de la Vallette, a grandmaster of the Knights of Saint John. He had planned the city's construction in 1566, a year after the order had withstood the onslaught of the Great Siege of Malta. Not surprisingly, Valletta was laid out with defense in mind and still felt like a fortress. Its backstreets were narrow and shadowed, even at midday.

As I walked toward the National Museum of Archaeology, housewives lowered baskets from their apartments down to produce sellers on the sidewalks below, as if too busy watching for marauders to leave their posts for the grocery store.

A major reason why Malta is frequently floated as a site for Atlantis is that it is home to some of the oldest stone monuments in the Mediterranean region. Judging from the exhibits I saw at the archaeology museum, seemingly every time a new road was cut in Malta, an important prehistoric site was uncovered. Malta's earliest settlements have been dated to 5200 BC and some of its more impressive stone temples predate the Great Pyramids of Egypt by a thousand years. The architectural style of these megaliths is unlike that seen anywhere else.

I was primarily interested in the cart ruts. An entire room was devoted to them at the museum, including a life-size diorama of imitation grooves cut into fake stone, surely one of the world's least interesting exhibits not sponsored by an agricultural council. A video playing on an endless loop showed the world's preeminent cart rut expert, Dr. David Trump, standing at a spot known as Clapham Junction, ignoring (from my perspective, anyway) the controversy over whether they were the canals of Atlantis and asking instead whether they had been worn into the stone by wheels or by the runners of sledges. On the video Clapham Junction looked like a shopping mall parking lot after a heavy snowstorm, covered in deep intersecting tire tracks.

On my way out of the exhibit I noticed a display named "The Significance of Cartruts in Ancient Landscapes." One of its screens flashed a message that seemed to have been written by someone wearing a monocle and a too-tight ascot:

> The current intellectual debate over cart-ruts in the Maltese Islands is markedly divided between those who base

their arguments on an academic/scientific basis and others who divert from the ethics of academia and delve into speculative tabloid sensationalism.

I told Mifsud about this oblique challenge to his sleuthing the next day when he picked me up in front of my ex-brothel lodgings in his Opel Corsa. He wasn't surprised. "People don't like amateurs to meddle in archaeology. They think, why don't you stick to your medicine?" He said he had archaeologist friends who admitted they agreed with some of his unorthodox ideas but couldn't go on record publicly.

The Mediterranean rainy season had just begun, and the sky darkened quickly as we drove. Mifsud fiddled with the radio looking for a weather report. Almost everyone in Malta spoke English, and most people spoke Italian, too, but the Maltese language sounded nothing like either language, or any other I'd ever heard. "Our language is basically Semitic," Mifsud explained. "Originally it was Phoenician, and then we integrated with Muslims. There was no written form until about 1700."

We were heading toward the southwest coastline, where the most impressive megalithic temples are located. "Colin Renfrew, a professor of archaeology at Cambridge, established that the Maltese temples are the oldest in the world. He suggested that they are arranged in groups—one of them is aligned with the equinoxes," Mifsud told me. I'd seen an interview with Renfrew in which he seemed sincerely baffled by the fact that Malta's temples were virtually unknown despite the radiocarbon dating showing they were the oldest known free-standing structures in the world.

Mifsud's theory rested on the idea that thousands of years ago Malta had been much larger—large enough to hold a plain of Atlantean proportions. "Plato describes channels that are all over the plains, yes?" He pulled over—the Maltese drive on the left—and pointed to a rock bluff jutting out of the Mediterranean about two miles off the coast. "That island is called Filfla. The Turkish military used to use it for target practice. There are cart ruts that lead there from the main island. That shows that Filfla was occupied before the sea rose."

We pulled into the parking lot of the museum next to the Hagar Qim temple. "It looks like we'll get some rain," Mifsud said, opening the hatchback. "We'll do the museum first. I'll bring the umbrella."

Mifsud bounded up the steps to the museum and had already paid our admissions by the time I caught up to him. The first exhibit caught his attention. "There it is! The lizard!" He took a very expensive-looking camera out of his backpack and snapped a photo of a photo of a *Podarcis filfolensis*, a species of lizard found only on the Maltese islands and the nearby Pelagian islands. In his Atlantis book, Mifsud makes a convincing case that the lizard's dispersal proved the islands had once been connected as one landmass. Even Tony agreed that this was solid evidence.

We next stopped in front of some spirals carved into ancient stones. They looked a lot like the concentric circles on the Tartessian stele that Richard Freund had made so much of, but Mifsud paused only to point out, proudly, that while the legendary archaeologist Arthur Evans had said that Maltese spirals were imitations of those on Crete, the opposite now seems to be the case.

The next room held a tabletop scale model of the megaliths. Mifsud noted various impressive features. "These are the temples of the gods. The two main ones represent the sun and the moon. Let's go see them for real!" He placed a hand on my arm. "It's about five hundred meters walking uphill. Is that okay for you? Are you fit?"

We made the hike up to the temples, which were covered by what looked like a circus big top with open sides, there to protect the megaliths from the elements. The pockmarked limestone had been eroded by exposure to the salt air. "Since they were excavated the temples have been nearly eaten away," Mifsud said. What remained was fascinating, though.

The two temples of Hagar Qim and Mnajdra were each believed to have been constructed at least five thousand years ago. Their walls are rounded and the structures are subdivided into several rooms. Remnants of ancient animal sacrifices—like those the ten princes of Atlantis performed on their pillar of orichalcum—have been found near multiple altars. Some of these had been constructed with astronomical alignments. At sunrise on the summer solstice, Mifsud told me, a thin beam of light illuminates one of the temples at Mnajdra. Very *Raiders of the Lost Ark*.

"The sun rises and it just *shoots* down here!" Mifsud said. "I've seen it; the sun shines right here onto the altar."

"Wow. So do you think this was Plato's Temple of Poseidon?" These magnificent buildings were more ancient than Stonehenge, almost three thousand years old when Plato was in Syracuse, less than a hundred miles away on Sicily. Trade between the two islands had gone on since before recorded history, so ancient lore could easily have spread in either direction.

"Was this the Temple of Poseidon? Mmm, no." Mifsud believed that the megaliths remaining on Malta had been those Plato described in the *Critias* as the "many temples built and dedicated to many gods," not the main buildings at the center of Atlantis. "The greater part of Plato's island lies on the seafloor," he told me.

The sky was threatening and we had yet to make our most important stop, so we hurried back to the Corsa and sped off down the coastal highway. Gigantic raindrops started to fall, first steadily splashing the windshield like water balloons, and then in buckets. In two minutes the steeply inclined road became a river, and we were pushing against the current. Mifsud turned to me and said in what I imagined was his concerned clinician's voice, "I think perhaps we shouldn't go outside, with the lightning. Probably not a good idea to be driving, either." We turned onto an unpaved private road and parked in the middle of a barren, rocky area. "I'm sorry but I don't think we will be able to see the ruts up close," he said. "Maybe you can get a look from here, yes?"

The Corsa's windows had steamed up completely; we might have been in a submarine. I rolled down my window halfway and my lap was immediately drenched. I thought that I could sort of see something off in the distance, maybe. Mifsud hummed as he flipped through a much-annotated book about the cart ruts. I asked a few questions about how Malta matched up, or didn't, with Plato's descriptions of Atlantis. Where the evidence was strong, as with the local preponderance of ancient bull cults that might relate to the sacrificial ceremony performed by the kings of Atlantis, he expounded. When the evidence was weak, as with the concentric circles, he downplayed. When he didn't have an obscure ancient source to back up his theories, he had inventive solutions. I asked about the black, red, and white stone Plato had described in Atlantis.

"My daughter the architect pointed out to me one day, 'Daddy, that rock is red because it faces north and grows lichen. That rock is black because of fungus. And the new stone from the quarry is white!'" Not a bad explanation, except virtually all the building stone on Malta seemed to be the same color: yellow.

"What about the elephants?" I asked.

"The elephants! Yes! But I can't talk about that because it's in my next book." Mifsud had shown me the outline for the book on his iPad, a constellation of documents and photos and notes compressed onto one slim device. My own Atlantis library, like Tony O'Connell's, now filled an entire office. I asked again about his 2200 BC date.

"The Eumalos manuscript cites specifically the date 2200 BC, which was the reign of King Ninus of Babylon. That date was confirmed for me by carbon dating."

When Mifsud had mentioned 2200 BC at dinner with Tony, the date had sounded familiar. Doing a little web research on my lumpy bed at the ex-brothel, I remembered why. A group of scientists at Columbia University had demonstrated that the powerful Akkadian Empire in Mesopotamia had collapsed due to sudden climate change. The resulting drought had lasted three hundred years and had been preserved in the epic poem "The Curse of Akkad," which lamented,

> For the first time since cities were built and founded,
> The great agricultural tracts produced no grain,
> The inundated tracts produced no fish,
> The irrigated orchards produced neither syrup nor wine,
> The gathered clouds did not rain.

Like most such works, "The Curse of Akkad" had long been considered fiction, even though a similar poem had been written in Egypt around the same time. Mifsud believed that the unexplained societal collapses around the Mediterranean circa 2200 BC—including the one in Malta—were related to the fall of Atlantis.

"Eumalos also gives the precise location of Atlantis, between Sicily and Libya," Mifsud continued. "It would be right in the middle here." Mifsud took my pen and notebook and scribbled a map of the western Mediterranean. I was amused to see that his physician's handwriting was utterly illegible. He handed the notebook back to me. Malta/Atlantis was at the center, roughly equal in size to Italy and Africa, according to the sketch—the proper place and proportions from a Maltese point of view.

"One piece of evidence, maybe not," he said. "Two pieces, maybe not. But if all the evidence converges in Malta . . ."

"Then Malta must be Atlantis," I said.

"Basically, I'd say that if there *was* an Atlantis, Malta has to be it."

This struck me as a very sensible perspective. Mifsud thumped a finger on a page in his cart-rut book. "Aha! See this?" He read aloud a passage stating that the ruts had been used for "transport of general agricultural and marine produce."

A red pickup truck pulled alongside us. Mifsud rolled down his window and shouted over the rain back and forth in Maltese with the driver, a teenage boy.

"That's the farmer's son. He wants to lock the gate." I hadn't realized we were on a farm. "What do you think? Do we take the risk and have a look?" Mifsud already had one leg out the driver's side door.

We jogged out into the rain and onto a rocky moonscape pitted with divots. Clapham Junction, as it turned out. The ruts were indeed interesting, though a bit haphazard. They also seemed to have been carved exclusively in parallel pairs, probably by the constant friction of wheels or sled runners. They were a tiny fraction of the sizes Plato gave, perhaps large enough to float single-file armadas of bath toys.

These were hardly the only problems with Mifsud's theory. The cornerstone on which it was built, the manuscript written by Eumalos of Cyrene, had been linked by an eminent Maltese historian to a dubious "Atlantis stone" identified as a hoax in the 1830s. (A disagreement between Mifsud and a German researcher over this controversy later broke out on the Atlantipedia.) At the very least the manuscript written by Eumalos seemed suspiciously perfect.

Mifsud's hypothesis stood astride the line between crazy and just crazy enough to work. I probably should have pressed him on the

Eumalos thing, and I definitely should have taken Tony's advice and pushed him harder on the cart ruts.

But in the moment, watching Mifsud standing there proudly smiling in the pouring rain, holding his hands up as if he'd just solved the mystery for me, I couldn't help but think: If there was an Atlantis, why shouldn't this be it?

CHAPTER SIXTEEN

The Minoans Return

Knossos, Crete (ca. 1900)

Here was the problem: In terms of corroboration with Plato's story, other rumored locations offered vastly more physical evidence than Malta. So much, in fact, that for a brief period a lot of reputable scientists believed that Atlantis had been found. Some still did.

In 1883, as Ignatius Donnelly's newly published *Atlantis: The Antediluvian World* was establishing the mid-Atlantic as the likeliest location of Plato's sunken island, a meeting took place in Athens that decades later would shift the focus of Atlantological studies back toward Greece.

The host of this social engagement was Heinrich Schliemann, discoverer of Troy and Mycenae, who welcomed into his custombuilt neoclassical mansion Arthur Evans, a young English newspaper reporter recently chased out of the Balkans for stirring up opposition to the Austro-Hungarian Empire. A year later Evans would be appointed keeper of the Ashmolean Museum at Oxford University, where he developed an interest in prealphabetic writing. This led him to the relic-rich island of Crete. An inheritance enabled Evans to acquire land and a permit to dig at a site near the city of Herakleion that had long intrigued scholars of ancient history.

Schliemann had tried and failed to purchase it earlier. Considering Schliemann's interest in myths, Crete would have been an obvious stop. According to legend, it was on Crete that King Minos had built an inescapable labyrinth beneath his palace at Knossos. Inside this maze lived the Minotaur, the half man, half beast who fed on the flesh of sacrificial Athenian youths and maidens.

When the team Evans hired began excavating on March 23, 1900, he had a particular prize in mind. In his work at the Ashmolean, Evans had collected several ancient examples of what he believed was an unknown form of Cretan script, written in clay. On the eighth day of excavations, one of Evans's laborers found an entire clay tablet inscribed with similar writing. By the end of that first season, more than a thousand complete and partial tablets had been discovered. Evans spent the next four decades trying, and failing, to decipher the mysterious script that he had named Linear B.

The Linear B inscriptions were overshadowed by the discovery of an enormous palace, the hub of a sophisticated ancient culture. Its main building comprised hundreds of rooms built on several levels, a cabinet of archaeological wonders untouched for thirty-five hundred years: fragments of gorgeous wall paintings; large *pithoi*, or urns; a sophisticated plumbing system; more tablets inscribed with a second, previously unknown variety of indecipherable writing. A large chamber decorated with frescoes of griffins and anchored by a carved gypsum chair was dubbed the Throne Room. The entire structure had been severely damaged by some sort of natural disaster around 1450 BC. Taking inspiration from his hero Schliemann's discovery at Troy, Evans declared that he had found Knossos, the palace of King Minos. Many centuries after their mysterious disappearance, Evans reintroduced to the world the people he called the Minoans.

According to legend, Minos's wife had been enchanted by Poseidon into mating with a bull and had given birth to the Minotaur.

The bull theme seemed to be everywhere at Knossos, engraved into gemstones and gold signet rings, in ceremonial bull's head–shaped vessels known as rhytons, and especially in the dramatic frescoes that covered the palace walls. One such painting, now among the most famous artworks from antiquity, is the Bull-Leaping Fresco, which depicts three young Minoans engaged in an activity that might make the steeliest matador wet his skintight pants. One girl stands in front of the bull, grabbing its horns, while another stands behind the animal, arms outstretched. The third youth, evidently a male acrobat, appears to be in the middle of executing a front flip over the beast.

The bull theme at Knossos matched up with other Minoan finds. A pair of exquisite gold cups, known as the Vapheio Cups, had been discovered in a Bronze Age tomb just south of Sparta. One vessel was elaborately decorated with scenes similar to that in the Bull-Leaping Fresco. The other showed the netting of wild bulls. The second tableau echoed Plato's description of the animals that ran free in the Temple of Poseidon in the center of Atlantis and the ten kings who "hunted the bulls, without weapons but with staves and nooses."

In February 1909, an article appeared in the London *Times* proposing that Evans's finds might be connected to Atlantis. The anonymous writer argued that the Minoan empire had been "a vast and ancient power" so great that "it seemed to be a separate continent with a genius of its own." Yet for unknown reasons the powerful maritime empire once centered at Knossos had collapsed during the Late Bronze Age. "It was as if the whole kingdom had sunk in the sea, as if the tale of Atlantis were true."

The author of the article later revealed himself to be K. T. Frost, a young professor at Queen's University in Belfast. Frost's initial reluctance to attach his name to his hypothesis may have been for professional reasons. The opinions of the late Benjamin Jowett, the Oxford tutor and classics scholar whose new translations of Plato's dialogues sparked a sort of Platomania in Victorian Britain, were still hugely influential in all Platonic matters. Jowett had been one of the first academics who felt the need to tamp down the urge to take Atlantis seriously. In his introduction to a new translation of the *Critias*, he stated firmly that Plato had intended the Atlantis tale to be an allegory of the Persian Wars. "We may safely conclude that the entire narrative is due to the imagination of Plato," he wrote.

Frost published a second essay four years later under his own byline. This time, he stressed the near certainty of a relationship between ancient Crete and Egypt. Minoan pottery had been found in Egypt, and representations of long-haired visitors wearing loincloths—typical signifiers of Cretans—appear in tomb paintings at the Theban Necropolis in Egypt. In one painting, the foreigners carry bull-themed gifts. To Frost, this was strong evidence that firsthand reports of the Minoan collapse had reached the Egyptians. "It is not impossible," Frost wrote, "that Solon went to Egypt and learned what was in fact the Egyptian version of the overthrow of the Minoans, although he did not recognize it as such." From this tale Solon might have composed notes for an epic poem, never completed, "the plot of which Plato knew and adapted to his own use."

Frost was less tentative in declaring that Plato had never intended the Atlantis story to be taken as historical fact. It was "geologically certain," he wrote, that the most famous element of Plato's story had to be fiction, since no vast island had been known to suddenly sink into the sea since the end of the last Ice Age.

Frost died in World War I, and little was done to advance his theory until the 1930s, when the young Greek archaeologist Spyridon Marinatos began working on the north coast of Crete. Marinatos noticed that some ancient structures seemed to have shifted when hit by a tremendous force. "What really piqued my interest," he later wrote, "were the curious positions of several stone blocks that had been torn from their foundations and strewn toward the sea." Even more intriguing was "a building near the shore with its basement full of pumice."

In 1937, Marinatos traveled to the Netherlands as a visiting professor at Utrecht University. There he had access to the extensive Dutch colonial records regarding the explosion of Krakatoa in the Indonesian archipelago on August 27, 1883. Krakatoa's eruption had been heard more than two thousand miles away in Australia and ejected enough pumice to blot out the sun for a hundred miles in all directions. The deadliest effects of the blast came from the waves that followed—hundred-foot-high walls of water moving at speeds greater than fifty miles an hour toward oblivious coastal towns on the islands of Java and Sumatra. "In places they raged inland for one thousand yards and were still thirty feet high," Marinatos wrote. More than thirty-six thousand people died, most of them victims of the tsunami.

In 1939, Marinatos published an article in the British archaeological journal *Antiquity* that suggested that parts of Crete had been similarly destroyed by aftereffects of the eruption of Thera (or Santorini), a volcanic island roughly midway between Knossos and Athens. This explosion, he wrote, had pulverized part of the island, burying much of the rest in ash one hundred feet deep, obliterating the culture of the Therans and unleashing tidal waves and ashfall that smothered Crete. The distance from Thera to Crete is only seventy miles. Thera's eruption, Marinatos estimated, had been four times as powerful as Krakatoa's. When the volcanic cone collapsed into the sea, it could have created massive waves moving at two hundred miles an hour. Marinatos dated the cataclysm to 1500 BC. His theory had raised a fascinating new possibility—that the "great and widespread catastrophe" caused by the eruption of Thera had suddenly ended the Minoan civilization that had built the extraordinary palace of Knossos.

A great sea power disappears suddenly due to a natural disaster—Marinatos certainly saw the possible correlation with Plato. He titled a 1950 essay expanding on his Minoan hypothesis "On the Legend of Atlantis." The word *legend*, Marinatos explained, "means something mixed of historic and imaginary elements and above all something which became a glorious but dubious tradition," as opposed to a fable, which is fabricated. "Plato's imagination could not possibly have conjured up an account so unique and unusual to classical literature," he wrote, turning Benjamin Jowett's earlier opinion on its head.

Marinatos believed the likeliest "historical core of a legend" in the Atlantis tale was that "a piece of land becomes submerged." The most obvious example of such a sunken land was Thera. Marinatos thought that the Egyptians, faced with the sudden unexplained absence of their Cretan trading partners, had merged that disappearance with reports they might have received of a sunken island. Plato's placement of Atlantis in a spot beyond the Pillars of Heracles, he felt, was an embellishment inspired by the sixth-century Phoenician sailors who circumnavigated Africa and returned with details of its mysterious Atlantic Coast. Marinatos hypothesized that perhaps the mysterious Sea Peoples had first attacked Mycenaean Greece and were repulsed before regrouping to invade Egypt. This might have inspired an oral tradition of the Athenians defeating a vast sea power.

Marinatos was uncommonly willing to view the Atlantis portions of the *Timaeus* and *Critias* as worthy of scholarly analysis. He wisely sidestepped any discussion of Plato's enigmatic numbers, other than to venture that the 1500 BC explosion of Thera transpired about nine hundred years before Solon's visit to Saïs, "which the Saite priest projected tenfold into the abyss of the past." Because of his growing stature as one of the world's leading archaeologists—he had also by this time identified the famous mountain pass at Thermopylae, where three hundred Spartans had held off thousands of Persian invaders—none of his peers protested when Marinatos concluded that while the Atlantis tale wasn't strictly factual, it had likely sprouted from a kernel of real history. To use the Hollywood vernacular, Plato's Atlantis had been based on a true story. Marinatos knew well the value of publicity, even if he had to drop the problematic name of Atlantis in order to catch the press's interest. The brilliantly noncommittal title of a slim book he later published shortly before his death, *Some Words About the Legend of Atlantis*, may be an indication of his attempt to have his baklava and eat it, too.

CHAPTER SEVENTEEN

The Front-runner

Santorini, Greece, 1967

In the early 1960s, the respected Greek seismologist Angelos Gala-nopoulos began tweaking Marinatos's theory and refining it into what has become known in Atlantology as the Minoan Hypothesis. Minoan pottery had been found beneath the ash of Santorini, demonstrating a relationship with Crete. Galanopoulos proposed that the two had once comprised the single political entity that Plato describes as Atlantis. Plato's capital city, with its concentric rings, matches Santorini's distinctive bull's-eye shape. One ancient name for Thera, Galanopoulos noted in his book *Atlantis: The Truth Behind the Legend*, was Strongyle, which means "round." Galanopoulos argued that the rings Poseidon carved around Atlantis had actually been, prior to Thera's eruption, "natural channels surrounding the central cone." Nea Kameni, the relatively new and still-growing volcanic island at the center of Santorini's donut-shaped caldera, had replaced an identical island that once held the temple of Poseidon. The shipping lane that bisected Plato's circles ("from the sea they bored a canal . . . fifty stades in length," Critias tells his friends) Galanopoulos believed was largely man-made and could still be seen in a sharply defined gap between modern Santorini's two main islands. Santorini was filled with red, white, and black stone, just as Plato's Atlantis had been. "The coincidences," Galanopoulos wrote, "are too many and too strong to be accepted as accidental."

Perhaps the most clever element of Galanopoulos's hypothesis was his explanation for Plato's fantastic-seeming numbers. In translating the story for Solon, he wrote, the hieroglyphic symbol for 100 was mistakenly replaced with the sign for 1,000. With his simple mathematical trick, Galanopoulos eliminated the biggest anachronisms in Plato's tale. Not coincidentally, his elegant solution also placed the disappearance of Atlantis at about 1500 BC—or almost exactly the time Marinatos pegged for the Thera explosion. By those same calculations, the fertile Atlantean plain shrank from two hundred miles long by three hundred miles wide down to twenty by thirty, which fit neatly into central Crete. (Plato's thousand-mile-long canal enwreathing the plain was thus shrunk to a more manageable hundred miles long.) As for the matter of Santorini's location far from the Atlantic Ocean, Galanopoulos argued that Plato's words had been misinterpreted. "The identification of the Pillars of Hercules with the Straits of Gibraltar need not be taken too literally," he explained, while shifting them to a convenient spot on the jagged southern edge of the Peloponnesus.

To me, this multiple-of-ten business seemed too much like a magic bullet. A very skeptical Tony O'Connell had shown me a page from a history of numbers that pretty clearly demonstrated the hieroglyphic symbols for 100 and 1,000 looked nothing alike. Still, I figured I should double-check with an authority and so e-mailed Janet Johnson, a University of Chicago professor of Egyptology, who is arguably America's leading expert on the ancient Egyptian language. She explained that a priest would likely have been writing in the hieratic or demotic script, which was more cursive than the hieroglyphs used in monuments—and illustrated in Tony's book. "In both of those writing systems," Johnson wrote me, "the 9 of 900 or 9,000 would look much the same; the difference would be in the 'tail' marking the hundreds or thousands. A practiced scribe would not likely make a mistake, but a Greek reading over his shoulder might, I suppose."

I checked Johnson's *Chicago Demotic Dictionary*, and it was true. To my unpracticed eye the symbols for hundreds and thousands were virtually indistinguishable. When I showed Tony, even he agreed that a nonnative scribe taking down the words of the priest at Saïs or reading Solon's notes might have mixed up the two.

The folkloric evidence for a catastrophic event in the eastern Mediterranean around the year 1500 BC is surprisingly strong. As Werner Wickboldt had pointed out to me in Braunschweig, the Parian Marble dates Deucalion's flood to 1528–27 BC. The fourth-century Christian scholar Saint Jerome dated the flood to 1460 BC. In *The City of God*, St. Augustine placed Deucalion's flood during the lifetime of Moses, very loosely dated to the span between 1557 BC and 1437 BC. Galanopoulos believed that the Thera cataclysm not only had inspired the myths of Deucalion and Atlantis but also was the source material for the story of God parting the Red Sea to allow the Israelites to escape from Egypt, found in the book of Exodus.

The name of the waters the Israelites crossed, according to Galanopoulos, has traditionally been mistranslated; it was not the Red Sea but the Sea of Reeds, a coastal lagoon "to the east of the Nile Delta." Typically before a tsunami makes landfall—such as following the 1755 Lisbon earthquake—the sea briefly withdraws from the shoreline. Galanopoulos argued that as the sea receded following Thera's post-eruption tsunami, the Israelites sprinted across a five-hundred-yard-wide gap to dry land. The waters then returned with explosive force as the Egyptians attempted to pursue them.

Not satisfied with connecting Atlantis to just one of the Bible's most important events, Galanopoulos also proposed that all ten of the plagues of Egypt described in the book of Exodus could be traced to the Thera explosion, especially the darkening of the sky (from the ash cloud), the violent hailstorm (a meteorological product of rapidly falling temperatures), and the Nile turning to blood ("iron oxide in the ash would dissolve in the waters and color them red").

As Juan Villarias-Robles had explained to me in Madrid, the 1960s were the dawning of what's sometimes called the New Archaeology, a shift away from hunting for relics and interpreting old tales and toward using more scientific methods. Willard Libby received the 1960 Nobel Prize in Chemistry for his work on radiocarbon dating, also known as carbon 14 dating, which as the Nobel Committee's citation correctly predicted, soon revolutionized the fields of "archaeology, geology, geophysics, and other sciences." It was inevitable that the methods of the New Archaeology would also make their mark on the less reputable science of Atlantology.

James Mavor, a research specialist at the prestigious Woods Hole Oceanographic Institute in Cape Cod, met Galanopoulos by chance in 1965 while on vacation in Athens. At that time Mavor was working on what he called "the most exciting project of my career," helping to design and build a deep-sea research submarine named *Alvin*. Mavor was entranced by Galanopoulos's hypothesis and offered to help procure the latest scientific equipment to prove it.

A year later, in August 1966, *The New York Times* published a story under the headline ATLANTIS SEARCH SHIFTS TO AEGEAN. Mavor had arranged for the 210-foot research vessel *Chain* to visit Santorini to take geophysical soundings of the caldera that might prove Galanopoulos's hypotheses about a man-made channel and naturally formed rings. The results were inconclusive but promising. The press seemed to have gotten a different impression. A follow-up story in the *Times* quoted Galanopoulos as saying that "most convincing proof" had been located in the form of what the reporter described as "the outline of a wide moat . . . 1300 feet underwater in the submerged part of Thera Island." Mavor, though not an archaeologist, also did a bit of searching on land and found what he later described as "unmistakably Minoan" potsherds and walls.

Mavor prepared for a 1967 return to Santorini expecting to lead a multidisciplinary team that would include two superstars. Jacques Cousteau, the dashing red-capped, cigarette-puffing French ocean-ographer planned to bring his research vessel *Calypso* to aid in the underwater exploration of the caldera. The other big-name specialist was Spyridon Marinatos, whose controversial essays about the Thera eruption and its possible connection to Atlantis had fired Galanopoulos's imagination. By this time, the charismatic Marina-tos was one of the world's preeminent archaeologists. But though he was attached to the promising Santorini project, Marinatos was ac-tually more interested in Helike. This important Golden Age Greek city south of Athens had vanished overnight in 373 BC due to a well-documented earthquake and flood. This similarity to the lost island described by Plato—who was living in Athens at the time—made Helike a perennial candidate as a proto-Atlantis. For Marinatos, the allure of finding an entire intact city was irresistible. He was indeed about to make such a discovery, just not at Helike.

Mavor's follow-up expedition seemed at first to be cursed. Perhaps the grandiose name he chose, the 1967 Helleno-American Multi-Disciplinary Scientific Investigation of Thera and Quest for the Lost Atlantis, was an act of hubris too great to escape divine punishment. In April, the Greek military raised a coup and took control of the country. A few weeks later, Cousteau was forced to drop out when the Six-Day War erupted between Egypt and Israel, closing the Suez Canal. Ten days before work was scheduled to begin in Santorini, Mavor admitted to his partners that he had been unable to obtain any of the backing that he had promised. ("No ship, no submarine, no scientists, no equipment, no money," one member of the team drily recalled.) He had been able to procure a sophisticated seismograph and magnetometer but was unable to get accurate readings from either.

Meanwhile, Marinatos surveyed an ash-covered field near the fishing village of Akrotiri, saw something in the landscape that looked promising, and said, "Dig there." His laborers almost instantly began to recover Minoan-style architecture and pottery. During six extraordinary days of excavation, diggers found large storage jars filled with remnants of wine and oil, kitchen utensils, loom weights, animal bones, frescoes, stone walls, and holes where disintegrated wooden beams had once held up two- and three-story buildings. An absence of human remains led to a working hypothesis that the residents of the buried city that came to be known as Akrotiri—or if Galanopoulos and Mavor were correct, Atlantis—had heeded seismological warnings and escaped doomed Thera before its final cataclysm. But indisputably Marinatos had found a wealthy maritime city of unknown proportions, a "Bronze Age Pompeii."

The American media eagerly credited Mavor with the discovery of Plato's lost city. "Two years ago, I couldn't find a single archaeologist interested in the Atlantis story," he told *Time* magazine in an article that, like most international news coverage, didn't mention Marinatos. "Now several admit there may be some connection." Greek newspapers reprinted information from the American press. Marinatos, whose friends in Greece's new military junta had promoted him to inspector general of the Antiquities Service, was not pleased; not only was his work at Akrotiri going unsung, but also Mavor was using his preliminary findings as solid proof that Atlantis had been discovered. Marinatos was willing to suggest that Thera's explosion might have inspired Plato's myth, but to claim the islands were one and the same was "irresponsible," he said. A few months later *The New York Times* published a final, short news story headlined U.S. SCIENTIST LET OUT IN DISPUTE OVER THERA DIG. Mavor had been informed by letter that his services were no longer welcome on Santorini.

When the psychic Edgar Cayce prophesied that Atlantis would rise again around 1969, he was in a sense correct. Mavor, Galanopoulos, and the Trinity College classics scholar John Luce all published books that year, each using the finds at Akrotiri to argue for the Minoan Hypothesis in a slightly different way. (Cayce may also have foreseen the singer Donovan's top-ten single "Atlantis," with its goofy lyrics inspired by Ignatius Donnelly's diffusionist ideas, which was also released in 1969.) Even the august *New York Review of Books* weighed in with two extensive (and dismissive) reviews of this Atlantis literature, a sign of the Minoan Hypothesis's popularity.

The momentum from this burst of publicity carried forward in the following decades. Jacques Cousteau finally made it to Santorini and in 1978 released a documentary titled *Calypso's Search for Atlantis*. (Guess what? He didn't find it, either.) Many more documentaries and books ensued, all of them following to some degree the story line that the Thera explosion had ended the Minoan civilization on Crete, which inspired Plato's story. Here, within an area that Plato would have been familiar with—the island was a likely stopping point on voyages he made to Crete and Egypt—was a scientifically documented occurrence of a sophisticated island civilization disappearing almost instantaneously due to a natural disaster.

These versions tended to accentuate the generally positive—the bulls, the tricolor stones—while sweeping inconsistencies under the rug. I found Galanopoulos's argument for the Pillars of Heracles to be particularly weak, and his numbers theory wasn't entirely convincing, either. There was also a problem with chronology. Further excavations on Crete showed that the Minoan empire had survived, in an ever-diminishing state, for a couple of centuries after the Thera blast before its sudden disappearance around 1200 BC, when the chaotic events of the Late Bronze Age collapse—war, famine, earthquakes—snuffed out one great Mediterranean society after another, including the Mycenaean Greeks.

In his book *Voyage to Atlantis*, Mavor expressed his faith "that in due course all manner of artifacts will be laboriously collected" from the ruins of Akrotiri, and the evidence would prove Galanopoulos's Minoan Hypothesis once and for all. Some fascinating buildings and relics had been discovered there in the half century since, enough to inspire new speculations about Atlantis, but archaeological work tended to progress glacially. For now there was one irrefutable fact: the explosion of Thera. Somewhere under all that ash, or at the bottom of that deep caldera, might lie the answer to the Atlantis question.

CHAPTER EIGHTEEN

Scientific Americans

Woods Hole Oceanographic Institute, Cape Cod

The more I read about the Thera explosion and the Minoan Hypothesis, the more I kept circling back to Werner Wickboldt's mention of the Parian Marble and Deucalion's flood. Solon describes the flood near the start of the *Timaeus* when trying to convey the great antiquity of Athens; the Egyptian priest cuts him off and explains that the Greeks have short historical memories due to their cyclical misfortune with natural disasters. "There have been, and will be again, many destructions of mankind rising out of many causes," he explains. "The greatest have been brought about by the agencies of fire and water." The priest mentions the flood again in the *Critias* when he describes an "extraordinary inundation," accompanied by earthquakes that transformed the shape of the Acropolis in Athens by washing away its soil.

The myth of Deucalion will sound familiar to anyone who's read the book of Genesis. Deucalion was the son of Prometheus, the Titan infamous for stealing fire from the gods. Prometheus learned that Zeus was planning to annihilate humanity with a flood and advised his son and his son's wife, Pyrrha, to build an ark to withstand the inundation. When the waters subsided, the ark came to rest on

Mount Parnassus. The earth's only two survivors gave thanks to Zeus, who instructed them to throw stones over their shoulders to repopulate the earth. Deucalion's stones became men, and Pyrrha's women.

There are a few differences between the stories of Deucalion and Noah, such as the lack of animals in the Greek version, but by and large the tales are similar enough to suggest a common origin. A centuries-long chicken-or-egg debate over which story came first became moot in the nineteenth century with the discovery of the *Epic of Gilgamesh*, a series of Babylonian stories about a king who seeks immortality, inscribed on twelve stone tablets that dated to the late third millennium BC. King Gilgamesh seeks the wisdom of Utnapishtim, a survivor of the great flood, whom the gods have granted eternal life. Utnapishtim explains that he was guided by a deity to build a boat so that a small remnant of people and animals could survive a coming flood. When the waters receded, the boat landed on a mountain; only when a raven was dispatched and did not return did the passengers feel safe to disembark.

It seems probable that all these stories of a Great Deluge were based on tales of ancient disasters that had been passed down orally through the generations. But were they the product of one flood or many? And might they tell us anything about the floods Plato wrote of?

Because the global warming trend that began with the onset of the Holocene period around 9700 BC roughly coincided with Plato's date of 9600 BC, many antiestablishment Atlantologists like Rand Flem-Ath have theorized that the torrents of water unleashed by this glacial melt could have been the source of Plato's flood myths. But serious scientists have also seen a connection between the big thaw and the preponderance of ancient flood narratives. The renowned oceanographer Robert Ballard—probably best known for locating the *Titanic* on the floor of the Atlantic Ocean—found the shoreline of what had likely been a freshwater lake four hundred feet beneath the Black Sea. Freshwater shells Ballard collected from the area were carbon-dated to around 5000 BC. The discovery bolstered a controversial hypothesis floated by two Columbia University scientists, William Ryan and Walter Pitman. They argued that the rapidly rising Mediterranean had spilled over the Bosphorus, pouring two hundred times the daily volume of Niagara Falls into what had been a lake, creating the Black Sea. Ballard believed that accounts of such a traumatic event, which would have inundated any lakeshore settlements, could have been passed down orally from generation to generation, essentially creating the Noah's ark tale.

One obstacle blocking any connection between the Thera explosion and ancient flood myths has been researchers' inability to agree on a hard date for the blast. Radiocarbon dates of charcoal samples have been stacked up against evidence of narrowed tree-growth rings (a result of reduced sunlight after the blast ejected ash into the atmosphere), which were compared to dated pottery samples. The technicians favored a date in the early 1600s BC; the specialists with dirt under their fingernails stood firm at 1500 BC. The hundred-year gap was important. A date of 1600 didn't line up nearly as well with the evidence for Atlantis.

Alexander MacGillivray, an archaeologist with the British School of Athens and codirector of excavations at Palaikastro, a major Minoan site in Crete, had recently published a long paper summarizing all the collected evidence. He had come down firmly in favor of the 1500 BC date for the Thera explosion. After Skyping MacGillivray at his home on a small vineyard near Athens, I asked the disembodied head that filled my laptop screen if there was any connection between Deucalion's flood and Thera.

"In terms of the mythology and the history, it tends to go together pretty well. Deucalion's flood appears in Greek history. It's the beginning of the Heroic Age and the rise of Mycenae and the heroes who go off and fight the Trojan War." In his long poem *Works and Days*, the Greek poet Hesiod identifies the Five Ages of Man: the Golden Age (when men lived peacefully among the gods), the Silver Age (when men turned away from the gods), the Bronze Age (a violent time ending with Deucalion's flood), the Heroic Age (when men fought noble battles like the Trojan War), and the Iron Age (Hesiod's own time, an era of lawlessness and evil). Egyptian chroniclers placed the flood of Deucalion during the reign of Pharaoh Thutmosis III, MacGillivray told me, which matches the 1500 BC date perfectly.

"So the Greeks never forgot that Poseidon sent this wave against all of Greece and, essentially, caused this great disaster. This massive flood comes all the way up to the foot of the Acropolis in Athens. Which is exactly what the Theran tsunami would have done." MacGillivray had been unable to find any tsunami research that had been done on the Greek mainland, but the latest modeling at Palaikastro indicated a wave fifty feet high. Another study showed that the Thera tsunami had traveled as far as modern Israel.

This was interesting. A point that often gets forgotten is that in the *Timaeus*, the priest tells Solon that in the same "violent earthquakes and floods" that obliterated Atlantis, "your entire warrior force sank below the earth all at once." I asked what MacGillivray thought about the Minoan Hypothesis.

"I'm pretty happy with what Plato gives us," he said. "The Egyptian priests told him that we should be looking beyond the Pillars of Hercules." In other words, outside of the Mediterranean.

MacGillivray had half-jokingly sent a tweet to filmmaker James Cameron a couple of weeks earlier suggesting that he might search for the lost civilization in his custom-made submersible *Deepsea Challenger*, with which he'd just dived a world-record thirty-six thousand feet to the bottom of the Mariana Trench. Another possibility, MacGillivray said, would be the oceanographer Ballard. "Finding the

Titanic in the middle of the Atlantic Ocean is like finding a grain of sand," he said. "If you can find that, you should be able to find substantial architecture."

As it turned out, the next person I called worked with both James Cameron and Robert Ballard. If anyone should be able to explain how to find something lost under the ocean, it would be David Gallo, the director of special projects at the Woods Hole Oceanographic Institute. An expert in deep-sea research, he had helped find the sunken Nazi battleship *Bismarck* in fifteen thousand feet of water and in recent years oversaw the 3-D mapping of the *Titanic*, also two and a half miles under the sea. In 2011, he led the team that located Air France Flight 447, which had vanished over the Atlantic on its way from Rio de Janeiro to Paris with 228 passengers aboard. A French executive for the plane's manufacturer, Airbus, asked why Gallo's team at the WHOI had been called in to conduct the search, had responded, "Because no one else in the world can do it."

Several e-mails I sent to Gallo vanished into the abyss, until late one night a reply popped up in my inbox. "Mark, just got out of two days of Atlantis meetings," he wrote. "Let's talk."

A few weeks later, I drove up on a sunny day to Cape Cod in Massachusetts, where Gallo conducts business when he's not at sea. The main WHOI campus, with its shingled buildings and manicured lawns, could still pass for its former role as the Gatsby-ish family compound of an especially wealthy New England businessman. Gallo's light-filled office on the second floor had a gorgeous view of Nantucket Sound. He had given one of the most popular TED Talks of all time, an inspirational multimedia presentation about the unexplored wonders of the oceans. When I arrived, he was just exiting a meeting to discuss an upcoming voyage to Antarctica to search for the wreck of Ernest Shackleton's ship *Endurance*. On his large desk he had an eclectic stack of Atlantis books, ranging from scholarly monographs on the Thera eruption to Rand Flem-Ath's *The Atlantis Blueprint*. He wore a turquoise polo shirt, a neon Swatch and fluorescent pink running shoes. Together with his seaman's suntan he seemed to glow from within like a bioluminescent jellyfish.

Archaeological technology has moved far beyond the rudimentary gadgets James Mavor brought to Santorini in the 1960s. The emerging field of satellite archaeology can now spot even underground structures from four hundred miles above the earth. An American team has mapped the ancient Egyptian city of Tanis, which long ago had been silted over by the Nile's shifting current, without lifting a shovelful of dirt. Other archaeologists have used remote sensing technology to find long-vanished temples in the jungles of Cambodia and Belize. In 2013, a team of scientists using an airborne 3-D mapping system called lidar penetrated the dense rain forest canopy in Honduras and located what are likely the ruins of Ciudad Blanca, a legendary lost city that countless explorers have died searching for since the sixteenth-century Spanish conquistador Hernán Cortés heard tales of its incredible riches. Perhaps the most promising area of all was deep-sea exploration.

"A bazillion people are out there looking for a bazillion different things" under the sea, Gallo said as we sat down at a round table covered with large color printouts of seafloors. "Bin Laden's corpse. Sir Francis Drake's coffin. Amelia Earhart's plane. Jeez, talk about spending a lot of money on something where there's nothing." Almost anything underwater was possible to search for. The issue was cost. "A deep-ocean expedition is about $1 million a month for starters," he said.

Finding stuff like Air France 447 is what had made Gallo famous, but it wasn't his primary job. "We're a scientific organization, so mostly when we're mapping we're looking for geology or biology or something from the natural world. If you're making a very detailed map of the seafloor or the ocean floor, anything that's human-made should fall out of that. Like on the bottom of the Atlantic there are incredible underwater dunes and sediment waves and currents and other stuff and then plunk in the middle, there's *Titanic*. We have a whole new suite of robots that cover a lot more ground with a lot better resolution and these would be perfect to go look in the deep Med. Even at a distance of about a mile you can see something the size of a cinder block if conditions are right."

Gallo suggested we drive down to the wharf to take a look at some of his cool new gadgetry. His latest obsession, he explained as we walked to my car, was finding a Minoan shipwreck. "We're in the process of putting together an expedition to go look in earnest for one of those," he said. Finding the first Minoan wreck, with an intact load of cargo, was "the Holy Grail of deep-sea archaeology. I can't understand why we don't know more about that era. I think there are some big surprises headed our way.

"A major problem with underwater archaeology in the Mediterranean is that much of the sea is relatively shallow. It's been picked over for centuries by divers and fishermen scooping up artifacts." More recently, fishing trawlers harvesting bottom-feeders like cod and scallops have scoured the seafloor. Robert Ballard had seen trawling furrows more than five hundred meters down off the coast of Malta.

"But the deep Med can go down four thousand–plus meters," Gallo said. "So that part's pretty much unexplored. We'd like to look between Crete and Santorini to see if we can find one of these Minoan wrecks. The other thing is, at the bottom of the Med there are these things called brine lakes. They look just like lakes on land but they're at the bottom of the ocean. Brine lakes have no oxygen and no sunlight. It's basically pickle juice. So any kind of organic matter that falls into there should be preserved incredibly well."

This was where Atlantis came in. Gallo had first heard of the

Minoan Hypothesis when a friend asked if he'd be willing to meet with her father, who turned out to be Prince Michael of Greece. "We went to a coffee shop in New York City and he started to unroll his idea of Atlantis and, oh man, it was like that scene in *Amadeus* where Salieri is talking to the priest. I left in a bucket of sweat."

In his recent meetings about an expedition to search for a Minoan wreck, the Atlantis connection had, naturally, come up. James Cameron, an adviser to WHOI—the group's undersea work had inspired his film *Titanic*—was gung ho about the possible connection. Not everyone at Woods Hole shared his enthusiasm. I assumed this had something to do with memories of James Mavor, the WHOI specialist whose long scientific career was overshadowed by his obsession with Atlantis.

"We made a deal among ourselves that we wouldn't talk about Atlantis while we are discussing [Minoan wrecks] because of the hype, you know, people living with mermaids at the bottom of the sea," Gallo said. "I don't think that's fair. I think we ought to be able to let people know that there's a plausible link between Atlantis and the Minoans."

The search for a Minoan ship was temporarily on hold due to lack of funds. As a related project, Gallo was trying to arrange for equipment to map the ancient city of Akrotiri, still buried under several layers of ash. Almost half a century after Marinatos had found it, only a tiny percentage of Akrotiri has been excavated. Guesses about what surprises might still be waiting varied widely. "Maybe beneath the vineyards of Santorini there's a giant chest of rubies and the controls of the earthshaking machine," Gallo said, laughing.

We parked in downtown Woods Hole at WHOI's sister campus. One of the institute's research ships was docked in preparation for a long voyage to the West Coast. A burly man with a ponytail wearing a Harley-Davidson T-shirt walked past dragging a duffel bag on wheels. "He's sure got the look of a crew member," Gallo said as he ushered me through the front door of a brick security building outside the marina. Two nice elderly ladies were on desk duty. "I forgot my ID badge again," Gallo said, patting the pockets of his jeans and slowing down only slightly. "This is Mark. He's a foreign spy with bad intentions." As the door closed behind us I heard a faint cry of "David, wait . . ."

We paused for about ten seconds to peek through the windows of a large shed. "Here's something you might like," Gallo said, standing on tiptoe. Inside, laid out carefully on tables, were large yellow cylinders, the autonomous underwater vehicles (AUVs) used to find Air France 447. "This stuff is top secret technology. Cool, huh? Let's go see Atlantis."

Or rather, *Atlantis*, WHOI's state-of-the-art 274-foot-long research vessel. Serious scientists may not always like the idea of searching for Plato's sunken island, but they sure do like naming things after it: a space shuttle, an asteroid, an impact crater on Mars. We walked up and down staircases and across catwalks, poking our heads into tiny cabins and rooms crammed with electronics. The ship had multiple winches and cranes, an enormous globe-shaped GPS receiver, six science labs, a full-service cafeteria that seemed to be unusually well stocked with Tabasco sauce and protein bars ("a lot of companies hear about us and just send boxes of stuff," Gallo explained), and beds for twenty-four crew members. I kept expecting to bump into Jacques Cousteau. At the end of our tour we finally reached the latest iteration of *Alvin*, the round little three-man submersible that Mavor had helped design. Its pincers were protected with boxing gloves, giving it the aspect of a chubby kid trying to defend himself. Maybe it would have to. James Cameron had just donated *Deepsea Challenger* to WHOI, which put *Alvin* in line for a demotion.

The AUVs Gallo had shown me were capable of sucking up terabytes of information, which was then processed into single images. Gallo wanted me to see some of the results. We crossed a road and walked to the WHOI's village campus, which seemed pretty ram-shackle compared to the one Gallo worked at. At the end of a long parking lot we finally reached what looked like a windowless double-wide trailer. This was the office of William Lange, WHOI's tech-nical wizard. Lange was famous in oceanographic circles as one of the first people to lay eyes on the submerged *Titanic* in 1985. Gallo paused before we ascended the steps to the door. "I need to warn you: Billy's a little prickly. But he is a genius."

The building was dimly lighted by fluorescent bulbs and com-puter screens and crammed with audiovisual equipment; its interior reminded me of the mobile TV command center parked outside a stadium during a major sporting event. At the front of the main room was the largest LCD screen I had ever seen.

Lange was reclining in an office chair in front of his computer. He had gray hair and a gray beard and wore a gray shirt and black jeans. Next to Gallo's neon glow he looked like a nocturnal forest creature caught outside his burrow. His right hand was wrapped in a bandage of some sort, so he shook my hand warily with his left.

"I told Mark that we don't normally like to use the term *Atlantis* because it sets in motion a whole bunch of stuff that probably has no basis in reality. True?" Gallo said.

"True," Lange said, leaning back and staring at me.

"And that there is a plausible link between Thera and the Mino-ans and what Plato talked about as being Atlantis," Gallo said. Lange looked displeased. "A *plausible* link, Billy," Gallo added. "Plausible."

Lange folded his hands over his belt buckle. He had scowled when Gallo said the word *Atlantis*.

To break the uncomfortable silence, I asked Lange what he thought of Gallo's plan to search for a Minoan ship. To my surprise, he seemed to think Gallo's ambitions were too small.

"I don't want to go down the ancient astronaut route or all that nonsense," Lange said, leaning back farther and boring into my eyes, "but I'm totally convinced there's a portion of our history that's missing. The sea level has changed significantly in the Mediterranean in the last ten thousand years. A significant part of our history and culture development is four hundred feet down. Worldwide." As a result, the river mouths where settlements tend to be built have shifted over time, sometimes dramatically. The mouth of the Hudson River is now located a hundred miles west of where it was prior to the end of the last Ice Age. "Waterways—lakes, rivers, oceans—were the highways back then. Where would you have a city or settlement? You'd have it where a river intersected the ocean. And those aren't where they used to be anymore. The economic capitals of multiple cultures potentially disappeared in a very, very narrow time span."

Lange pointed out that a recent discovery of a stone axe in Crete had suggested that humans may have been sailing the Mediterranean one hundred thousand years ago. "If you go back and project what was going on in the Med from 3000 to 7000 BC, or five thousand to nine thousand years from us right now, there's a lot of building going on, especially on islands. That's when Santorini, Malta, Crete, Cyprus, even the Canaries—they all have big megalithic structures there that really don't make a lot of sense. I'm hoping that by looking at some of these ancient shorelines we'll be able to find some submerged structures that would've survived."

Gallo prodded the reluctant Lange into unrolling a gigantic black-and-white photo that covered a large tabletop. "This is probably the highest-resolution data we have for any part of the ocean," Lange said. Near the center of the image was a tiny white wedge. The bow of the *Titanic*. "My dream is to do with Akrotiri what we've done with *Titanic*," he said. He hoped to combine ground-penetrating radar with high-resolution underwater images "to put Akrotiri in scope and see how big it was."

It sounded like a massive undertaking. If the roll-out of Google

Ocean had made Atlantologists' pulses race, a map of greater Akrotiri might result in heads exploding. "How could you even begin to plan such a project?" I asked.

"We could do it in a week if we had the money," Lange said.

"Why don't you show Mark some of the 3-D stuff you've been working on?" Gallo said.

"It's not ready yet," Lange said. He had returned to his chair and was reclining to the point where he appeared to be awaiting a molar extraction, but after the *Titanic* demonstration the edge in his voice had disappeared.

"Aw, come on, Billy." Gallo turned to me. "I haven't even seen this stuff."

Lange pursed his lips as he thought it over. Finally, he called across the room to a young associate. "Beth, can you kill the lights and get the glasses?"

Beth left and returned with dark glasses for everyone. We put them on and stared at the enormous screen.

"This is the highest resolution underwater imagery ever collected," Lange said as the lights dimmed. He turned to Gallo. "We're getting toward immersion, right?"

The footage was staggering. We watched as schools of porpoises chased what looked like millions of fish. We passed over a propeller airplane, covered in decades of marine muck. A gigantic, pulsating jellyfish crossed the screen, followed by the colorful spiral of a nautilus paddling by. Everything looked as if you could reach out and touch it.

"You. Have. Got. To. Be. Kidding. Me," Gallo said.

I asked if, hypothetically, this technology could be used to locate an underwater city.

"There's a bigger story, and it's not that one city disappeared," Lange said. "It's that a hundred cities disappeared."

At the end of his TED Talk, Gallo quoted Marcel Proust: "The true voyage of discovery is not so much in seeking new landscapes as in having new eyes." The prospect of using this technology to find whatever was lurking under Santorini's ash and its surrounding waters was tantalizing. Maybe there really were a hundred cities waiting to be found, any of which might have inspired a story of a watery cataclysm.

I needed to find only one.

CHAPTER NINETEEN

Kalimera!

Santorini, Greece

When I arrived in Santorini, my to-do list had a single item on it: Find George Nomikos. I wasn't entirely sure why I needed to find him. I'd gotten his contact information from the Greek tourist board in New York City. Usually when a writer contacts a country's travel council, the people in that office bend over backward to provide far more information than the writer can possibly use, most of it relating to spas and horseback riding. Then they follow up so many times that the words *restraining order* must sometimes be deployed.

The Greeks played hard to get. Phone calls, e-mails; for weeks, I tried—and failed—to connect. Finally, as I was preparing to leave for the airport, a nice fellow named Chris called back and assured me that whatever it was I needed to do in Santorini, George Nomikos would take care of it. George and I exchanged e-mails and he promised to get in touch shortly before my arrival, but he hadn't by the time my flight landed at Santorini's tiny airport. I awoke on my first morning in Greece wondering what I was going to do with myself.

At 8:55 my phone rang. "*Kalimera*, Mark! That's how we say 'good morning' in Santorini! I'll pick you up in ten minutes. We'll have coffee at my café!"

A few minutes later I was riding shotgun in George's white Volkswagen hatchback. George was in his early thirties, handsome, deeply tanned, with perfectly groomed black hair. His prosperous belly bulged a bit behind his pressed pink oxford. We drove through the narrow streets of Fira, Santorini's main town, searching for a place to park as George waved at, shouted *"Kalimera!"* to, or stopped to shake hands with every other person we passed. After about ten minutes, we finally backed into a very illegal spot blocking the driveway of a hairdresser's shop. "It's okay; I got my hair cut here the other day," George explained. He shouted *"Kalimera!"* to the shop's owner and waved. We were about fifty yards from my hotel.

We walked through the tight passageways of Fira's whitewashed old town to George's café, Character. (The English word derives from the same ancient Greek word.) George shouted *"Kalimera!"* to the half dozen young, attractive staff members and ordered coffees for us on the terrace. The view was spectacular and, at first glance, utterly Atlantean in its circularity—totally worth the five bucks George charges for a cappuccino. It's like looking down into a half-filled gigantic teacup from a perch on the rim. At the center of this annular basin, surrounded by deep blue water, is the island of Nea Kameni, roughly where Angelos Galanopoulos believed the Temple of Poseidon and Cleito had once stood. Steep cliffs surround most of the caldera, on this day dwarfing two gigantic cruise ships parked near shore. For many boats, dropping anchor is pointless. The Thera blast had been so powerful that the water in the four-mile-wide caldera was more than a thousand feet deep.

"Okay, Mark, so we can't see the ruins at Akrotiri today," George said, leaning back in his chair and adjusting his sunglasses. "There's a strike. I know you only have two days here, so if there's still a strike again tomorrow"—his tone seemed to imply this was a possibility roughly on par with the sun rising in the east—"I have a friend who works in the laboratory there, cleaning artifacts. He can sneak us in through the back door." George looked down at his phone on the table. "Right now I'm waiting for a call from Mr. Doumas."

This was news. Because my communication with the Greek tourism board had been so sketchy, the only request I'd been able to get through was that I wanted to meet someone working at Akrotiri. If Atlantis was Santorini's number one legend, Christos Doumas was probably runner-up. He had worked as second-in-command to Spyridon Marinatos himself and had taken over when his mentor suffered a stroke and died at Akrotiri in 1974. Doumas had been leading the excavations of the buried city for nearly four decades. If anyone had an up-to-date opinion about its connection to Plato, it would be Doumas.

George and I finished our coffees and took a walk through the claustrophobic maze of Fira's shopping district. Archaeologists might still be debating Santorini's status as Atlantis, but the local merchants had obviously long since made up their minds. We passed an Atlantis Hotel, an Atlantis restaurant, and several shops selling Atlantis T-shirts. For a guy who ran a busy café, George sure seemed to have a lot of side projects: He stopped to show me some guidebooks he had published, some calendars that used photos he had taken, and two or three coffee shops that sold a popular brand of espresso he imported. George grabbed a pumice stone from a basket outside one shop and handed it to me. "Good for the feet," he said, pantomiming a scrubbing motion. I reached for my wallet but the shopkeeper waved me off. Only when we were back in George's car did I understand his indifference. Many of Santorini's roads had been carved through volcanic pumice more than twenty feet deep.

I finally determined that George held some sort of elected office in town, something like a city council member, but I never did find out specifics. Nor could I suss out his opinions on Santorini's relation to Plato's Atlantis other than a general feeling that it was good for tourism. (His English was pretty solid but his linguistic strengths pertained to the hospitality business; my Greek consisted entirely of "*Kalimera!*") Every few minutes, the chirping pop song of George's ringtone emanated from his pocket. He'd check who was calling and slip the phone back into his jeans.

The strike had shut down Santorini's many museums as well, so we didn't have much to do except drive around the island, which seemed to please George immensely. Santorini isn't particularly large, and George wanted to make sure I saw every inch of its tephra, the thick white layer of volcanic boulders, ash, and cinders that covers its surface like frosting on a cake. We drove through George's village from every conceivable direction—"There's my grandmother's house; there's the store where I used to buy candy; there's my cousin; *Kalimera! Kalimera!*"—and saw some of the island's best-known sights. We visited the famous red sand beach and the equally famous black sand beach; we drove up to the mountaintop monastery; we gazed down at an open-air pumice mine that had provided raw material for the cement that built the Suez Canal; we passed through picturesque tomato fields and vineyards, beneficiaries of the island's rich volcanic soil. We drove through, over, and around a lot of tephra. We made our way north toward Oia, a whitewashed town perched atop the cliffs at the northern tip of Santorini's crescent and by general consensus the prettiest spot on an island renowned for its beauty. We visited a few more stores featuring George's various wares, including the Atlantis bookshop, passing along the way several brides in white gowns posing for photographs. I asked George why they all seemed to be Asian. "Santorini is very popular with the Chinese," he said. "They come all this way for weddings and they *don't even drink!*" He pounded the steering wheel to underscore this lunacy.

We descended the steep, curving two-lane road to Oia's harbor, where George had arranged for his pal Dimitris to take us out on his speedboat. Over the years I've noticed that people who live on small islands tend to fall into two categories—those who dream of escaping someday and those who couldn't possibly imagine living elsewhere. George and Dimitris, like Anton Mifsud on Malta, belonged wholeheartedly to the second group. Dimitris was big and bearded and smiled a lot. With a cigarette dangling from his mouth he looked like a friendly Russian heavyweight gone to seed.

We circled the caldera clockwise, slapping through choppy surf. Wind stood my hair on end, and salt spray dried and crusted in a film on my glasses. I looked over at George, who was returning some phone calls. Not a hair was out of place. Occasionally, he cupped his hand over the mouthpiece and pointed at something, saying, "Mark, take a picture of that."

Dimitris steered the boat toward Nea Kameni, Santorini's central island. As we approached, he scrunched up his nose. "You can smell now—like a bad egg," he said. Near the shore, sulfur had tinted the water shamrock green. On the island, tourists were marching around a smoldering crater. Geologically speaking, Nea Kameni is a newborn, having first appeared in 1707 and expanding through occasional lava growth spurts ever since. Though the volcano had been relatively quiet for more than sixty years, restaurateurs had recently noticed their wineglasses clinking together, the result of new tremors. Geologists had in recent months determined that a new "magma balloon," a name perhaps a shade too jolly for the first sign of an inevitable volcanic apocalypse, was growing beneath Santorini's caldera.

Back on shore, George took me to Dimitris's waterfront restaurant and ordered enough food and wine for eight people. We finished only about two-thirds of it. Oia is famous for its sunsets, and we waited for the sun to start its descent toward the sea, as happy as a Chinese wedding party, if somewhat less sober. My eyelids began to droop. George's phone trilled. He glanced down, sat up straight, and took off his sunglasses. He had a brief, somewhat formal-sounding discussion in Greek with the other party.

"Mr. Doumas would like to meet us for dinner," he said, placing his phone solemnly on the table. "Mark, thank you for making this possible. To meet Mr. Doumas is a great honor for me."

Between the time George dropped me off and then picked me up for our dinner date with Doumas, I drank a very large coffee and reviewed my notes about Akrotiri. If anything, the archaeological discoveries following the Marinatos dig in the 1960s had only made it a stronger candidate for Atlantis. At the time of its burial, Akrotiri had been a thriving port city whose citizens enjoyed the prosperity of their maritime trading successes. Two- and three-story houses were built on narrow cobbled streets. Remains from storage chambers demonstrated gourmet tastes for foods both domestic and imported. A sophisticated plumbing system carried wastewater away from homes into pipes under the paving stones. Neat piles of debris and evidence of recent structural repair work seemed to indicate that Akrotiri was cleaning up from an earlier seismic shock when the Thera blast occurred. The earthquake-followed-by-catastrophe sequence paralleled the demise of Plato's Atlantis.

The most revelatory finds had been the frescoes found adorning the walls of nearly every home. These had been preserved to a remarkable degree by their burial in ash. George had given me a pamphlet written by Doumas in which the scholar described the painting and pottery of the ancient Therans as showing Minoan influence, but displaying a looser, less formal style. One intricately detailed fresco wrapping around three walls of a second-story room could have been a panoramic snapshot taken thirty-six hundred years ago. A fleet of oared ships carrying warriors, escorted by dolphins, sails between two towns. Well-dressed crowds have assembled in both, the smaller one bidding farewell and the larger one, which resembles Akrotiri, greeting the arrivals. It seemed possible that the scene captured a pre-eruption voyage between Crete and Thera.

Around eight that night, George and I drove to the southern end of Santorini, to a quiet restaurant looking out onto the infinite blackness of the Sea of Crete. George arranged for a table on the terrace where we could hear the gentle waves rolling onto the shore. Then we waited. And waited. After about forty-five minutes George nervously called Doumas, who was so absorbed in some work that he had forgotten about dinner. A few minutes later we watched a tiny, bespectacled figure slowly materialize from the direction of the Akrotiri ruins.

"I must apologize again; I was preparing slides for a presentation tomorrow and I lost track of time," Doumas said, taking a seat across from George and me. His excellent posture and pouf of white hair gave him the bearing of a wise eagle. He spoke English with the perfectly clipped cadences of a British aristocrat and used words like *whilst*. Two women approached the table, smiling and leaning in to give him a kiss. "You see, all the ladies love me," he said, and as further proof a gray-haired matron in a black dress and apron burst out of the kitchen and smothered Doumas with affection. When she departed, Doumas said, "She was the cook at our dig here," with Marinatos in the 1960s. "She was fourteen years old. Now she has grandchildren."

George poured dry Santorini white wine for the three of us, and Doumas warily inquired about my research. As the world's leading living expert on the world's number one Atlantis candidate, he was called on frequently to appear in documentaries and such, only to find out later that his words had been twisted or used out of context.[9] He was visibly relieved when I told him that I wasn't necessarily trying to prove that Santorini was Atlantis. I was more interested in trying to find out why so many others had tried to do so.

"Well, first of all because Santorini's present shape recalls the shape of rings," he said. "Akrotiri is the best example of a Bronze Age city in the Aegean that is so well preserved, and it is a revelation because of its high standard of living. This, combined with the shape of the island, makes people imagine things."

"But didn't Marinatos see a correlation between Thera and Atlantis?" I asked.

"Marinatos said that after the eruption of the volcano, obviously contacts between Crete and Egypt were interrupted. And therefore there was created a legend that an island disappeared and so on. But he says on the other hand, if this was known to the Egyptians, why does no source in Egypt mention it? We know a lot about the ancient world, thanks to the Egyptian sources, but there is nothing like that in the Egyptian literature."

Had I been less intimidated and afraid of embarrassing George, who was sitting quietly with his hands folded, like an altar boy listening to a homily, I might have argued that whether or not the disappearance of Thera appears in the Egyptian chronicles was, like most things Atlantean, open to interpretation. I might also have noted that Marinatos had sometimes indulged ambiguity for the sake of drawing attention (and money) to Akrotiri, to the degree that people still argued about whether he'd said Thera was Atlantis or not.

Doumas saw no point in equivocating. When he started working at Akrotiri in 1968, a friend who owned the island's only hotel had called to ask if Doumas would adopt a neutral stance on the question

---

9 Perhaps the one thing that every scholar I spoke with for this book could agree on was that at some point they'd been interviewed by a documentary crew that neglected to mention they were making a film about Atlantis.

of Atlantis in order to attract visitors. "I said I was a scholar, not a tourist agent," he said. The sour look on his face made clear that forty years later he was still irked by the hotelier's nerve.

Doumas has never been exactly shy about voicing his skepticism about Atlantis, either. He'd expressed plenty of doubts into a microphone at the inaugural Atlantis conference in 2005, at which he'd been invited to give the keynote address. He started his remarks by calling Atlantis "science fiction," a description that must have confused a crowd largely comprised of people hoping to find Plato's lost land. In the version published in the conference proceedings, he concluded with a quotation in French and an appeal to his fellow scholars to "stop pursuing chimeras."

Over dinner, Doumas was no less dubious. "Those who support a view that Santorini was Atlantis say, 'Well, it was a mistake,'" Doumas said. "Instead of 900 they wrote 9,000. No. Plato was firm; he was clear. It was nine thousand years before. And of course in the tenth millennium such a culture never existed. It is the postglacial period. Plato has also written about the Cave of the Ideas, yes?" Plato's Allegory of the Cave, one of the most famous passages in the *Republic*, is where Socrates describes a hypothetical group of prisoners chained underground who experience reality as a set of flickering shadows on a wall. Meanwhile all the colorful, three-dimensional wonders of the sun-filled world transpire a few meters beyond. The scene nicely illustrates one of philosophy's primary conundrums: the wide gap between the small slice of existence that we're able to perceive through our senses and any sort of objective truth. "So why don't we identify the Cave of the Ideas and try to find it?" Doumas asked.

To Doumas, the story of Atlantis was simply a tale that Plato cooked up to illustrate the political theories in the *Republic*. "He wanted to present to his fellow Athenians that for a society to be in harmony, in peace, it has to respect certain rules. And as soon as these rules are not followed, then the gods are against you. It's exactly the same thing like in the myth of Sodom and Gomorrah, in the Bible. It's no different. So why do people not try to find Sodom and Gomorrah?"

"Actually," I said, trying not to sound disrespectful, "I'm pretty sure people are looking for Sodom and Gomorrah at this very moment."

"They are; I know," Doumas said, shaking his head. "People are crazy."

While Doumas and I chatted, George continued filling our wine-glasses and quietly ordered a massive spread of seafood. Plates of mussels and shrimp and tiny fried fish arrived in waves until the tabletop was so crowded we had to keep our hands in our laps. Doumas nibbled at a few things and apologized for not being able to indulge more enthusiastically. He'd recently suffered a heart attack. He was nearing eighty years old and with the Greek economic crisis the budget for Akrotiri excavations had been cut to zero. I got the sense that his naturally low reserves of bullshit had long since been burned through.

"If you look at the occupation, or the specialty, of those who are in favor of Atlantis, you will realize that they have nothing to do with classics nor history nor archaeology. Nothing. Somebody's an engineer, another is a geologist. Well, when Praxiteles made the famous statue of Hermes in Olympia, he called the sandalmaker of Olympia to check if there was anything wrong with the sandals. This sandalmaker came and, admiring, said, 'I think if the head of the statue was a little bit further left, or if the hair . . .' So Praxiteles said, 'Shoemaker to your shoes.' Don't get involved in other people's affairs. I don't say these people are crooks. I think because they are not specialists in the field, maybe they really believe these things."

"So why do you think people still get so excited about finding it?" I asked. I was a little drunk at this point—maybe more than a little— and Doumas had just dismissed about a year's worth of research I had done. I suddenly felt emotionally committed to the search for Atlantis. I was looking for an honest answer.

"If you remember, the title of my paper at the 2005 conference was 'The Utopia of a Utopia.' Atlantis is a utopia. Everyone would like to live in such an ideal city. It's a dream."

I didn't do much dreaming when I crawled into bed after midnight. Around 6:00 A.M. I woke up unrested, still unsettled by my talk with Doumas, and severely hungover. My mouth felt as if it had been stuffed with volcanic ash, and the words of the physician Eryximachus from Plato's *Symposium* swished around my throbbing brain: "If I have learned anything from medicine, it is the following point: Inebriation is harmful to everyone."

I cursed George's gift for hospitality, pulled on some clothes, and went out in search of coffee. The only place open was a small, open-air restaurant catering to the fishermen who sold their daily catch at a small stand across the street. Seafood was perhaps second on the list of things I didn't want to think about, behind dry Santorini white wine. After two double espressos, I decided to sweat out the prior day's overindulgence by walking down the 586 steps from Fira, on the rim of Santorini's bowl, to the water.

The zigzagging trip to the bottom was peaceful and pretty enough that I wished I'd brought my camera. Out ahead of me, Nea Kameni smoldered in the center of the caldera. Doumas's doubts had made me more skeptical than ever that any temple of Poseidon had ever occupied the same space. The return trip to the top was far trickier. Every two minutes a small team of mules came charging down the steps like the bulls at Pamplona, shitting everywhere, followed by a mule tender with no sympathy for anyone who lacked the good sense to pay him for a ride to the top. I finally reached the summit, soaked with sweat, smelling of yesterday's wine from the waist up and barnyard from the ankles down. George called, sounding less than fresh himself. He suggested we push our scheduled visit to Akrotiri back a couple of hours. "No strike today, Mark," he croaked. "Meet me at my café at eleven."

By noon, George was wheedling complimentary passes from the ticket sellers at Akrotiri. (I recognized the universal hand gestures signifying "This guy is a travel writer; can't we come in for free?") Visitors have to enter a modern building, covered by a new steel-beamed roof, in order to see the ancient buildings dug out of the earth. (The site had only recently reopened after a seven-year hiatus because part of the old roof had collapsed and killed a tourist.) Even on a hot sunny day the ruins felt spooky, recently deserted. They looked like abandoned sand castles. Walking down the excavated streets made me feel creepy, like I was visiting a crime scene. No human remains had yet been found. Doumas believed that future excavations might find large numbers of bodies once the area near the former port was cleared. His hypothesis was that the people of Thera had been waiting to escape on ships when the island blew sky-high.

We circled the ruins for an hour, George snapping plenty of high-resolution photos for future projects. The frescoes had all been removed and shipped off to the national museum in Athens. There were no Atlantis revelations to be found here.

"Mark, you look like you could use a glass of wine," George said, patting me on the shoulder. Ten minutes later we were seated on the terrace of a winery of which George was, I wasn't shocked to learn, part owner. After two glasses of dry white, our hangovers lifted. In a pleasant haze, I met some more of George's cousins. We ate a huge lunch at Character Café, polished off a bottle of Santorini rosé, and watched the sun sink over the caldera, the most gorgeous sunset I'd ever seen. But just thinking of the blast that had formed a thousand-foot-deep hole gave me chills.

In the *Odyssey*, Homer writes of the importance of *xenia*, or "guest-friendship," the ancient Greek tradition of offering hospitality to strangers who are far from home. I thanked George for showing me *xenia*, but he said he didn't recognize the word and changed the subject to restaurants that I should check out in Athens, where I was heading next. Perhaps I was butchering the pronunciation. Early the next morning, when I checked out of the hotel, the owner handed me my bill, along with two shopping bags stuffed with postcards, calendars, books, dried fava beans, olive oil, and wine.

"*Kalimera!*" he said. "George left these for you."

CHAPTER TWENTY

Triangulating Pythagoras

Plato's Academy, Athens (ca. 360 BC)

If Christos Doumas was correct, the Atlantis tale was solely a literary invention, like the Cave of the Ideas, created to illustrate the political model Plato placed at the center of what is probably the most influential work in the history of philosophy, the *Republic*. Near the start of the *Timaeus*, Socrates reminds his friends that "the chief theme of my yesterday's discourse was the state—how constituted and of what citizens composed it would seem likely to be most perfect." He then expresses a desire to see his ideas brought to life, in a story about how Athens "when at war showed by the greatness of her actions and the magnanimity of her words in dealing with other cities a result worthy of her training and education." This is Critias's cue to start telling the story he heard of the war between Athens and Atlantis.

But what was Plato's ideal state? Strange though it may seem today, one of the Cradle of Democracy's greatest citizens was no populist. His noble lineage predisposed him to negative feelings toward democracy, which he wrote "distributes a sort of equality to both equals and unequals alike." Average citizens were easily swayed by rhetoric; a majority had repeatedly voted in support of the disastrous military campaigns of the Peloponnesian War against Sparta, which ended with the defeat of Athens in 404 BC, including a reckless invasion of Syracuse that ended with the loss of thousands of Athenian soldiers and two fleets of warships. Following the war Athens was briefly ruled by a brutal oligarchy installed by the Spartans. When democracy was restored, Socrates, who was himself no populist, was prosecuted for the crimes of "refusing to recognize the gods of the state" and "corrupting the youth of Athens." Socrates was found guilty by a majority vote and sentenced to death. He chose to die by drinking hemlock rather than escape into exile. In Plato's beautiful dialogue the *Phaedo*, one of the witnesses to Socrates's death presumably speaks for the author when he says, "My own tears came in floods against my will."

Following the death of Socrates in 399 BC, Plato escaped Athens to travel widely for a decade, stopping in Libya, Italy, and Egypt, all three of which, of course, later appeared in his Atlantis tale. In 390 BC, he began a long stay in southern Italy and Sicily, a period during which he encountered two men who would greatly influence the path of his life and thinking. In the city of Taras (now Taranto), he met Archytas, a statesman who led his city according to the principles of Pythagoreanism. This school of philosophy, founded by the Greek expatriate Pythagoras around 530 BC, held that mathematics provided a key to unlocking the mysteries of the universe. Plato's conversations with Archytas seem to have left him a convert to the Pythagorean veneration of numbers.

In Sicily, Plato met the dictator Dionysius I, a very different type of ruler. Dionysius controlled the powerful city of Syracuse absolutely. Plato liked dictatorships even less than he did democracies, an opinion he shared freely with Dionysius. The king responded by having Plato arrested and (according to one version of the story) sold into slavery. By luck, a friend of Plato's was at the auction and purchased his freedom.

Having completed one of history's most fruitful study-abroad trips, Plato returned to Athens in 387 BC and founded the Academy on a plot of land about a mile from central Athens. He was already predisposed toward authoritarianism by his aristocratic roots, but the execution of Socrates by referendum seems to have cemented the military oligarchy of Sparta in Plato's mind as the least-worst model for a society. Plato provides a framework for such a society in the *Republic*.

In the *Republic*, the character Socrates compares running a large state to steering a large ship. To do so by majority rule invites calamity. "The true pilot must give his attention to the time of year, the seasons, the sky, the winds, the stars, and all that pertains to his art if he is to be a true ruler of a ship," Plato writes. And just as trained navigators are the only ones suited to captain ships, only rulers trained in philosophy are capable of governing. The very best ruler would be both a philosopher and a king, or what Plato calls a philosopher-king.

Socrates also describes one of Plato's most important philosophical concepts, the Theory of Forms, by which the world is divided into two regions—that which we can intuit through our senses and a higher, abstract perfection (the forms) that exists outside of space and time. This latter idea is where we get the Platonic ideal, the unattainable model.[10] We see a spindly legged animal with a long face and mane and we think "horse," but that animal is merely a flawed example of the form of a horse.

Plato's ideal city-state in the *Republic* more closely resembles Sparta

---

10 One Platonic ideal that Plato didn't invent was Platonic love—that is, nonsexual friendship. The term was originally coined by the Renaissance scholar Marsilio Ficino, as a purified interpretation of a speech Socrates gives in Plato's *Symposium*, in which, as Rebecca Newberger Goldstein writes, the philosopher "passionately urges them to transform the erotic longing that tends to fixate on particular boys into an equally passionate longing for abstract truth."

than Athens. All classes were expected to live austerely. Children were to be raised communally; no child would know the identity of his parents and vice versa. Men and women who possessed desirable characteristics would be encouraged to breed. Rigid state control of education would be essential. Children's exposure to literature would be limited—Homer in particular was to be banned—so as not to expose them to tales that featured poorly behaved gods or soldiers who showed doubt or remorse.

Stories, Plato knew, were much more than entertainment. Used properly, they could be powerful tools.

If classics scholars are correct in estimating that Plato wrote the *Timaeus* and *Critias* around 360 BC, his writing would have been colored by a disastrous real-world attempt to create a model society like that of the *Republic*. One might think that after being sold into slavery at the end of his first extended visit to Syracuse (just imagine the nasty TripAdvisor review he could leave today), Plato would have sworn off the place. But when Dionysius I died in 367 BC, his brother convinced Plato to return to Syracuse to train the new ruler, Dionysius II. Under Plato's tutelage the young dictator might develop into a philosopher-king.

If Plato was hoping to use the *Republic* as a training manual, his expectations were wildly unrealistic. In book VII of the *Republic*, Socrates explains that good philosopher-kings will require, in addition to extensive work in mathematics, five years of study in dialectic and fifteen years of practical training in governing. A true philosopher-king should be prepared to rule by age fifty—not exactly the sort of advice a young dictator is eager to hear. Whatever soured Plato's second extended visit to Syracuse, he ended it under house arrest. When Plato's old Pythagorean friend Archytas, the widely respected leader of nearby Taras, received word that Plato was being held captive, he dispatched a rescue ship.

Archytas was himself a mathematician, famous for devising a nifty formula to double the size of a cube. (He seems to have been a most extraordinary man; among his achievements he is also credited with inventing a toy bird that could fly—possibly history's first robot.) Some scholars believe he was the model for the philosopher-king in the *Republic*. It seems quite likely that his ideas were on Plato's mind during the composition of the *Timaeus*, Plato's attempt to impose order on a chaotic world. The Pythagorean basis of the *Timaeus* would have been obvious to anyone studying at the Academy. The school's curriculum was based on the four disciplines of the Pythagorean quadrivium: arithmetic, geometry, astronomy, and harmonics. Aristotle even wrote a book, since lost, about the relationship between Archytas's works and the *Timaeus*.

One thing I had noticed about the Atlantologists I'd met was that while almost all of them took Plato's numbers quite seriously, none had much considered the possible influence of his Pythagorean thinking. Perhaps this is because the Pythagoreans themselves were such an odd bunch.

Though we can't be completely certain that the historical figure Pythagoras even existed—some historians think that he was invented, and there is a general consensus that all mathematical discoveries made by Pythagoreans were routinely attributed to their founder—classical sources paint him as a brilliant, charismatic philosopher from the Greek island of Samos. He may have traveled to Egypt, where he could have picked up some basic geometry, and eventually settled in Crotona, on the front part of the Italian boot's instep. It was here that the Pythagorean Order was founded, a religious community (*cult* might be a more accurate description) based on his teachings. The Pythagoreans were secretive and wrote nothing down, but there is no doubt that their core beliefs blended two basic ingredients that do not mix well today—mathematics and mysticism.

Pythagoras is famously credited with saying, "All things are numbers," an idea that fascinated not only Plato but also Aristotle. In his *Metaphysics*, Aristotle wrote of the Pythagoreans that "in numbers they seemed to see many resemblances to the things that exist . . . fire, earth, and water," but also justice, soul, reason, opportunity, "and similarly almost all other things." The discovery of mathematical formulas such as the Pythagorean theorem about 3-4-5 right triangles or that the sum of sequential odd integers starting with the number 1 always adds up to a square (i.e., $1 + 3 + 5 + 7 = 16 = 4$ squared) must have felt like divine revelations. It was as if bit by bit they were unraveling the binary code behind reality.

The Pythagoreans were equally well-known for their esoteric dogmas. Chief among these was a belief in the transmigration of souls, or reincarnation. Austerity was prized. Property was held in common. Women were considered equal to men. Pythagoreans were vegetarians—the term *Pythagorean diet* was commonly used to describe abstinence from meat until the nineteenth century—possibly because of their belief in transmigrating souls. Their list of dos and don'ts was long and strange. Never touch a white rooster. Always remove the right shoe first but wash the left foot first. Do not leave the impression of one's body in the bedclothes upon rising. And never eat—nor even touch—beans.

As often occurs with charismatic religious leaders, Pythagoras himself became the subject of various astounding stories, many of them involving animals. He was said to have once persuaded a bear to give up eating meat. On another occasion he heard a dog yelping as it was being beaten and intervened, insisting that he recognized the animal's bark as the voice of a reincarnated friend. Aristotle noted that Pythagoras was believed to have a golden thigh, had traveled to the underworld, and was reported to have been seen in two different cities at one time.

If all things were numbers to the Pythagoreans, those same numbers were also, to a certain extent, living things. They had personalities and meanings beyond representing amounts. The number 1, for instance, represented reason and indivisibility. The number 2 represented opinion and imperfection, 3 represented harmony, and so on. Odd numbers were male, even numbers female. Numbers were represented by groups of monads, or dots, which is why 9 is still called a "square" number—it would probably have been depicted as three identical rows of three pebbles. The most perfect number of all was 10, which was the sum of 1 + 2 + 3 + 4 and would have been represented like this:

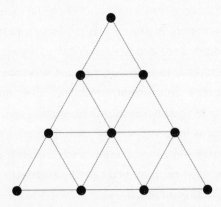

This figure was called the sacred tetractys, and it would have been packed with meaning for a Pythagorean. Not only does this equilateral triangle have three equal sides, but also the four rows correspond to four of the fundamental concepts of geometry: a point (zero dimensions), a line (a one-dimensional segment between two points), a plane (a two-dimensional shape, in this instance a triangle), and a polyhedron (a 3-D solid that occupies space, in this instance a pyramid). The Pythagoreans believed that numbers gave off vibrations, an idea that is still popular with numerologists, who proudly cite Pythagoras as their founder. It should come as no surprise that the Pythagoreans were really into pentagrams, which they apparently used as symbols of health.

But what might strike us as a particularly modern goofball idea—is there any term more self-evidently flaky than *good vibrations?*—seems to have instead emerged from one of the greatest mathematical discoveries ever made. Historians agree that this discovery had a major influence on Plato, and on the *Timaeus*. Which means that it might help explain Atlantis, too.

According to Pythagorean lore, one day Pythagoras was walking past a metalworker's workshop. From within he heard the surprisingly harmonious sounds of hammers beating iron on anvils. The philosopher entered the shop to discover the source of this concordance. Within he learned that when two hammers, one twice the weight of the other—a six-pounder and a twelve-pounder—struck metal simultaneously, they were in perfect harmony. The key was the ratio of their weights, 1:2. Pythagoras later re-created the same effect by plucking two strings, one twice the length of the other. (Musically inclined blacksmiths should not attempt to replicate these results at home. Subsequent tests have shown that the hammer demonstration doesn't actually work, but the string does.)

What Pythagoras had found was the octave. Because there are seven notes to the CDEFGAB musical scale, two notes eight places apart will have the same pitch, like the first and last *do* in the sequence *do, re, mi, fa, sol, la, ti, do*. The higher note has twice the frequency of the other. Pythagoras also noted that the twelve-pound hammer and the eight-pound hammer (a 3:2 ratio) produced the sweet harmony of what musicians call a perfect fifth. The twelve-pounder paired with a nine-pounder (a 4:3 ratio) created what's now known as a perfect fourth. As if these discoveries weren't enough proof of having tapped into the supernatural world, the ratios 1:2, 2:3, and 3:4 would likely have been represented like this:

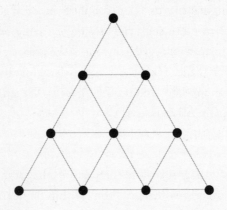

Pythagoras had uncovered a mathematical foundation for the most ephemeral of human pleasures, music. No wonder he thought all things were numbers.

From here Pythagoras, according to tradition, looked into the night sky and speculated that the distances between the celestial bodies above (the visible planets, the moon, the sun, and the stars) might adhere to the same ratios. Aristotle reported in his *Metaphysics* that the Pythagoreans believed that the orbits of the heavenly bodies produced a sound. This cosmic harmony, which humans other than Pythagoras (allegedly) didn't hear, became known as "the music of the spheres." This idea would prove to be so enduring that it would serve as the inspiration for Johannes Kepler's work on the third law of planetary motion more than two thousand years later.

Perhaps the most important influence of Pythagorean celestial harmony was on Plato's *Timaeus*, his own attempt to explain the cosmos. The very first words of the dialogue, spoken by Socrates, set the Pythagorean tone by echoing the sacred tetractys: "One, two, three . . . Where is number four, Timaeus?" In a surprisingly short amount of time, Plato moves through the first part of the Atlantis story to his description of the Divine Craftsman creating the universe from a set of blueprints. Plato proposes that this universe is both the sum total of all matter and a living being, animated by something he calls the World-Soul.

By now you're asking yourself, *What the hell does all this have to do with Atlantis?* Well, Plato shifts abruptly from extreme obscurity to odd precision by defining the exact proportions into which the Divine Craftsman divided this raw World-Soul material. The measurements are given as 1, 2, 3, 4, 9, 8, and 27. The scholar Crantor—who studied at the Academy in Athens not long after Plato's death, wrote history's first known commentary on the *Timaeus* and believed that the Atlantis story was literal history—suggested that it might be helpful to arrange the numbers like this:

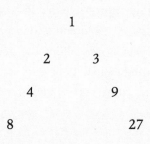

A few things about this schema are notable. Let's set aside the number 1 atop the pyramid because for the Pythagoreans 1 was the symbol of the universe and was a sort of super number from which all others derived. The remaining numbers to the left are evens; to the right are odds. The first number on each side is a prime, followed by its square, followed by its cube. Look closely and you'll also see that the basic Pythagorean harmonic ratios are there—1:2, 2:3, 4:3, and 9:8. Plato goes on in the *Timaeus* to explain—somewhat—what he's up to, using math to show that the Divine Craftsman was weaving Pythagoras's invisible source code of the universe, the harmonic scale, into the very fabric of the cosmos. Somehow, the World-Soul is also simultaneously formed into a long band that the Craftsman cuts lengthwise into two strips, which he formed into two linked circles. One of these circles he subdivided into seven other circles. These were the orbits of the five visible planets, plus the moon and the sun. The choice of seven is not coincidental. There are seven notes in the CDEFGAB scale.

There is a lot more of this type of stuff in the *Timaeus*, but that's enough for now. All we need to keep in mind at this point is that Plato wrote the numbers-packed *Timaeus* and *Critias* after hanging around with Archytas, and that their message wasn't aimed at twenty-first-century readers armed with world maps and satellite photos. Plato wrote the *Timaeus* and *Critias* as lectures to be delivered to his students at the Academy, who were studying a Pythagorean curriculum. It seems highly improbable that Plato would have written a dialogue named for the Pythagorean philosopher Timaeus, filled it with numbers and speculations about the geometric basis of the universe—and then sandwiched it between the two parts of the Atlantis story in which the numbers were intended to be taken literally.

Plato, center left, with his prize pupil Aristotle, center right, from Raphael's *The School of Athens*. In his left hand Plato holds a copy of the *Timaeus*, the original source of the Atlantis story. The seated figure, lower left, is generally believed to be Pythagoras. The tablet at his feet shows mystical numbers that influenced Plato's writings. *(Courtesy of Wikimedia Commons)*

Ignatius Donnelly, a US congressman and the author of history's second-most-important work on Atlantis, *Atlantis: The Antediluvian World* *(Courtesy of the Library of Congress)*

Tony O'Connell, founder of the online *Atlantipedia* and expert on all matters related to the lost city *(Courtesy of Tony O'Connell)*

Richard Freund, archeologist and star of the documentary *Finding Atlantis*, with a prehistoric Spanish concentric-circle stele *(Courtesy of Associated Producers, Ltd.)*

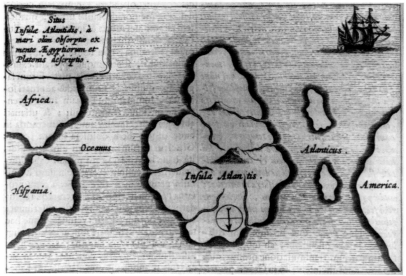

A speculative map from Athanasius Kircher's *Mundus Subterraneus* (1666), often cited as evidence that ancient sailors voyaged to Atlantis *(Courtesy of the Library of Congress)*

The pharaoh Ramses III repulses the invading Sea Peoples, as recorded in hieroglyphics at Medinet Habu, his mortuary temple in Egypt. *(Rendering by Jean-François Champollion, courtesy of the author)*

Rainer Kühne, the German physicist whose article in the journal *Antiquity* launched a new wave of searching for Atlantis *(Courtesy of Associated Producers, Ltd.)*

Juan Villarias-Robles, the Spanish historian and anthropologist whose multidisciplinary team investigated Kühne's hypothesis *(Courtesy of Juan Villarias-Robles)*

The Lisbon earthquake of 1755 destroyed Portugal's capital and echoed Plato's description of Atlantis's end—massive tremors followed by devastating floods. *(Courtesy of the Jan T. Kozak Collection, NISEE)*

George Nomikos on the island of Santorini, sometimes known by its former name, Thera *(Courtesy of George Nomikos)*

Santorini's unique bull's-eye shape and deep caldera have led some to believe the volcanic explosion that created it inspired Plato's story. *(Courtesy of George Nomikos)*

Santorini's ancient city of Akrotiri, discovered in 1967 under several meters of volcanic ash, bears striking similarity to Plato's description of Atlantis. *(Courtesy of the author)*

For a brief period in the 1960s, the search for Atlantis was treated as legitimate scientific news. *(The New York Times, September 4, 1966)*

Dr. Anton Mifsud believes he has found a twenty-three-hundred-year-old source that proves Atlantis was located in Malta. *(Courtesy of Anton Mifsud)*

The enormous canals Plato described in Atlantis may have been modeled on Malta's mysterious ancient cart ruts. *(Courtesy of the author)*

The Strait of Gibraltar, which the ancient Greeks called the Pillars of Heracles—the end of the known world *(Courtesy of Olaf Tausch/Wikimedia Commons)*

The sixth-century BC Greek philosopher Pythagoras discovered the mathematical ratios behind musical harmonies, evidence that numbers were the hidden code of nature. *(Courtesy of the author)*

Details Plato gave about the ancient Acropolis in Athens, once believed fictional elements of the Atlantis story, were confirmed by twentieth-century archaeology. *(Courtesy of the Library of Congress)*

Geophysics professor Stavros Papamarinopoulos, who has analyzed Plato's use of myth and history in the Atlantis tale for more than forty years *(Courtesy of Stavros Papamarinopoulos)*

Papamarinopoulos argues that the concentric rings of Atlantis may have been a natural formation, similar to the Richat Structure in Mauritania. *(Courtesy of NASA)*

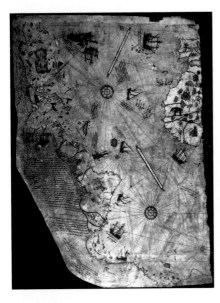

The Piri Reis map, created five hundred years ago by an Ottoman admiral, is seen by some as evidence of an Atlantis located in Antarctica. *(Courtesy of Wikimedia Commons)*

Michael Hübner, whose statistical analysis of details in the Atlantis story concluded overwhelmingly that Plato's island had sunk near Morocco's Atlantic coast *(Courtesy of the author)*

The naturally formed circle located by Hübner near Agadir, Morocco. Its measurements are strikingly similar to those Plato gave for Atlantis's ringed city. *(Courtesy of the author)*

The ocean impact of a meteorite (many times larger than the one that caused Arizona's Meteor Crater, shown here) could have unleashed worldwide devastation recorded in flood stories such as Atlantis, Gilgamesh, and Noah's ark. *(Courtesy of NASA)*

CHAPTER TWENTY-ONE

The Cradle of Atlantology

Athens

When Plato returned to his hometown of Athens for good, having failed to put his ideas into practice in Syracuse, it's likely that he fine-tuned the ideas that formed the *Timaeus* and *Critias* by strolling the grounds of the Academy with a promising, if somewhat literal-minded, young student from Macedonia with a penchant for untangling complex ideas during ambulatory conversations. That pupil was Aristotle.

Because they are the two most important thinkers in the Western canon, and because their general philosophies were so different—Plato the dreamer asking, "What if?" and Aristotle the realist asking, "What is?"—they are often portrayed in contrast to each other. Aristotle, the story goes, having been passed over to run the Academy upon Plato's death, went home to Macedonia to tutor Alexander the Great and returned years later to open his own rival school, the Lyceum, which played Yale to the Academy's Harvard. For Atlantology, one consequence of this insubordination, cited in almost every semiserious Atlantis book and documentary, is Aristotle's quote "He who invented it also destroyed it."

When I raised this issue with Tony O'Connell, he insisted that I take a look at the work of Thorwald Franke, an independent Atlantis researcher in Germany. Franke was diligent about his philological research, to the extent that he had self-published a nifty bit of textual detective work, *Aristotle and Atlantis*, that examined the sources of Aristotle's supposed doubt. (Franke believes Sicily was the original inspiration for Atlantis but didn't mention this in the Aristotle book.) Franke argues convincingly that the Aristotle quote can be traced to a conflation of two similar-sounding passages in one of the key works of ancient geography, Strabo's *Geographica*, published early in the first century AD. Over the years a misinterpretation hardened into fact.

What I found even more interesting in Franke's book was his argument that not only hadn't Aristotle objected to the idea of Atlantis, but also in many of his works he seems to confirm some belief in its veracity. In his *Meteorology*, he describes the shallow sea outside the Pillars of Heracles as clogged by mud, and Franke notes that "in the context of a geophysical work that deals with matters such as earthquakes and floods, one might have expected from Aristotle an explanation for this phenomenon." Since there is none, Franke writes, it is reasonable to assume this mud west of Gibraltar was common knowledge. Aristotle supports Plato's description of the Deucalion flood as a regional, catastrophic event, and—crucially— affirms his teacher's ideas that knowledge is discovered and lost repeatedly in cycles and that "mythical traditions are remnants of knowledge from before the last cultural demise," Franke writes. Franke concludes that while none of this proves the existence of Plato's Atlantis, we can deduce from Aristotle's "eloquent silence" that at the very least the second-greatest Western philosopher didn't consider the lost island an outright fabrication.

Modern Athens seemed to be going through its own cycle of catastrophes. A few days before my arrival, Syntagma Square, which I belatedly realized on the train from the airport was about a Molotov cocktail's throw from my hotel, had been packed with fifty thousand angry protesters, many chucking rocks at the police, who responded with tear gas. They had come to show their displeasure with the German chancellor, who was in town to squeeze further cuts from the Greek budget. What I found in Syntagma when I emerged from the subway after dark was something less dramatic but sadder—a large park across the street from Greece's parliament populated by homeless people sleeping on the ground. Stray dogs sniffed around for edible scraps and didn't seem to be finding much.

In the morning, I stepped over the sidewalk campers outside my hotel and walked a couple of miles, crossing under a highway and over a set of train tracks, to the original site of Plato's Academy. As a scenic monument to one of the most important pieces of real estate in intellectual history, it falls a little short of the Platonic ideal. The sign warning away nongeometers has long since disappeared, along with just about everything else. In Plato's time the spot had been a peaceful grove with shrines, a gymnasium, and areas dedicated to lectures and debate. Today, it consists of a few stone foundations that have been excavated inside of a public park in a somewhat shabby neighborhood northwest of the Acropolis. Plato died at a wedding feast in 347 BC, and his body had been buried on the grounds of the Academy, according to Diogenes Laertius's *Lives of Eminent Philosophers*. Which means that theoretically his grave is within the confines of the park, but like so much about Plato, the location of his final resting spot remains a mystery.

The day was hot and the park was nearly deserted. In Plato's time, scholars throughout the Mediterranean gathered at the Academy for communal meals and ontological discourse. The only group I saw was unwashed men huddled atop the stone remains of an ancient foundation, hiding from the noon sun and drinking large cans of Alfa beer. Their possessions were stuffed into plastic shopping bags that had been stowed between gaps in the ruins. Several stones had been tagged with graffiti. My search for an ancient olive tree under which Plato was said to have led discussions with students was no more successful than my hunt for his tomb. Later I read that someone had pulled down the tree to use for firewood.

I walked back toward the city center and an outdoor souvlaki joint that George Nomikos had recommended, ordered a large Alfa of my own, and pulled out my copy of *The Atlantis Hypothesis: Searching for a Lost Land*, the collected papers delivered at the first International Conference on the Atlantis Hypothesis in 2005. This compendium is, to put it mildly, eclectic. It opens with Christos Doumas's essay dismissing Atlantis as a chimera and closes with one by Stavros Papamarinopoulos, the organizer of the conference, making an entirely cogent and convincing argument for its reality. Scattered in between are articles on everything from Freudian interpretations of the Atlantis myth to the effects of sea-level change on coastal geography following the last Ice Age. The essay I was searching for, however, was about another of the great lost cities of ancient Greece, Helike, and its possible influence on Plato.

The accepted history of Helike's sudden end is strikingly similar to the story of Atlantis. During the winter of 373 BC, this prosperous capital of the city-state of Achaea, situated on a coastal plain near the Gulf of Corinth, disappeared in a single night. For five days prior to the event, the historian Aelian wrote, inhabitants of the city had noticed that "all the mice and martens and snakes and centipedes and beetles and every other creature of that kind left in a body" and fled for higher ground. A huge earthquake struck Helike during the night, destroying houses and killing most of its residents. When day broke, the stunned survivors attempted to flee but were drowned by a massive wave that overwhelmed Helike and erased almost any evidence that a city had existed. The Greek geographer Strabo wrote that the "whole district together with the city was hidden from sight; and two thousand men who were sent by the Achaeans were unable to recover the dead bodies." In the city's sacred grove devoted to

Poseidon, only the tops of the trees were still visible. Ten Spartan ships at anchor nearby were also destroyed.

Like Atlantis, Helike had a strong connection to Poseidon. When the Greek geographer Eratosthenes visited the site about 150 years after the catastrophe, he spoke with ferrymen who described a bronze statue of Poseidon that remained standing, visible just beneath the water's surface in a *poros*, an archaic Greek word that's usually translated as a narrow passage of water. In its hand the statue held aloft a small sea horse that threatened to snag fishermen's nets. The second-century-AD Greek geographer Pausanias wrote that the destruction of Helike had been the work of a vengeful Poseidon, a punishment by the god of earthquakes against the people of Helike for refusing to give a statue of himself to a group of supplicants who had voyaged from Asia Minor.

Despite the abundance of historical accounts, physical evidence of Helike is scarce. Spyridon Marinatos spent more than twenty years searching for the lost city; just months before his breakthrough at Akrotiri, he had predicted to a reporter that Helike, which because of its sudden disappearance might contain unimaginable bronze and marble sculptures from the classical era, would be "almost surely the most spectacular archaeological discovery ever made." Even after Akrotiri became world famous in 1967, Marinatos continued to pursue Helike until his death seven years later.

At the moment Helike vanished in 373 BC, Plato would have been in Athens, less than a hundred miles away, teaching at the Academy. He had likely written the *Republic* by this time and may have been pondering how to expand on some of its ideas in what would become the *Timaeus*. News of an important Greek city with ties to Poseidon being almost instantaneously demolished by an earthquake and resulting sea surge would surely have reached him. If the Atlantis tale was indeed the first example of historical fiction, as some have proposed, then the disappearance of Helike would have been obvious source material. The eminent Plato scholar A. E. Taylor wrote of Atlantis that "the account of its destruction is manifestly based on the facts of the great earthquake and tidal wave of the year 373 which ravaged the Achaean coast."

Employing the standard interpretation of *poros* as a narrow passage of water, Marinatos sought the lost city on the seabed of the Gulf of Corinth. Others, including Jacques Cousteau, turned up to try their luck. (Cousteau actually came twice, to no avail.) It was only when a young classics scholar paused to question the meaning of *poros* that a breakthrough was made.

That scholar, Dora Katsonopoulou, invited me to meet her at the new Acropolis Museum in Athens. It occurred to me as I waited outside for her to arrive, looking up at the hilltop ruins, that when Plato wrote the *Critias* these temples were younger than the Empire State Building is today. Katsonopoulou, now in her fifties, was easy to spot from fifty yards away—effortlessly glamorous, with long dark hair and a red scarf.

We took the escalator to the museum's third-floor café, where a wall of windows provided a breathtaking panoramic view of the Acropolis, the afternoon sun illuminating the geometric perfection of the ruined Parthenon. Heads at other tables turned in our direction, trying to figure out if Katsonopoulou was someone important, which she certainly was to anyone interested in Atlantis. We ordered coffees and split a piece of apple pie. By this time I'd met enough Atlantologists for coffee that my Pavlovian response to the scent of roasted beans was to start asking questions about concentric circles, but Katsonopoulou preempted me by explaining how she had gotten involved in hunting for lost cities.

"I was a graduate student getting a PhD in classics at Cornell University, back in '85 or '86," she said. One day her adviser phoned and said someone from the astrophysics department was interested in Helike and wanted to speak with her. Steven Soter was a well-known scientist who, among other achievements, had cowritten Carl Sagan's *Cosmos* documentary series. While helping a colleague research ancient literature about the possible causes of earthquakes, he had become fascinated by Helike. Katsonopoulou knew the story well—she had studied ancient Greek and had grown up on the Peloponnesus near the rumored site of Helike. She had heard tales of its disappearance as a child. Soter and Katsonopoulou organized the Helike Project to conduct an archaeological search for the lost city. In 1988, following the strategy employed by their predecessors, they conducted a thorough sonar survey of the muddy waters of the Gulf of Corinth. They found nothing.

After this failure, Katsonopoulou went back and reviewed Eratosthenes's account of his visit, focusing on the detail of the statue sunk in the *poros*. She realized that the ferrymen whom Eratosthenes had interviewed were not transporting people across the larger gulf, but rather across "a sort of lake or lagoon that was connected to the sea," she told me. Today, the spot occupied by this *poros* is dry land, covered with a thick layer of sediment. "So I said we should look on land, not in the sea," she said, pointing her fork at me. "And I was right!"

In 2000, having moved their search inland, the Helike Project team dug four trial trenches and began finding evidence ten to twenty feet beneath the ground—ceramics, masonry stones, and a bronze coin from the fifth century BC. Predictably, the BBC marked these discoveries by airing a documentary titled *Helike: The Real Atlantis*.

A waiter brought another slice of pie to the table, unsolicited. Katsanopoulou arched an eyebrow and waved him away. I asked how the just-completed archaeological season at Helike had gone. "Amazing! Very exciting! In one trench we found a very impressive destruction layer, as we call it in archaeology. It means you don't have the remains of walls or buildings, but you have . . . like someone just hurled everything! I suspect that this is the layer of the 373 earth-quake."

Such a violent dispersal would require extremely powerful seismic activity. Sedimentological analysis, still pending, could prove a tsunami had followed. Naturally, I steered the topic toward Atlantis. How closely were the two related?

"I think for Plato, Helike is the model of the destructive phenom-enon," Katsonopoulou said. "The same things are described, the sea and the tsunami and how the city disappeared from the face of the earth. Exactly what our sources say about Helike. Poseidon was the patron god of Helike and the patron god of Atlantis and also the god of earthquakes and underground waters. Poseidon destroyed He-like, and he probably destroyed Atlantis—in both cases for being im-pious. In *Critias*, Plato's text stops abruptly at the end. I believe that the continuation would have been for Zeus to ask Poseidon to come in and punish Atlantis."

Another waiter came bearing apple pie. Katsonopoulou threw her hands up and said something sharp to him in Greek. He scurried away. She shook her head, took a sip of coffee, and continued.

"Another amazing thing is that Plato was alive at the time of He-like and lived very close, in Athens. One of the ancients tells us that the Spartan admiral who tried to take Plato into slavery in Syracuse—to sell him, in fact—this Spartan admiral was in Helike the night of the catastrophe and drowned there. That makes it even more plau-sible that Plato knew about this event and that it could serve as a model."

There was an even more direct personal link from Helike to Plato. One of the primary sources about the city's destruction had been a student of his at the Academy, Heraclides. The whole Atlantis story might have been cooked up at a faculty-student mixer just a mile or so from where we were sitting.

"Would you be shocked if they found a real Atlantis?" I asked.

"Yes, I would, to tell you the truth. Because so far from the evidence known to us I don't find any good grounds to support the idea that it did exist. I find it quite plausible that Plato had reasons, including political reasons, to create such a story that involves the Athenians." She stirred her coffee and tilted her head slightly to the side. "On the other hand, we cannot absolutely exclude the possibility." Katsonopoulou adjusted her scarf and waited a few seconds to see if I found this diplomatic answer satisfactory. "You're asking if I think it existed?"

"Yes."

"I cannot say yes. I would be quite, um, cautious." She seemed to be not quite satisfied with this response.

"Skeptical?" I suggested.

"Yes! Skeptical."

Katsonopoulou's theory certainly made sense, if one was looking to explain the disappearance of a sophisticated city connected to Poseidon. It definitely accounted for what Marinatos had called the "one fundamental fact" of Plato's story, that "a piece of land becomes submerged." A story based on Helike worked perfectly with Doumas's idea that the whole point was to illustrate the political ideas in the *Republic*. Looking out at the world's most famous ruins, though, I couldn't help but think of Alexander MacGillivray's description of a flood that had reached the foot of the Acropolis. When it came to trashing cities with natural disasters, Poseidon had a long rap sheet.

Just one floor down from the café is a reconstruction of the sculpture that once decorated the west pediment of the Parthenon. At the center of the triangular scene are the figures of Poseidon and Athena, who according to myth had long ago competed to be the patron of Attica, the city-state of which Athens was capital. Poseidon struck his trident into the rock of the Acropolis and created a saltwater spring. Athena planted the first olive tree. Athena was chosen as victor and patron, and the city was named in her honor. The furious Poseidon retaliated by sending a massive wave to flood all of Attica.

Tony O'Connell had noted a serious problem with the theory that Plato's story was simply a political fable dipped in historical detail, intended to illustrate the ideas of the *Republic*: The good guys, the Athenians, suffer the same watery punishment as the bad guys, the Atlanteans. Virtue, rather than being rewarded, drowns right alongside evil. If there was a kernel of truth hiding behind all the myths—and I was almost certain there was, maybe even a big one—it might help unscramble the message Plato had been trying to send. And I was pretty sure I knew the one person on Earth who could help me locate it.

CHAPTER TWENTY-TWO

Well, That Explains Everything

Patras, Greece

As I was talking on my cell phone in the café of the Patras bus station, the world's most respected Atlantologist slipped in quietly and took a seat at the table across from mine. He looked about sixty, wore sunglasses and a navy polo shirt, and scrolled through his text messages as if he had nothing more on his mind than catching the eleven thirty local to Thessaloniki. He made no attempt to catch my attention, and if I hadn't Googled a photo of him the night before I probably wouldn't have noticed him, let alone known who he was.

Stavros Papamarinopoulos could've been a character in a John le Carré novel. He held a government job that gave him access to arcane knowledge understandable only to a select group. He spent long stretches of time in Paris. He had arranged for us to meet in the unfashionable port city of Patras, which required me to ride a bus for four hours in each direction from Athens; I later learned that he kept an apartment in Athens. He had replied to perhaps half of the many e-mails I had sent him, and then only briefly and enigmatically. He hadn't responded at all to the text messages I'd sent this morning informing him of my arrival time. He believed that 70 percent of Plato's tale had been proven, a number that seemed preposterous until I read his essays. He had organized three international conferences on the subject of Atlantis and edited three thick volumes of papers, yet was perhaps the world's only Atlantis expert who had never appeared in a BBC documentary.

"Stavros?" I finally asked.

"Yes, Mark," he said, pocketing his phone. "It's good to meet you." He stood and motioned toward the door. "Let's get a taxi. The students are on strike at my university today. It's stupid because they will have to do makeup work on Saturday. But today I'm locked out of my office. I have arranged a place for us to talk. We have much to discuss."

Papamarinopoulos is a professor of geophysics at the University of Patras, one of the best universities in Greece. "My job is to find ancient cities through geophysics, by means of software and computers," he explained as we rode along the coast in the backseat of the taxi. His accomplishments were impressive. He had helped Dora Katsonopoulou find Helike using magnetometry to map beneath the site and conducted seismic surveys to prove that a fantastic-seeming story from Herodotus—that the Persian king Xerxes had ordered his men to dig a canal across the Mount Athos peninsula wide enough for two warships to pass each other—was true. He had once talked an Olympic Airways pilot into carrying two thousand pounds of geophysical equipment to Egypt when he supervised an unsuccessful search for the tomb of Alexander the Great in Alexandria. "If it was there, we would have found it," he said with a shrug.

The taxi stopped in a commercial district of Patras. We rode a tiny elevator up to the suite of offices of Papamarinopoulos's friend, an economist, who introduced himself as Yannis and then went off to buy coffees for everyone. Papamarinopoulos and I sat down on opposite sides of a conference table in the front room. It was a sunny Mediterranean day, and through the open windows we received the cicada buzz of motorbike traffic and a hint of a breeze from the

Ionian Sea, a few blocks down the hill. Papamarinopoulos removed his sunglasses; he had a kind face and the sunken eyes of an exhausted man.

Most Greeks I'd met looked worn-out by their recent economic troubles, and Papamarinopoulos certainly had his own: The government had been gradually cutting his salary since the economic crisis began. He had also spent decades suffering the insults—implied and direct—of his academic peers. Dora Katsonopoulou described her fellow archaeologists' reactions to Papamarinopoulos's Atlantis theory as "very hostile," which was probably an understatement. A prominent French historian had once mocked him openly at an assembly in Athens. When Christos Doumas had condescendingly suggested to me that sandalmakers would be better off leaving archaeological questions to the professionals, he was referring to Papamarinopoulos.

"I'm going to ask you a question," Papamarinopoulos said, leaning forward across the table. "Who defined science?"

"Plato did, in the *Phaedrus*," I said. I didn't mention that I'd learned this about two hours earlier while reading one of Papamarinopoulos's essays on the bus from Athens, but I suspected that he knew. In the *Phaedrus*, Plato has Socrates explain how a subject can be isolated, then divided into smaller chunks and analyzed until it becomes understandable.

"Very good! Since you know that, you know at least part of the personality of Plato." He pronounced the name *Plah-toh*, which seemed to give it even more gravitas than usual. "Plato also defined mythology. He differentiated between genuine and fabricated myths. It is advisable then to ask if Atlantis is a genuine or a fabricated myth."

The word *myth* is slippery because it has multiple meanings. The most common one, at least among nonspecialists, is something that is generally perceived to be true but is actually false. (Such as when Kermit explains in *The Muppet Movie* that contrary to popular belief,

a person can't get warts from touching a frog.) What Papamarinopoulos calls a fabricated myth is an invented story, the sort of tale
that Plato in the *Republic* says is useful for instructing children. At
the end of the *Republic*, Socrates tells the Myth of Er, in which a soldier returns from the land of the dead. The moral of this fabricated
myth is that only the souls of those who live virtuous lives as outlined in the *Republic* will find eternal peace.

The definition of *myth* that matters to folklorists (and Atlantologists like Papamarinopoulos) is this: a very old story, often containing
supernatural elements, that explains an event or phenomenon from
the distant past. These sorts of myths often include real historical
truths, such as the Trojan War myth that led Heinrich Schliemann
to Turkey. This is what Papamarinopoulos calls a genuine myth.
Plato, in addition to stating several times in the *Timaeus* and *Critias*
that the Atlantis story is true, also says that "the fact that it is no invented fable but genuine history is all important."

The respected classics scholar John V. Luce, a rare Atlantis possi-
bilist in an otherwise suspicious field, noted that Plato always used
the term *logos* when writing about Atlantis, rather than *muthos* (or
mythos). A *logos* is an account of something that occurred, and its use
typically refers to logical, fact-based thinking. A *mythos* is a traditional story that seeks to explain things that have no rational
explanation—long-ago historical events for which there are no records. A myth might explain the existence of evil or the creation of
the world. "Myth is about the unknown," Karen Armstrong explains
in *A Short History of Myth*. "It is about that for which initially we have
no words."

To tease out the possible kernel of truth in Plato's Atlantis tale,
Papamarinopoulos approached the story from an unconventional
direction. The most vivid and memorable elements of Plato's Atlantis story are those that describe the rise and sudden fall of a mysterious lost civilization: the huge navy, the concentric rings, the

magnificent temples, the catastrophic watery end. Papamarinopou-los instead began by taking a hard look at what Plato said about Ath-ens. "In the *Republic* Plato presents an imaginary Athens," he told me, referring to the ideal state ruled by a class of guardians. "But in the *Critias*, he presents a real Athens. One completely unknown to him."

This raised an obvious question: How could Plato write about an Athens that was completely unknown to him? Because, Papamari-nopoulos said, the information had been passed down to him orally through many generations, via a chain that included Solon two hun-dred years earlier. "The Athens in the Atlantis tale is proved as a reality by geological and archaeological science," he said.

Prove is a pretty risky word to use in relation to Atlantis. It is inter-esting, though, how Plato piles up what seems at first to be a lot of irrelevant detail about Athens in the Atlantis story. He describes how the Acropolis had once been the site of a fortified Mycenaean castle, very different from the Golden Age collection of stone tem-ples and buildings. In those ancient times, Critias explains, warriors spent winters living communally in simple structures located on the north side of the rock outcropping. These soldiers drew water from a single spring that "gave an abundant supply of water" but was choked off when a massive earthquake hit Athens. That quake was accompanied by torrential rains that swept most of Greece's fertile soil into the sea, leaving behind "the mere skeleton of the land." These natural disasters, the priest at Saïs told Solon, were so severe that only "a small seed or remnant" of the population survived. Written language died out, for as the priest at Saïs said, when "the gods purge the earth with a deluge of water, the survivors in your country are herdsmen and shepherds who dwell on the mountains, but those who, like you, live in cities are carried by the rivers into the sea."

Until fairly recently, the Athens half of Plato's tale was largely ignored by Atlantologists. Ignatius Donnelly, who seems to have crammed every fact he could find about ancient history into *The Antediluvian World*, mentioned Athens just once in his four hundred–plus pages of argument, and the Acropolis not at all. In his groundbreaking 1913 article linking Atlantis with the Minoans, K. T. Frost wrote, "The whole description of the Athenian state in these dialogues seems much more fictitious than that of Atlantis itself." John V. Luce's scholarly book *Lost Atlantis: New Light on an Old Legend* summarizes every single detail in the *Timaeus* and *Critias* related to Atlantis *except* for the parts about Athens, which the author dismisses with a note explaining that the "detailed account of Athens and Attica" has been "omitted as only marginally relevant to the identification of Atlantis."

Yet Plato's precise descriptions of the ancient Mycenaean city—the evidence of which had been buried for several centuries at the time he wrote, and of which no written records remain—have been shown to be remarkably accurate. In the 1930s, the Swedish-American archaeologist Oscar Broneer was excavating at the Acropolis when he located a subterranean spring that had evidently been smothered by the debris from an earthquake. Relics found in the bottom of the spring dated to around 1200 BC. "They found pottery in this well from the early twelfth century, the Mycenaean period," Papamarinopoulos told me. "That defines the time framework." Mycenaean-era housing similar to that used by Plato's ancient warriors has also been uncovered on the northern slope of the rock, exactly where he placed it in the *Critias*. Even the story of the shrinking Acropolis might have had some truth to it. I later asked Michael Higgins, coauthor of the definitive *Geological Companion to Greece and the Aegean* if it were possible, as the priest told Solon, "that a single night of excessive rain washed away the earth and laid bare the rock." Higgins replied that the meaning of *acropolis* (which means "high place") might have changed over time. The rock outcropping on which the buildings sit actually juts out from the base of a much larger elevated area. As for storms, "You know the Greek climate. It is indeed possible that much soil and loose matériel could have been removed during a single storm."

The disappearance of written Greek, Papamarinopoulos believed, was another crucial historical event mentioned only by Plato, and only inadvertently. Historians generally agree that around 1200 BC Greece entered what is sometimes called its Dark Ages. Near that date, several Bronze Age civilizations around the Mediterranean, including that of the Mycenaeans, mysteriously collapsed. Use of the Linear B script that Arthur Evans had uncovered at Knossos, and which had also turned up at various sites throughout Greece, stopped abruptly around the same time.

Up until the 1950s, most classical scholars concurred that pre-Homeric Greeks were illiterate. Then in 1954 the London architect and former World War II cryptographer Michael Ventris stunned the world by demonstrating that one of the two mysterious scripts that Arthur Evans had found on the tablets at Knossos, Linear B, was in fact the earliest known written form of Greek. (One of the names Ventris deciphered was *Poseidon*.) The Linear B script, it emerged, had been brought to Crete by Mycenaean invaders. When literacy once again become widespread in Greece several hundred years later, the Greeks had adopted an entirely new alphabet containing vowels, derived from the Phoenician one, which had only consonants.

"Plato said the Greeks were giving Greek names to their offspring," Papamarinopoulos said. "Obviously they were speaking Greek, because if you speak Greek, you write it. But what sort of Greek? It was Linear B. He talks about the Linear B writing before the discovery of archaeologists in the modern period, before the decipherment of the Linear B!"

For Papamarinopoulos, this meant one of two things. Plato

either invented uncannily precise details about Mycenaean-era Athens, which was extremely unlikely, or he was passing along truthful information that had been passed down to him orally. "Therefore, 50 percent of *Timaeus* and *Critias* has proved data," he said. "It has maybe some inaccuracies, some exaggerations, but the core of this information has been proved. To ignore this 50 percent is completely unscientific." Any professor dismissing Plato's story of Atlantis and Athens as fiction was guilty not only of poor scholarship, but also of academic malpractice, he said. "Science, as defined by Plato, has the conduct of honesty."

Papamarinopoulos argued that most Atlantis doubters, poisoned by their bias, have subsequently been led astray by laziness. Such people "take for granted Atlantis as a gigantic island in the middle of the Atlantic Ocean," he said, exasperated. This was a result of their perfunctory reading of Plato's work in ancient Greek. Much as Dora Katsonopoulou revitalized the search for Helike with her reinterpretation of *poros*, Papamarinopoulos argued that the search for Atlantis hinges on Plato's use of the ancient Greek word *nesos*, almost always translated as "island."

"I know ancient Greek," he told me, leaning back in his chair. "I read and I write ancient Greek. In the sixth century, when Solon lived, *nesos* had five geographic meanings." He began to count off on his fingers. "One, an island as we know it. Two, a promontory. Three, a peninsula. Four, a coast. Five, a land within a continent, surrounded by lakes, rivers, or springs." By this definition, not only would Hawaii qualify as a *nesos*, but so would Utah, Florida, California, and Minnesota. For the 2008 Atlantis conference Papamarinopoulos had written a paper demonstrating that Pharos Island (aka Pharos Nesos), home to one of the Seven Wonders of the Ancient World—Alexandria's four-hundred-foot-high lighthouse—had actually been a peninsula. The land bridge I'd crossed on the bus from Athens that morning was an even clearer example. The name *Peloponnesus*, arguably Western history's most famous peninsula, literally means "Island of Pelops."

"So if Atlantis wasn't in the middle of the Atlantic, where was it?" I asked.

Papamarinopoulos shook his head. "Before we go to that," he said, rising from his chair, "I want to answer a question—is there anybody else who mentions Atlantis before Plato? It's a classic question." Christos Doumas, among others, had stressed the significance of there being no references to Atlantis in the voluminous Egyptian archives. "May I close the window? It's noisy."

The room was suddenly as quiet as a library. Papamarinopoulos lowered his voice. "The experts and romantic archaeologists"—the Indiana Jones types who focus their efforts on finding precious artifacts and intact ancient structures—"are trapped by this question," he said as he returned to his seat. "They try to find the word *Atlantis* in other cultures and they fail to find it. So what do they conclude? That there is no Atlantis, that it exists only in Plato's mind. They don't realize that Atlantis is a name *invented* by Plato." Plato is pretty explicit on this point. In the *Critias* he explains that the priest at Saïs gave Solon names in Egyptian form. Solon then translated these names into Greek. Assuming that Plato really did receive the tale via Solon, he would have Hellenized the names.

"So who were the Atlanteans? Plato gave one name to a coalition of different nations that came and invaded the eastern Mediterranean. Twice. With a difference of thirty years. Plato doesn't say two invasions; he talks about one. We don't know which one. But we have the names of these people written in hieroglyphics in Medinet Habu, in a victorious granite stele." Rainer Kühne had mentioned Medinet Habu. It's one of the archaeological treasures of Egypt. It was built as the mortuary temple of the great pharaoh Ramses III, who reigned from roughly 1186 BC to 1155 BC. Its walls contain some of the most spectacular hieroglyphics in existence.

"So who were they?" I asked.

"It's interesting. All these countries were traditionally enemies for centuries, before the two invasions. The Libyans. The ancestors of some of the Italians. Others from the Middle East. But also *others* with peculiar boats. How do you call these in English?" He made a rowing motion.

"Oars?"

"Oars. They did not have oars. These people also had, in the front and the back of their boats, a bird, like a duck. And if you don't have oars in the Nile and the wind is not favorable to you, your boat with a duck becomes a sitting duck! The Egyptians got them as prisoners and divided them into two categories. The punishment was unbelievable!" He brought his palm to his brow and laughed. "One group lost their hands. The other lost their penis!"

Shelley Wachsmann, a professor of biblical archaeology at Texas A & M University, had identified these boats as coming from central Europe. "So this coalition of Sea Peoples may also have had central Europeans and perhaps western Europeans," Papamarinopoulos said. "And we have paintings of the warriors that connect them with certain northwestern European cultures." Long pause. "Of which Spain is perhaps a part."

Papamarinopoulos believed that the *nesos* Plato wrote of was not an island, but a giant peninsula, encompassing all of mainland Europe west of Italy. I may have let out a small groan.

"If you follow Plato, you go exactly to the Iberian Peninsula because this is where the text leads you. Literally! He describes a valley that is flat and elongated, surrounded by mountains. These mountains are the Sierra Nevada and Sierra Morena. The valley has the same position and orientation. It fits exactly with Plato's description. Like a puzzle piece."

So we were back to Spain. Hoping to convey skepticism through body language, I took a huge, slow swig of my tepid coffee, realizing too late it had been made Greek-style, with an inch of grounds at the bottom of the cup. "So the Pillars of Heracles really were at Gibraltar," I finally said, dislodging bits of coffee from my teeth with my tongue. "Did you consider other possible locations?"

"Of course! There are eight others. None of them has a Gadeiriki peninsula." This was a new twist on the Gades/Cádiz clue from the *Critias*. *Gadeiriki* is a diminutive variant of *Gadeira*, the ancient Greek name for Gades/Cádiz; the suffix denotes a small peninsula. *Gadir* is the old Phoenician name meaning "walled city," such as the one situated on a tiny spit of land northwest of the Rock of Gibraltar. Plato wrote that Gadeirus, one of the ten twin sons of Poseidon, "obtained as his lot the extremity of the island toward the Pillars of Heracles, facing the country which is now called the region of Gadeira in that part of the world."

Atlantis doubters have seized on the tortured geography in this sentence as evidence that Plato must have invented such a place. There are no islands west of modern Cádiz, so it would be impossible to stand on one while looking back toward Cádiz and the Pillars. Such a location would *need* to be in the Atlantic Ocean.

But if the entire Iberian peninsula is counted as a *nesos*, then just up the coast from Cádiz is another lost city that could have been the original Atlantis. Tartessos.

Plato evidently had no firsthand knowledge of Tartessos. Other ancient Greek writers mention it by name and—possibly—by description. It took me several weeks after returning home to untangle all the threads of Papamarinopoulos's explanation of pre-Platonic evidence, so here's a watered-down version. Several Greeks who lived in the centuries before Plato and were familiar with details of the western Mediterranean, including Homer and Hesiod, described an obscure circular shape that was believed to be the work of

Poseidon. This "circularity," as Papamarinopoulos called it, was once located on the Atlantic coast of Andalusia.

There was certainly a history of seismic activity in that area. The wave that barreled through Cádiz during the 1755 Lisbon earthquake has been estimated at more than sixty feet tall—comparable to the height of 2011's devastating Fukushima tsunami. If Juan Villarías-Robles's estimates about the Azores-Gibraltar Transform Fault are correct, the location Papamarinopoulos suggests would have gotten walloped.

"In Greek there is a word *cymatosyrmos*. It is a better word than the Japanese *tsunami*," he said. "Because *tsunami* means simply a wave in the coast. *Cymatosyrmos* is a train with wagons. Imagine a train with wagons, rushing with some hundreds of kilometers per hour of velocity, one after the other. Those are the extraordinary floods that followed the extraordinary earthquakes. So whatever was there in the coast was in a day and night destroyed. That is the catastrophe that destroyed Atlantis."

Papamarinopoulos believed that Plato had given the name *Atlantis* to a place with three distinct elements: the giant *nesos*, the horseshoe-shaped plain that fit like a puzzle piece, and the concentric rings. He thought the rings had been located "in the southern part of the valley going out into the Atlantic Ocean"—before being buried by sediment.

The creation of these rings, Papamarinopoulos told me, was likely the product not of superhuman labor but of an earlier natural disaster. "There are three ways of interpreting this system of concentric circles," he said. "First, a concentric volcano, like Santorini or Kilimanjaro." I had just seen Santorini's bull's-eye-shaped circularity. Mount Kilimanjaro, in Tanzania, is a dormant volcano with a three-ringed crater at its peak.

Another prospect was an impact crater, a circular depression caused by a high-velocity object from space—like a meteorite—crashing into a planet's surface. The moon's face is pocked with round impact craters, some large enough to be seen on a clear night with the naked eye. There are plenty of craters on Earth, too. They're just a lot harder to spot because of the effects of erosion and the Earth's gradually shifting crust. Meteor Crater in Arizona, three-quarters of a mile across and 550 feet deep, is only fifty thousand years old, young enough to have survived the ravages of time.

The third possibility was a geologic formation known as a mud volcano, caused by pressure from below the Earth's surface. "Steam and methane escape sometimes and produce concentric circles," Papamarinopoulos explained. Like most geologic concepts, this one is a little hard to convey with words, but I'd seen a photograph in one of the Atlantis essay collections of a possible mud volcano, the Richat Structure in Mauritania. For anyone interested in Atlantis, the image is jaw-dropping: a twenty-five-mile-wide set of naturally formed concentric rings that look like ripples from a stone tossed into God's koi pond.

Depending on the local geology, Papamarinopoulos said, the creation of all three types of crater can result in the formation of black, red, and white rock, as well as hot and cold springs, just as Plato said existed in Atlantis. Several craters, some of them circular, have been located underwater in the Bay of Cádiz near the spot where Tartessos is believed to have vanished. (One of these craters is quite close to shore but seems thus far to have attracted less interest from geologists than from people interested in crater-causing extraterrestrials.) Whatever the type of crater, Papamarinopoulos said, it was something that the Atlanteans "found in nature and they added on it. They did some engineering or built monuments or whatever. It doesn't take supertechnology to do these things. If you know how the Egyptians built giant things, you can see how other people could do it. So the ancient Greek visitors in this area saw this thing and they interpret it as Poseidon's work. Later writers presented it with different mythological variants."

Papamarinopoulos wasn't especially concerned with the Saïs priest's claim that "the island was larger than Libya and Asia put together." The territory of Atlantis's empire could have included most of the western Mediterranean. Or he could have meant that Egypt was describing the size of the threat they felt on their borders. The next part of Plato's text, however, had always confused me. Atlantis, he wrote,

> was the way to other islands, and from these you might pass to the whole of the opposite continent which surrounded the true ocean; for this sea which is within the Straits of Heracles is only a harbor, having a narrow entrance, but that other is a real sea, and the surrounding land may be most truly called a boundless continent.

"Plato did not use the word *ocean*; he called it a *panpelagos*, an infinite sea," Papamarinopoulos said. "When he goes into the hypothetical crossing of the *panpelagos*, then you have a continent." Contrary to popular belief, Plato never uses the word *continent* to describe the vanished Atlantis. But he uses for the first and only time three adverbs to describe the boundless continent across the *panpelagos*: *totally*, *correctly*, and *truly*. "If you go west of Atlantis," Papamarinopoulos said, "you find—totally, correctly, and truly—a gigantic land. And it is your country."

I stopped scribbling in my notebook midsentence and looked up. "What? Plato was talking about America?"

"Absolutely. Plato says also that Atlantis had relationships with other islands, which could be any of the five meanings of *nesos*. It is a very crude way of presenting the two Americas and Antarctica together. Plato is the very first person who mentions the existence of this land. Other historians, the *real* historians, say nothing about this land."

Had we shaken hands and said good-bye five minutes earlier, I'd have departed Patras convinced that I'd found the answer to the Atlantis mystery. We suddenly seemed to be veering into *Ancient Aliens* territory. "I suppose there are other sources besides Plato that talk about these crossings?"

"Wait! Let me finish, Mark! In Paris, I met a woman, Michelle Lescot-Layer, a member of the Musée de l'Histoire, who in the early 1980s had found minute pieces of nicotine in the mummy of Ramses II. Her results produced a world sensation! She got many enemies."

"Uh-huh."

"Later, I communicated with Svetlana Balabanova in Munich, who analyzed ancient mummies and found 30 percent had nicotine and cotinine and cocaine." Cotinine is a by-product of the body metabolizing nicotine. "Balabanova also produced a world sensation and many enemies."

"Uh-huh."

"I would accept that *Nicotiana tabacum* could be found as a wild species in South Africa. I find it rather unlikely that the Egyptians knew it, brought it to Egypt, cultivated it, and used it in ceremonies. But it is a possibility. But there is *no* possibility to find cocaine anywhere else but in South America."

It was true that Svetlana Balabanova had published such studies in the 1990s, but she had been pilloried by mainstream historians and archaeologists after doing so. Two decades later, attempts to repeat her experiment had been inconclusive. Balabanova stood behind her results and the argument had reached a stalemate. "Cocaine mummies" was a favorite topic of alternative history websites. Was it possible that the mummies had been contaminated? As for Lescot-Layer's findings, skeptics had raised the possibility of nicotine-based insecticides having been used in museums. Judging from my personal experience with Egyptians, heavy smoking was also not exactly unknown in the greater Cairo area. I floated this possibility.

"I cannot imagine they can do it deeply into the internal organs!" he said. "How much can you contaminate it?" Even if nicotine were ruled out, though, cocaine was still unexplained. Coca was definitely indigenous to South America. "This proves trade with America since at least the tenth century BC. Someone was going there in prehistoric times and knew where they were going. Repeatedly."

As further evidence of ancient sea crossings, Papamarinopoulos cites several sixteenth-century maps that seem to show accurate depictions of the South American and Antarctic continents. Strangely, even though the sixteenth century was the greatest in history for worldwide exploration, the depictions of these continents became less accurate as the century progressed. To Papamarinopoulos, the reason was clear—an earlier civilization had mastered longitude long before its official discovery in 1773. It was a paradox of progress. The further cartographers moved away from their ancient maps and the destruction of Atlantis, the less precise their work became.

CHAPTER TWENTY-THREE

"You Don't Buy It"

Patras, continued

Papamarinopoulos seemed to sense that he was pushing the limits of my skepticism. He suggested a brief lunch recess. We took the mini elevator downstairs and walked a few blocks through the empty afternoon streets of downtown Patras. I asked if he had seen Richard Freund's *Finding Atlantis* documentary, which leaned so heavily on Kühne's original theory about Tartessos but didn't mention any of Papamarinopoulos's work. He hadn't, though he had communicated with Freund during preproduction. "I sent him all the papers I did at the geological society. He told me, 'It would take me two months to read all this.'"

Once we'd ordered lunch, I asked if there were parts of the Atlantis story that he hadn't been able to explain. He nodded yes.

"Is it the elephants?" I asked.

The elephants were tricky. Some Atlantologists claimed Plato was referring to mammoths or dwarf elephants, fossils of which have been found on the islands of Cyprus, Sicily, and Malta. Tony O'Connell had shown me a theory that explained the presence of elephants in Malta as a transcription error. Someone had mistakenly written *elephas*, Greek for "elephant," rather than *elaphos*, Greek for "deer." Except that Plato uses the elephants to illustrate the abundance of space in Atlantis, describing them as "the largest and most voracious of all" animals.

Papamarinopoulos wasn't worried about the elephants. "The elephants exist in the zone of influence of Atlantis," he said with a shrug, meaning that they were just across the Strait of Gibraltar in North Africa.

"No, I have two weak points," he said. "The canals and the size of the valley. The size, maybe it's a mistake with the numbers." This referred to Plato's incredible ten-thousand-stade perimeter. "The other thing which is a weak point for me—for the time being—is this." He took my pen and drew a pattern of intersecting lines. "The checkerboard canals. We have not found this *yet*, but maybe in the future we can do it with satellite image processing. I can't do everything. Now, I don't want to make you crazy, but you can find this matrix in Guatemala and Bolivia." He looked up and a half smile crept up the side of his mouth. "You don't buy it."

Of course I didn't buy it. Why would an enormous navy make its way from the altiplano of landlocked Bolivia, which, the last time I visited anyway, was *two hundred miles from the nearest ocean and two miles above sea level*, sail down and around the notoriously difficult-to-navigate Cape Horn, cross the Atlantic Ocean, navigate into the Mediterranean, and engage Athens in a war? How would you feed the gigantic navy you'd need? A high-altitude Atlantis also failed to explain an island sinking below the waves and leaving behind muddy shoals. I asked Papamarinopoulos his opinion of a similar theory, that some concentric circles found in northwest Louisiana indicated that the Atlanteans had traveled up the Mississippi River.

"Do you know what the person who says this says the motivation was?" he asked.

"Let me guess. Copper?" This was typically the second part of the

Atlantis-meets-the-Mississippi theory; the supposed terminus of the journey was Isle Royale, an island in Lake Superior, famous for its high-quality copper deposits. Millions of pounds of the metal seem to have been removed thousands of years ago, which no one has been able to account for. The natives of the Great Lakes region didn't use copper. Where unexplained phenomena met the search for Atlantis, wild hypotheses were sure to follow. This one could be traced all the way back to Ignatius Donnelly.

"Yes, copper!"

"But isn't the island of Cyprus basically one huge chunk of copper? Doesn't the name Cyprus *mean* 'copper'? Wasn't Cyprus about ten thousand times easier to reach from the Mediterranean than Lake Superior would have been?"

"Yes, but this is the purest deposit of copper in the world. And the Indians did not use it." Another half smile. "You don't buy it."

Nope. I still didn't buy it. "Where does that leave the nine thousand years?"

"Ah, now we come to the date! Serious *experts*"—he spat out the word—"take for granted the nine thousand years. They try to ridicule Plato, but they ridicule themselves! Solon talked only to the priests of Saïs. We know from the ancient Greek literature and from Egyptology that the priests used lunar calendars. So you take a solar year and divide it by 12.37, the number of full moons." If one does so, as Werner Wickboldt had demonstrated in Braunschweig, the date of the Atlantis disaster catapults forward from 9600 BC to around 1200 BC.

The revised date would not only yank Atlantis out of the murky, post–Ice Age era, but also conveniently place its end roughly alongside the destruction of Mycenaean Athens and the start of the Greek Dark Ages, as evidenced by the earthquake findings at the Acropolis: the time when cities and towns throughout Greece were abandoned and writing in Linear B ceased. In fact, Papamarinopoulos noted, "We have three collapses occurring—Atlantis, Athens, and Troy. Not in the same month, but in the same century."

The period around 1200 BC was one of sudden, and still unexplained, upheaval in the Mediterranean. The two great empires that had dominated the region, the Egyptians and the Hittites of Asia Minor, suffered vicious attacks. Egypt seems to have barely survived, while the Hittites vanished altogether. A letter survives from the king of Ugarit, an important port city in Syria, pleading with his trading partners in Cyprus to send aid to fight the mysterious sea raiders who have attacked his city. "The enemy ships are already here, they have set fire to my towns and have done great damage in the country," he wrote. Ugarit, too, was burned to the ground.

"Do you really think Solon got the story from the priest, undiluted?" I asked.

"I like this question of yours, saying do you trust only one priest?" Papamarinopoulos said, tapping a finger on the table. He summoned the waiter and ordered coffees. By this point in my odyssey I was mixing caffeine and strange conversations with the regularity of a Stieg Larsson character. "No, I trust the priests because they were the antiquarians of Egypt. And I trust Plato, who possibly deduced something from stories he heard from the Greek mariners in Syracuse" during his visits with Dionysius I and II. In one of his papers, Papamarinopoulos cites a fragment from Hesiod, written before Solon's time, that describes a sea route from Gadeira to Taras in southern Italy to Ionia in Asia Minor. Stories from beyond Gibraltar would surely have traveled east toward Greece. It's possible that Plato or Solon or both would have been familiar with these tales. As for the incredible numbers in Plato's story, Papamarinopoulos argued that they were the opposite of a mistake.

"You're dealing with a person who is a genius, Mark! A genius works in a way that we cannot understand. The large numbers of occupants in Atlantis, the large number of soldiers, the gigantic fleets, and all this. Plato, because he was a naughty boy, added mathematical exaggerations for his own purposes to this real story. Here, I will explain." He motioned for my pen again and began drawing on a paper napkin. He handed the napkin back to me and said, "I want you to keep this as a memento."

The picture he had drawn (and signed, and dated) was of three concentric circles, but not those of Atlantis. It was a graph that looked like an avocado cut widthwise. The innermost circle (the avocado pit) was the nucleus of a historical event. This was the *logos*. "It is like a signal, but it has a cloud of noise around it," he said. In order to get to the historic truth at the center of the story, one had to filter out the fantastic elements in the middle ring (the avocado's flesh). Papamarinopoulos called these fabrications the paramyths. The outermost, third ring (the rind) was composed of mathematical and musicological information invented by Plato.

"Plato likes you to dig, to search to find the mathematical theory," he said. He circled the outermost ring with the pen. "The thin black sector here is truth, but not historically, only mathematically. He tells you to try and play with the numbers. He invites you to decode it. And if you decode it, you will find something useless for historians and archaeologists but useful for mathematicians. He was obsessed with music. And with mathematics. Remember, the Greek language—the alphabetic Greek language—was used by an intelligent person three times. Written script, numbers, musical notes."

Incredibly, this seemed to be possible. A British philosophy professor had recently published a theory, quickly dubbed "The Plato Code" by the media, which claimed to have identified a twelve-note Pythagorean musical scale hidden in some of Plato's most famous works. The discovery, he told *The Guardian*, "unlocks the gate to the labyrinth of symbolic messages in Plato."

"So if I want to communicate with you in music," Papamarinopoulos said, "I would use the same symbols, and I will send you a poem with music. Or I will encrypt a mathematical formula through the same symbols. Or I will send a report from my work in Egypt as a script. So you have a language which could be used three ways."

The check arrived. I sat in stunned silence.

"You have questions on this?" Papamarinopoulos asked.

"I can't say I understand it entirely," I said. So he was saying not only were the enormous numbers exaggerations, but they also hinted at a secret code buried in the Atlantis story, which also happens to cryptically mention ancient sea crossings to America? Oh, and the Atlantis story was more or less true? One afternoon in Patras and I had enough material for my own BBC miniseries.

"One day is not enough to talk about this, Mark. I have lived with this for forty years! Atlantis might look like a tale for a child, but it isn't. Because it has layers with philosophical meanings, with mathematical meanings, musicology, even morality. But we take all that out and what we have left is the germ of the story."

Church bells rang six o'clock. We had been talking since noon. We stopped to get a beer at a noisy bar filled with college students celebrating their triumphant day on strike. I was jittery and mentally exhausted, and Papamarinopoulos looked wiped out, too. He leaned his head back against the wall and closed his eyes as we talked. I remembered the one question I'd forgotten to ask. Why are so many people interested in finding Atlantis?

He opened his eyes and turned to me.

"Because their minds are fired with a continuous fever," he said. "They get possessed by this."

CHAPTER TWENTY-FOUR

The Power of Myth

New York, New York

I suppose at this point it shouldn't come as a surprise that when I telephoned one of the world's leading experts on myth, hoping to get a little more clarity on Papamarinopoulos's three-ring logos/paramyth/naughty-boy-secret-mathematical-code diagram, we wound up talking about vampires. This was actually a good thing. Elizabeth Wayland Barber is an emerita professor of linguistics and archaeology at Occidental College and author of several books, including *When They Severed Earth from Sky: How the Human Mind Shapes Myth*, which she cowrote with her husband, Paul Barber. She was also a world-renowned expert on everything from prehistoric textiles to folk dancing and had once written a book with footnotes in twenty-six languages. After five minutes on the phone, I could tell she'd be delightful company on a long car trip. When I asked her if fellow archaeologists were a little reluctant to dip into mythology, she snorted and said, "A *little* bit? Uh, yeah."

It was Barber who had raised the subject of vampires, as a way to illustrate how myths are created. "The human brain demands explanations," she told me. "For my husband's first book he looked at all the original vampire descriptions from the archives of the Austro-Hungarian Empire," which existed from 1867 to 1918. "They would have an outbreak of vampires in some remote Transylvanian village. People don't like their neighbors digging up their relatives' corpses, so the central administration would send out a doctor to keep an eye on things and report back on what he saw." The doctors looked at the recently deceased and saw bodies showing early signs of decomposition. The peasants looked at those same corpses and saw engorged bodies with blood dripping around the mouth. When stakes were driven through the hearts of some of these suspected vampires, they groaned and bled.

"Bodies bloat" from gases that form during decomposition, Barber explained. "After rigor mortis, the blood liquefies again after some period of time and is forced out through any available cavities," such as the mouth. A stake plunged into a bloated corpse's chest can expel air past the voice box, causing the dead man to groan audibly. "So the peasants observed things quite accurately," she said. "But their *explanation* of what happened was completely off the mark." To get to the original kernel (or avocado pit) of truth, Barber subjects myths to something that she calls the Stripping Procedure: "In order to understand the true original events, we have to see clearly what the events are. In order to do that, we must strip the explanations from the story." Good-bye, Poseidon.

In the time before recorded history, Barber explains in *When They Severed*, the only way to transmit important information was through myth. Now that writing is the norm, "we have forgotten how nonliterate people stored and transmitted information and why it was done that way," she writes. "We have lost track of how to decode the information often densely compressed into these stories, and they appear to us as mostly gibberish." Humans are susceptible to what the Barbers call the Memory Crunch: Our brains have only so much storage capacity. "You're working in a very constricted channel when you're having to remember information," she told me. "The great advantage of writing is you can put it down and have it later; you don't have to remember it."

Yet the Barbers found multiple instances where information has been passed down orally and faithfully for up to thousands of years as long as three criteria are met. The information must be considered important enough to merit preservation, such as the massive volcanic explosion that formed Crater Lake in Oregon circa 5700 BC—a story that was still being passed down by the local Klamath Indians into the nineteenth century as the tale of an unpleasant visit from the Chief of the Below World. Second, the information must relate to something still visible to those who hear the myth (again, Crater Lake, which the Klamath had been taught to avoid so as not to incite the powerful subterranean deity). And third, the myth must be memorable; it has to be a good story. If the first two standards were uncertain in relation to Plato's Atlantis tale—we don't know if Plato was passing along ancient information—the third was an obvious match. The Atlantis story was certainly memorable.

Barber believes that the Thera explosion, which volcanologists have estimated to have been more than double the size of the Crater Lake blast, was large enough to have inspired myths in several ancient Mediterranean cultures. The myth of the flood that Poseidon sends against Attica is one possible result of the blast. "Poseidon is really the god of the great unchained forces of nature, whereas Athena is the goddess of what human beings can do to combat that: with *techne*, know-how. When Athena wins the contest for ownership of Athens, Poseidon is a bad loser and he sends a tidal wave that comes up all the way to the foot of the Acropolis." Once the supernatural battle-of-the-gods explanation is stripped away, what remains sounds like an account of an ancient tsunami. "There's only one wave that could have been that big," she said. Thera.

"We know from the geologists that the wind was blowing

southeast that day. That's very nice for Western civilization, because had it been blowing to the northwest, it would have wiped out the Greeks. As it was, they had a ringside seat of watching Thera explode. Hesiod talks about how the sea was so hot it boiled and the sound was so loud it was as though the sky had fallen and was hitting upon earth."

In Hesiod's *Theogony* (the name means "Birth of the Gods"), written about a hundred years before Solon, he tells the story of the epic battle between the gods and the giants. The Barbers cite fascinating research by the geology historian Mott Greene at the University of Puget Sound, who is a pioneer in the relatively new field of geomythology, which seeks out the geological phenomena, especially natural catastrophes, that have found their way into folklore. "Mott Greene was looking at Hesiod and the other Greek myths and saying, you know, each volcano erupts in its own way," Barber told me. "It has its own signature type of eruption, as a result of the kind of magma and the temperatures underneath it. So Thera has its style, Etna has its style, Stromboli has its style, and so forth." Greene noted a sequence of fifteen events in Hesiod that, based on a close examination of Thera's geology, closely parallel the Thera eruption. The early trembling of Mount Olympus corresponds with powerful earthquakes at Thera. Missiles screeching through the air correspond to the discharge of "pyroclastic ejecta," such as lava and volcanic rocks. Zeus's arrival hurling thunderbolts that scorch the earth corresponds with Thera's volcanic lightning.

The Egyptians, being farther away from the blast than the mainland Greeks, would have had a different perspective. Like the Greek seismologist Galanopoulos, Barber believes that the stories from Exodus—whether they took place at the same time as the Thera blast or were combined with other stories from various centuries—match up with the volcanic explosion. Darkness falls over Egypt for three days (possibly the result of ash in the atmosphere obscuring the sun), and the Lord sends a pillar of cloud by day followed by a pillar of fire at night, which echoes the appearance of an eruption at different times of day. The Hittites in Asia Minor had a myth of a giant who emerged from the sea to grow thousands of miles tall. He was vanquished only when scythed off at the base—a detail that mirrors the detachment of an ash pillar from its volcano once an eruption ceases.

Barber believes that Solon was the first Greek to take written notes "to stockpile information regularly for his own use." If he wrote down the story of an island that sank beneath the waves that had been told to him by an Egyptian priest, one of his descendants could very well have come across his musings decades later. After using her Stripping Procedure, we come away with an original source that is identical to Marinatos's theory: The Egyptians witnessed the natural destruction of the Thera eruption, followed by a disruption in their trade with Crete. The story of a rich, vanished island kingdom is passed along to Solon by the priests at Saïs.

I asked Barber, a student of ancient Greek, if she thought Plato had believed the story was true.

"Plato really treats it as though he believed that he had read this in his family archives and that he believed that Solon had indeed written it down from the Egyptian. I think Plato had a lot of respect for the written word, and if he found this in the family archives, I can just imagine the look on his face the day he found the thing. Like, 'Oh my God, look at this. This. Is. Amazing.' And that there were probably some hiccups in it, but that basically it was telling him something about the early world that had happened."

"Maybe it's a conflation of Thera and what Plato heard about Tartessos," I said.

"Or that the Egyptian priest had conflated. There are so many sources of possible hiccups in here. We just need to find a suitable inscription in Egypt, or a papyrus!"

The idea that such things might one day be found was not

impossible. While the great temples and statues that Herodotus described seeing in Saïs have long since disappeared—carted away by looters and builders—a British team has been excavating the old city with some success. An ancient garbage dump from the Egyptian town of Oxyrhynchus has yielded important papyrus fragments of Greek classics, such as the *Republic*, as well as previously unknown works.

"There are a couple points where Critias says, 'I know this is going to sound crazy, but this is what I heard . . . ,'" I said.

"Right right right right! And so Plato was taking it with a little grain of salt but basically thought that he had a valuable document there which told him some real, true things about the early world, even if he couldn't quite see all the details."

"So what would the purpose of Plato telling the story be? Assume it's from Solon. Why, and telling it to whom?"

"And he tells it at least twice. This presumably was something Plato was using to teach at the Academy. And calling on the things of greatest antiquity that he had within his grasp to make his point." According to another of Barber's key tenets, what she calls the Silence Principle, that audience would not have required an explanation of the sorts of details in the Atlantis story that befuddle us today. Such omissions lead to what she calls the Lethe Effect: "What is never said may eventually be forgotten entirely."

Did she have any recommendations on where I might go from here?

"Follow the details!" she shouted. "The devil's in the details!"

CHAPTER TWENTY-FIVE

Maps and Legends

New York, New York

Stavros Papamarinopoulos was hardly the first person to suggest that prehistoric sailors had crossed the Atlantic Ocean and returned with news of a distant land. Ancient writers prior to Plato described islands across the boundless sea. The conspiratorial theme "Who *really* discovered America?" had become a staple of pseudohistorical TV shows and controversial bestselling books. Even Spyridon Marinatos had once written coquettishly, "We are apt to underestimate the daring feats of ancient seafarers. Plato's narrative could be considered as the first reference to the existence of America."

When I started to hunt through the modern scholarly research concerning what I assumed would be a hot topic, what I found was disciplines collectively holding their fingers in their ears and saying "La la la, can't hear you." Part of the resistance is logical—archaeologists and anthropologists depend on "material culture" like midden heaps, burial sites, and pottery sherds, and none exists that proves the occurrence of early transatlantic crossings. (Extraterrestrial landing strips don't count.) As often as not, charges of hyperdiffusionism, the unforgivable sin committed by Ignatius Donnelly, would be hurled at anyone who tried to demonstrate that ancient seafarers had ever made round-trip visits.

Reigning scientific paradigms do not shift easily. In 1960, the explorer Helge Ingstad began compiling proof that the Viking Leif Eriksson had not only sailed to Newfoundland around AD 1000 but also established a short-lived colony there. Historians, deeply invested in the romantic story of Christopher Columbus, loudly dismissed Ingstad's idea until he eventually amassed an overwhelming amount of hard evidence. It didn't help Ingstad's case that his original hypothesis was based on interpretations of Norse sagas describing the settlement of Greenland and farther colonies in a place called Vinland.

Should anyone ever compile a list of anthropologists' least favorite twentieth-century Norwegian explorers, though, Ingstad is unlikely to place higher than second. The clear winner would be Thor Heyerdahl, who sailed west across the Pacific from Peru to French Polynesia in 1947 on the *Kon-Tiki*, a balsa wood raft he'd built. He believed the voyage demonstrated the likelihood that the South Seas had been settled by seafarers from the South American mainland. (This conclusion has not aged well; the overwhelming consensus is that migration occurred in the opposite direction.) In 1970, Heyerdahl crossed from Morocco to Barbados in the *Ra II*, a boat made of reeds. This time he demonstrated the possibility of Egyptian crossings during the Pharaonic period. The first voyage made Heyerdahl famous; his low standing among professional scholars was probably not enhanced by his directing an Oscar-winning documentary in which he also starred, his tanned and shirtless torso a silent rebuke to tenure-track bookworms. The *Ra II* expedition was, if anything, even less popular with mainstream academics, in part because any link between ancient Egypt and the New World—a clear echo of Ignatius Donnelly's argument—boosted the possible case for hyperdiffusionism.

Alice Beck Kehoe, an emerita professor of anthropology at Marquette University, was one of the few experts I could find who had an open mind about ancient sea crossings. Kehoe was both an ardent critic of the sort of hyperdiffusionism that Donnelly had promoted (which, in her book *Controversies in Archaeology*, she calls a "grossly racist ideology") and someone willing to write a textbook that asked the kinds of questions that might make bored undergraduates read ahead on the syllabus, such as this one: "Why did people in Afghanistan and Mexico and Utah make hundreds of little clay statuettes of naked women with fancy hairdos?"

Kehoe had compiled dozens of modern examples of small craft making transoceanic crossings. The British explorer Tim Severin, seeking to prove that an account of the voyage of sixth-century Irish monk Saint Brendan across the Atlantic and back was true, successfully re-created the journey in 1976–77 aboard a thirty-six-foot craft built using only tools and materials available in Brendan's day, including forty-nine greased oxhides. (Severin was particularly popular among Atlantologists, including Papamarinopoulos, because the only extant source for Brendan's story is a legend written down centuries after the fact.) Within a few years, a voyage that a century earlier had been considered so dangerous as to be suicidal had entered the realm of stunts. Men and women have since crossed the oceans in both directions aboard craft such as rowboats, dinghies, and kayaks. Two Frenchmen windsurfed the Atlantic on an oversize surfboard.

In some fields, such a preponderance of anecdotal evidence would open new areas of inquiry. It seemed to me that if a Japanese sailor could cross the eight thousand miles of the Pacific solo aboard a boat made from beer kegs, propelled by a sail made of recycled plastic bottles, perhaps the notion of experienced Greek or Phoenician sailors bringing back stories from a trip across the Atlantic wasn't so outlandish. I called Kehoe at her home in Milwaukee and asked if she ever tried to raise the subject of transatlantic crossings at professional conferences.

"Oh, consistently," she said. "It's totally taboo. If you bring it up at archaeology meetings, people give you this kind of cold stare and start looking for somebody else to talk to."

Just because hyperdiffusionism as an explanation for all New World progress is a racist theory, Kehoe argues, doesn't mean that pre-Viking contact never occurred. She sees in her colleagues' resistance the lingering influence of the Manifest Destiny doctrine, which supported the conquest of the American frontier by labeling its native occupants "merciless Indian savages." (The phrase is Thomas Jefferson's, from the Declaration of Independence.) According to this line of thinking, even if someone *had* managed to reach the shore of North or South America, they'd have been massacred immediately by bloodthirsty primitives. Dead men don't carry home tales of newly discovered continents.

This convenient theoretical obliteration of possible contacts allows historians to discount or ignore intriguing references in ancient literature. Stavros Papamarinopoulos interprets passages from the first-century-AD historian Plutarch as describing the ancient Greeks possibly founding colonies in America. The fifth-century-AD Neoplatonist scholar Proclus quotes an earlier historian's claim that "there were seven islands" in the Atlantic, as well as three larger ones. The last of these was inhabited by a people who, according to William Smith's *Dictionary of Greek and Roman Geography*, had "preserved from their ancestors the memory of the exceedingly large island of Atlantis, which for many ages had ruled over all the islands of the Atlantic Sea, and which had been itself sacred to Poseidon." By the sixth century BC, a century before Plato was born, the Greeks had heard reports of a discovery made by the Phoenicians, a large, fertile island with navigable rivers in the ocean outside the Pillars of Heracles. There are no islands between Spain and America with rivers of that size.

Kehoe suggests that the first sea crossings from the Old World to the New might have taken a longer route. "Mediterranean keel-bottomed boats were capable of crossing the ocean," she said. "But if you really wanted to get across the ocean in 1000 BC, you should've gotten yourself a Chinese junk or a Polynesian double-hulled canoe." The Polynesians, she pointed out, were able to voyage thousands of miles and locate the tiny speck of Easter Island centuries before Columbus sailed. It hardly seems possible that they never continued on to find the entire west coast of the Americas. Bones of Polynesian chickens have been excavated at a pre-Columbian site in Chile, and a sweet potato native to South America has been shown to have been introduced throughout Polynesia a thousand years ago. (In both places, Kehoe notes, the potato was called by the name *kumara*.) The geographer Carl Johannessen has tallied more than two hundred life forms that seem to predate Columbus's crossing. Some cultures even share supernatural concepts. Kehoe told me that long before 1492 both Mesoamericans and the Chinese looked at the full moon and saw the same thing: a rabbit pounding some sort of beverage in a mortar and pestle.

Kehoe believes that her colleagues had constructed an imaginary "unsurmountable barrier" of water between the continents. "American archaeologists are incredibly land-bound," Kehoe said. "They very rarely go out on the seas at all. People who go into archaeology do so because they're not interested in political science, they're not interested in mythology—they want to do science. They want to have quantifiable data. Some of us are also comfortable with history, but the majority are not. Like my husband. He didn't really like to read. He went into archaeology because he liked to go outdoors and dig."

Kehoe told me she considers the Atlantis story to be "a harmless parable for what Plato wanted to say about the fragility of civilization, that it can be totally overcome by natural forces." She felt the cocaine mummies are important, that long ago coca leaves had traveled across the Pacific to Egypt, part of the search for elixirs of life that obsessed the early alchemists. Her response when I asked her opinion of the Lake Superior copper hypothesis was a long chuckle of recognition. "There's so much copper in Eurasia," she finally said. "It doesn't make any sense."[11]

I decided to give Papamarinopoulos an incomplete on the transatlantic crossings and turned to the cartographic evidence. Renaissance maps, of course, were popular with Atlantologists as evidence of distant voyages made by ancient sailors. Rand Flem-Ath based his theory largely on the evidence of the 1513 Piri Reis map. Papamarinopoulos cited several others, in particular the Orontius Finaeus (or Oronce Finé) map of 1531. The striking thing about these maps is that they appeared to show accurate depictions of Antarctica many centuries before its first recorded sighting in 1820. "One must conclude that the Antarctic continent was discovered not by whalers and sealers of the nineteenth century," Papamarinopoulos wrote in an essay coauthored with the geologist John G. Weihaupt, "but by adventurers in or more likely before the sixteenth century." Moreover, South America appears to be drawn with more precision *before* explorers began making ocean crossings in 1492 than it would be for the century that followed. The implication was that potential blockbuster evidence of Plato's land across the *panpelagos* had been preserved in these ancient maps.

Gregory McIntosh, a historian who wrote the definitive history of the granddaddy of Atlantis-theory-inspiring maps, *The Piri Reis Map of 1513*, confirmed to me that the map is genuine and an extraordinarily important historical document. (The Oronce Finé map is

---

11 To be fair, when I asked Corby Anderson, a professor of metallurgical and materials engineering at the Colorado School of Mines, if it made any sense to transport heavy loads of copper across the ocean, he said, "There could be something to it, because high-grade copper is much easier to smelt and refine, and smelting technologies pre–500 BC were not very effective."

also real.) On this side of the Aegean the Piri Reis may be best known as exhibit A in certain Atlantological arguments, but the document is so revered in Turkey that it appears on national currency. McIntosh's expertise had made him a minor celebrity in Istanbul, and he'd just accepted a position teaching at the city's Piri Reis University. I asked him about the map's surprisingly accurate depiction of Antarctica.

"I've been looking at this map every single day for the last thirty years," McIntosh said. He explained that any map that converts the Earth's three-dimensional globe shape into a two-dimensional version is a projection, or an interpretation of how the world's geographic features might relate to each other on a planar surface. "There are six aspects of the spherical Earth that can be distorted or preserved when made into a flat map: sizes, shapes, directions, bearings, distances, and ratios. The Piri Reis map, as with *all* flat maps, does not maintain accuracy in all these aspects. In fact, the Piri Reis map, as with most Renaissance maps, *distorts* all of these aspects."

The world map most commonly used today is the Mercator projection of 1569, which captures geographic shapes accurately at the expense of size; those near the top and bottom appear far larger than they actually are. (Though the two landmasses appear similar in size on paper or Google Maps, Greenland is less than one-eighth the size of South America. In fact, it's smaller than either Brazil or Argentina.) Prior to Mercator, there was a lot less standardization and a lot more guesswork. "Today we think of maps as highly scientific representations, but five hundred years ago world maps combined actual geography with theoretical geography," McIntosh said. "Just because a Renaissance map shows a coastline doesn't mean anybody saw and surveyed that coast. More often, distant lands on early maps included graphic descriptions and visualizations based on written descriptions, ideas, and beliefs." In the case of Piri Reis, this would include the hypothetical Terra Australis Incognita, a giant southern landmass first hypothesized by Aristotle. A similar landmass, labeled "Terra Australis," appears on the Oronce Finé map. "The Piri Reis map is not any more or less accurate than any other map made at the time," McIntosh told me.

McIntosh got excited talking about the "fringe" that insisted these maps proved ancient knowledge. Many claimed that the Reis and Finé maps resembled Antarctica beneath the polar cap. And yet one can't even be sure what an ice-free Antarctica would look like, because if what McIntosh called "a quintillion tons of ice" were to melt, the isotonic rebound effect of the weight loss would raise the continent's elevation significantly, regardless of any resulting rise in sea levels. The process would completely change Antarctica's size and the shape of its perimeter. In either case, McIntosh stressed each time I cited a supposed similarity between one of the maps and Antarctica, "They don't look anything alike!"

"Not even a little?" I asked, rotating the copy I had on my desk to try to make a better match. Charles Hapgood had needed to do something similar in *Maps of the Ancient Sea Kings* to accentuate the similarities. McIntosh was right, of course. On both old maps, the tip of South America bumps against Antarctica, obliterating the chilly six-hundred-mile sea gap of the Drake Passage and the nine-hundred-mile-long crooked finger of the Antarctic Peninsula, either of which would have been hard to miss. There was a small problem of scale, too. On the Finé map, McIntosh pointed out, Terra Australis is nine times the size of the real Antarctica.

"What the fringe means by *accurate* is 'Gee, it looks the same to me,'" McIntosh told me.

Selective picking and choosing of evidence was, of course, a problem with every Atlantis location theory to some degree. Tony O'Connell had cautioned me about that from the get-go. I'd seen the sites in Spain, Malta, and Santorini, and while all seemed plausible candidates to one degree or another, the hypothesis behind each reflected the bias of its authors. I could empathize. My own journalistic objectivity about this project had long since evaporated. By this point I didn't just want to figure out why people were searching for Atlantis. I wanted to find it, too.

Plato's purpose in the *Timaeus* had been to impose mathematical logic on the cosmos, so it seemed appropriate to make my last stop in Morocco. There, I'd been promised, Atlantis had already been found strictly by the numbers.

CHAPTER TWENTY-SIX

Statistically Speaking

Bonn, Germany; and Agadir, Morocco

Even the most math-obsessed Greeks before Plato's time didn't study probability. They were more interested in the power of gods like Poseidon to determine their fates. To learn what the residents of Olympus might be thinking, ancient Greeks consulted oracles, shrines where prophets could answer questions and prognosticate based on contact with the supernatural world. The most famous of these was the Oracle of Delphi, where a priestess passed along cryptic messages from Apollo that time and again redirected the course of ancient history. In Plato's *Apology*, Socrates tells the story of hearing that the Delphic oracle had declared no man was wiser than Socrates himself. He took this to mean that he was wisest because only he understood how limited his knowledge was.

While oracles may have been handy, there's little doubt that Plato would have preferred statistics, with its magical-seeming formulas and bell curves that tease out the unseen patterns underlying the world. But it was Aristotle, the great taxonomist, who first classified events into three types: certain, probable, and unpredictable. As I packed my bags in Athens to fly to Morocco, I knew what Plato must've felt like to be stuck between Socrates and Aristotle. I knew what I didn't know about Atlantis, and I knew that there were some things I couldn't know. I also thought I might be zeroing in on some probable answers. First I needed to meet the one Atlantologist who had used statistical modeling to search for Plato's lost civilization, and got surprisingly definite results.

Back in Malta, Tony O'Connell had spoken so highly of Michael Hübner's work on Atlantis that I'd sensed Anton Mifsud was a little jealous. Hübner's theory was far and away the most objective I'd seen—he had located Atlantis strictly by analyzing the data he could glean from Plato's accounts. After watching Hübner's half-hour online video presentation, I understood why Tony had written in the Atlantipedia that "although there are still some outstanding questions in my mind, I consider Hübner's hypothesis one of the more convincing on offer to date." Hübner had pinpointed the Atlantic coast of Morocco.

I had first met Hübner in Bonn on my way to visit Kühne and Wickboldt. Hübner lived a few blocks from Beethoven's old house, on a pretty tree-lined street that in midautumn looked like a movie set for a European romantic comedy. He was a big man, well over six feet tall and bearish, with a long ponytail and a four-day growth of beard. He invited me into his one-bedroom apartment and immediately handed me a piece of tangible Atlantis evidence he'd brought back from Morocco: a chunk of rock that had red, white, and black striations like a slice of Poseidon's marble cheesecake.

Hübner brewed me an enormous cup of tea and offered me a selection of pastries on a platter before sitting down at his desk. The surface was crowded with two open laptop computers and a large microscope. Since science and philosophy have been moving in opposite directions almost since the *Timaeus*, I told Hübner I thought it was odd that an information technology specialist had taken an interest in Plato.

"One day I was carrying a washing machine and my back cracked," he explained in a voice that was surprisingly soft for a man built like a nightclub bouncer. "I was in bed for two weeks—even going to the toilet was . . . *ach*. I used the time in bed to read Plato." Like so many others before him, he was struck by the level of detail in the Atlantis story. Rather than just ponder the lost city as a *Gedankenexperiment*, he said, "I made an Excel file and put the entire text of Plato into it."

Because he was mathematically inclined, Hübner decided to locate the most probable site for Atlantis through a search procedure known as hierarchical constraint satisfaction. It was a statistical method of plugging variables—in this instance, data from the *Timaeus* and *Critias*—into a map overlaid with a grid. The more variables that matched a set of geographic coordinates, the higher the probability that particular square had once contained Plato's lost island. The overall effect was like a game of Battleship, with the location of Atlantis as the prize.

Hübner started with the assumption that Atlantis must be "within a reasonable distance" of Athens, which he set at five thousand kilometers, or about thirty-one hundred miles. (His point of reference was the forty-seven hundred kilometers that Alexander the Great reached in his farthest military campaigns.) Such an area encompasses virtually all of Europe, Africa north of the equator, and the Middle East. Hübner then mapped this zone onto a twenty-by-twenty grid, creating four hundred possible subareas in which Atlantis might have been located. From there, he worked his way through seven geographical clues that Plato gave. Each subarea was awarded points for being on a coast; for being situated on a large body of water that was connected to the Mediterranean; for sitting west of Egypt and Tyrrhenia (modern Tuscany); for having tall mountains to its north (Hübner found nine such locations in his master zone); for sitting outside the Strait of Gibraltar (he didn't consider any other candidates for the Pillars of Heracles); for containing elephants (not, as some Atlantologists have posited, mammoths, because the flora and fauna Plato describes indicate a tropical or subtropical climate); and—because Atlantis was planning to attack Europe and Asia, two of the ancient Greek world's three primary land masses—for sitting within Libya, or what we now call North Africa. (I thought this was the shakiest of his assumptions. Would the Maltese islands, which lay farther south than Carthage, have been considered part of Europe? Couldn't a distant land such as Tartessos be a possibility?) When Hübner tallied up his scores, one of the four hundred squares clearly stood out—a chunk of modern-day coastal Morocco, just south of the Atlas Mountains, known as the Souss-Massa region.

When Hübner added his regional and local constraints, the evidence was even more compelling. Perhaps the most appealing part of his hypothesis was his comparisons with Plato's strangely precise descriptions and measurements for the capital of Atlantis. Hübner had found a circular hill surrounded by three concentric *wadis*, or dry riverbeds. The measurements for the diameter of his outermost ring and the distance of his capital from the Atlantic Ocean varied by only about 10 percent from Plato's numbers. On paper, at least, he made a compelling case.

"You know perhaps Six Sigma?" Hübner asked, referring to the quality-control term in which 99.999 percent of a company's products are manufactured defect-free. Particle physicists must reach a Five Sigma level of certainty before they are credited with making a scientific discovery. He pointed to the map on his computer screen. "Well, if Plato's criteria are real, this is better than Seven Sigma."

If the numbers were on Hübner's side, time was not. When Hübner started visiting the area several years earlier following his lower-lumbar epiphany, it had been covered in ancient ruins built from colored stone, but these were rapidly being dug up and pulverized to make pigment for paint. The only archaeological expert on the area that Hübner was able to locate was a professor at the University of

Agadir, who showed little interest in the Neolithic ruins. European scholars had even less interest in a Moroccan site.

"I tried to get some German experts involved, but in my experience it's very hard to get scientists to look at this place," he told me.

"Why?"

"I think I made a mistake by mentioning Atlantis. They are afraid of getting contaminated."

Hübner had arranged for me to stay overnight at his father's house in a nearby suburb of Bonn, so we climbed into his red Volkswagen, which seemed a couple of sizes too small for him. On the way out of town we talked about his use of sources other than Plato. Hübner was an admirer of the works of Diodorus Siculus, a Greek born in Sicily in the first century BC. Diodorus was the author of the *Bibliotheca Historica*, a forty-volume universal history of the world from mythological times to his present. One of the fifteen volumes that remain deals with the history of North Africa. Diodorus wrote of a land bordered by the Atlas Mountains and the Atlantic Ocean, ruled by a king named Atlas. The land, which occupied the same space Hübner's calculations had zeroed in on, was called Atlantis.

"I don't think his work was much based on Plato because there are differences," Hübner told me as we merged into rush-hour traffic. Where Plato says that Atlas is the eldest son of Poseidon, Diodorus said he was the son of the Titan Iapetus. Tony O'Connell agreed that this indicated separate sources for the two Atlantis tales, a rare case of possible corroboration.

"The names Diodorus used were a little different, too," Hübner said, shifting gears. "He called the people the Atalantoi. *Scheisse!*" Hübner had been so involved in reciting his evidence that we had taken the wrong exit and were crossing a bridge over the Rhine. In Diodorus's telling, a tribe of women warriors called the Amazons lived in Atalantoi territory on an island within a large freshwater North African lake. The island was eventually destroyed by earthquakes, which caused most of the water to drain into the sea, leaving behind only a marsh.

Another ancient source that Hübner used, the second-century-AD writer Maximus of Tyre, also describes an area in West Africa that sounds a lot like the spot that Hübner had focused on. In this place, Maximus wrote, ocean waves had been known to rise "like a wall" and flood the coastal plain. The Souss-Massa was certainly susceptible to seismic disasters. A 1960 earthquake had leveled the regional capital of Agadir and killed fifteen thousand people.

When I'd first contacted Hübner, he'd briefly tried to explain where all his most important sites were located via GPS coordinates but soon sensed (correctly) that I would probably take a wrong turn at Marrakesh and vanish forever into the Sahara. He had agreed to meet me in Morocco to show me his evidence personally. To celebrate our forthcoming trip, his stepmother had prepared a traditional Moroccan tagine for dinner, and the smell of lamb and couscous followed us out onto the balcony, where we watched barges traveling up and down the Rhine. Hübner's father, a stern-looking older man with thick white hair and a bushy mustache, joined us. He told me that he had been a little boy at the end of World War II. "The American GIs I met after the war were very kind," he said. "They gave me a piece of chewing tobacco and I swallowed it."

Over dinner, we chatted about Hübner's hypothesis, which his family had evidently heard many times. He had a Pythagorean faith in numbers and no patience for ambiguous factors like Platonic allegories or fabricated myths. Either Atlantis was real and had almost certainly been located where he placed it, or it was complete fiction. "If my hypothesis was incorrect, the result would be a null set," he explained.

Near midnight Hübner drove back to Bonn, and his father and I sat quietly in the living room looking out the large picture window. The commuter train that I was going to be running for in a few hours rolled past along the riverbank. "I suppose Michael's been to Morocco eight or nine times to search for Atlantis," he finally said. "I know he thinks it's real. But . . ." He looked tired, and for a moment I thought he might have dozed off.

"But what if it *isn't* real?" he finally said.

At his apartment in Bonn, Hübner had offered me a little veteran advice about traveling to Morocco. "I wouldn't tell the people at the airport that you're a journalist," he said. "They lock those people up in Morocco." I'd figured out by then that Hübner was a little suspicious by nature, but even in the wake of the Arab Spring, his paranoia seemed overblown. About a week later, after a long day flying from Athens to Madrid to Casablanca—where crowds of people filled almost every foot of airport floor space, waiting for four flights that boarded simultaneously like rush-hour trains leaving Times Square—I arrived at Agadir Al Massira Airport around 1:30 A.M. as tired as I have ever been. I approached an open immigration window, handed over my passport, and waited for the stamping sound as I squinted into the atrium beyond hoping to spot a currency exchange.

"You speak English?" the man behind the glass asked.

"Yes."

"It says here you are a writer." Oops. "What sort of writing do you do?" he asked. "Are you a reporter? *Why have you come to Morocco?*"

The answer, "to find Atlantis," seemed inappropriate, so instead I mumbled something about vacationing and watched in silent terror as he slowly paged through my suddenly suspicious-looking passport: Ireland, Spain, Malta, Germany, Greece, now Morocco. My shoulder bag at this point contained two tape recorders holding hours of interviews that might require some explaining, several notebooks filled with similar material, and a laptop that if opened

would display a new file named ATLANTIS INTERVIEW NOTES—
MOROCCO. I could imagine the US embassy official roused out of bed
to handle this crisis. ("Male, traveling alone, looking for Atlantis? I'll
try to get back to you on that next week.") Mercifully, the agent silently handed back my passport and allowed me to pass through.

In the morning, I took one of Agadir's ubiquitous early-'80s-
vintage Mercedes taxis to Hübner's hotel in the foothills outside of
the city. (He didn't like Agadir, which caters to French package tourists who like sunbathing, and by the time I departed neither did I.)
The main thoroughfare, Avenue Mohammed V, became the N10
highway, and once we turned north onto dirt roads, the only time
the taxi slowed or stopped was to allow a herd of camels to cross. In
the hotel parking lot I told Hübner about my odd airport entry and
he seemed unsurprised. "Ja, they track you by your phone signal,
too," he said.

I have to assume that a moderately skilled secret police force
could have nabbed us at any moment if they wanted to: a sunburned
white guy with tortoiseshell glasses and a hulking white guy with a
foot-long ponytail, driving around the desolate foothills of the Atlas
Mountains in a gigantic Nissan Pathfinder 4 x 4, openly consulting
the map that Hübner had downloaded to his oversize laptop.

Probably the best-known attribute of Plato's Atlantis—other than
its unfortunate, watery demise—is its concentric rings. As Christos
Doumas had pointed out, the bull's-eye of Santorini has hypnotized
some people into thinking it might be Atlantis. (Hübner, naturally,
had data to back up his claim against other sites, including Santorini,
which met only twenty-three of his fifty-one specifications. "Bonn
applies to the same number of criteria," he said, dismissively.) Hübner wanted to show me the annular shape he had located almost
exactly where Plato said it would be. "If you use the measurement of
the Egyptian stade, it's about 211 meters long," Hübner said as we
drove to the site. "So Plato's fifty stades is about ten kilometers from

the sea." The place we were heading to was about twelve kilometers—seven miles—from the sea. Not perfect, by Hübner's Seven Sigma standards, but by Atlantology's usual benchmarks, remarkably close.

We pulled off the road and hiked up a dry hillside covered sparsely with thornbushes. Hübner walked with his head bowed, which I first took to be a tall man's habit from ducking under doorways. In fact, he was scanning the ground for clues. "Flint," he said, picking up a small shard of rock and examining it closely. "There used to be prehistoric stone tools all over here. Now there are almost none."

The day was sunny and hot, so we moved slowly up the incline, stopping frequently to look for flints. After about an hour we reached the top. Hübner had warned me that we wouldn't find a classic three-ringed structure, and it's true that when we arrived it took my eyes a minute to adjust. Once they did, I saw that we were on the lip of a sort of natural bowl. At its center was a small hill, similar to the one Plato had mentioned at the center of Atlantis's capital. Today this nucleus was occupied by a small cluster of plastic tarps, a makeshift campground for some nomadic Berbers.

"It is about five kilometers across here, very close to Plato's twenty-seven stades," Hübner said. "In the center there are the ruins of a triangular structure, with a perimeter of several hundred meters. You can see it on satellite photos. There was a round building over there last year. I hope it's still there." On Google Maps the ring looked like a sort of jagged donut encircling several poorly drawn primary shapes.

Hübner said that a few years earlier, thousands of ruined buildings had dotted this area, but fewer remained each time he returned. They were being carted off stone by stone to be crushed into the reddish pigment that seemed to paint nine out of ten structures in the Souss-Massa. Hübner wanted to slow or stop the destruction, but he was fighting a losing battle. The king owned all land in Morocco and hadn't shown much interest in preserving pre-Islamic ruins, Atlantean or otherwise. And by the standards of, say, the Acropolis, there wasn't much to see here, just dust and rocks and brambles. Plato had described a lush agricultural plain with two growing seasons. We were on the cusp of the Sahara desert. The landscape looked more like the surface of Mars than a thriving maritime port.

Hübner had a stomach bug, so we postponed our visit inside the annular structure and cut our day short. I returned to the Agadir waterfront, ordered a mint tea at the bustling Jour et Nuit café, and watched Moroccan couples walk up and down the promenade holding hands. If I squinted, I could have been in Miami. The 1960 earthquake had obliterated the old city, and the lack of historical architecture made it hard to imagine that this was actually a Phoenician settlement; as with Cádiz and Gadeirus (the second son of Poseidon, who ruled the land facing Atlantis, according to Plato), the name Agadir is derived from the Phoenician word for *wall* or *enclosure*.

The fifth-century-BC Carthaginian navigator Hanno described sailing through the Pillars of Heracles and passing down this coast, spotting a lagoon where elephants fed. About a day's sail beyond that point, he claimed to have founded five cities. Though these cities have never been definitively identified, the historian Rhys Carpenter guessed that two likely possibilities were a fertile valley to the east of Agadir, which Hübner planned to show me, and the island of Mogador. Mogador was renowned in ancient times as a source of indigo dye made from marine snails, a possible connection with the blue vestments worn by the princes of Atlantis.

Agadir certainly provided some of the most satisfying answers I'd yet found for Tony O'Connell's two main conundrums, the mountains and the muddy shoals. Plato wrote that Atlantis's plain was surrounded by mountains and stretched to the infinite sea (presumably the Atlantic Ocean). Those mountains sheltered Atlantis from northern winds. The Souss-Massa is protected from the northerly gusts of the Azores High by the twelve-thousand- and thirteen-thousand-foot peaks of the High Atlas range.

Herodotus reports that a Persian named Sataspes was dispatched by the emperor Xerxes to circumnavigate Africa. After passing through the Pillars and sailing down the west coast, "he encountered a race of little men who wore palm leaf clothing"—likely Pygmies—who "fled into the hills whenever he landed near them." Here, Sataspes told Xerxes upon his return, he had to turn back because "the ship was unable to move any further forward but remained fast in the water." Xerxes didn't believe Sataspes and "had him impaled," Herodotus wrote.

It wasn't hard to imagine Carthaginians, eager to keep the Greeks out of their western territories, passing these stories down a chain that led back to Athens, where they might have found their way into a tale about an island beyond the Pillars of Heracles that sank, "for which reason the sea in those parts is impassable and impenetrable."

Before sunrise the following morning I called down to my hotel's front desk asking for a taxi and was informed that none would be available all day. It was Eid al-Adha, the Festival of the Sacrifice, which honors Ibrahim's resolute obedience to the somewhat capricious Allah through his willingness to take his son Ismail's life. The previous night a waiter had explained the holiday by saying something that sounded like "tomorrow is day we kill the ship," which in New York would have earned him at the very least an unpleasant visit from Naval Intelligence. But the day's first incantatory calls to prayer, drifting through my open windows as dawn began to break, lured me outside, and I found that my hotel's desk person had not been exaggerating. For several minutes I stood on the edge of Avenue Mohammed V's six lanes, which had been jammed with traffic from morning to night the day before. Not a single vehicle drove by in either direction.

A few hours later, large groups of families dressed up in immaculately pressed and colorful robes began to appear on the sidewalks. I finally found a taxi driver napping in his vehicle down by the beach and persuaded him to take my fare. I'd made a date to meet Hübner at the gigantic Metro supermarket (also closed) on the outskirts of Agadir, and as we drove through the neighborhoods on the route, I understood what my waiter had been talking about. In every third or fourth doorway hung the carcass of a freshly killed sheep, an important part of the celebration.

I was reminded that the setting of the *Timaeus* and *Critias* was a gathering at the annual Panathenaia festival in Athens, which culminated in a ritual sacrifice. "The theme is very appropriate to the festival of the goddess," Socrates tells Critias of his plan to honor the event—a tribute to Athena—with his story of Atlantis. "And it's a considerable advantage that it happens to be a true account and not a fictitious tale."

Everything I'd done hinged on the truth or falsity of a statement about truth or falsity. Plato would've gotten a kick out of that.

Hübner and I drove the Pathfinder into the center of the annular structure, past where we'd seen the Berber camp the day before. Hübner explained that North Africa's native Berber (or Amazigh) people have inhabited a triangular swath of the Souss-Massa plain for at least five thousand years and call the region *island*, because it is isolated by mountain ranges on two sides and the Atlantic on the third. Young boys were chasing goats through the rocky landscape. Vegetation in this part of the Souss-Massa is so sparse that it isn't unusual to see trees loaded with goats, who climb onto any branch that will support their weight. Hübner's stomach was feeling better and he was in a good mood. He and his brother, Sebastian, had located hundreds of stone constructions inside this circle and just outside of it. "Plato said many cultures came together," he said. "There were so many buildings in the place we are going. Maybe it would have been like the New York City of the ancient world."

We stepped out of the SUV and started to walk, passing some stone circles and crossing over a sort of fence woven like a crown of thorns from thousands of prickly bushes. Hübner stopped frequently to pick up bits of stone, which he studied intently for flint-like qualities and then tossed back on the ground. It felt as if we were tracking some sort of beast that might have recently gone extinct. Though the pigment makers had evidently been digging like hungry squirrels going after tulip bulbs, the area was still filled with the remains of stone foundations of some sort—circles, ovals, rectangles. Hübner had once found a chunk of pottery near here that seemed to date from the Neolithic era, but beyond that, the area we were walking through was a complete mystery, in terms of who had lived here and when. Stavros Papamarinopoulos had made the not entirely helpful suggestion to Hübner that he should rent a helicopter for a few weeks to take aerial photographs of the entire area. "On the satellite you can see a large rectangular shape here, attached to a circle with cisterns in it," Hübner told me over his shoulder. "Maybe it was a megalith to mark a spring," like the hot and cold springs in Atlantis.

As in Doñana Park, the unique landforms visible from space were invisible in the monotonous landscape. It was impossible to tell that we were actually inside the giant ring. We lost the Pathfinder and walked up and down hills until we spotted it again. Rain started to fall. We got very wet. Hübner paused to pick up and examine approximately ten thousand individual flints, one of which actually came in handy when I used it to scrape red mud off my pants and notebook after falling down a slope leading to a small, bubbling pool of water. Ever on the lookout for clues, Hübner walked past me, inched himself close to the edge, and stuck his hand in to see if it might be one of Plato's hot springs. "It's cold," he said.

In an Atlantis documentary, our visit to the annular structure would be the moment when the camera zoomed out to show the ring we were walking around, and the narrator would ask, "But could this *really* have been Plato's Atlantis?" Hübner had located an abandoned circular settlement, roughly the dimensions Plato gave, outside of the Pillars of Heracles. His numbers matched up pretty well with Plato's, but so did Werner Wickboldt's. They couldn't both be correct. Like Anton Mifsud, Hübner had inventive explanations for some of Plato's details. The shiny orichalcum, Hübner hypothesized, had actually been a metallic paint made by mixing copper-colored mica and lime. (An Egyptian pharaoh, he told me, was said to have had his floors painted with a mixture of gold and lime.) No matter how hard I hinted, I couldn't get Hübner to admit that his criteria might be in any way flawed or tainted by selection bias. When I asked about the million-strong army of Atlantis, which was not part of his data, he answered, "All I can say is that Atlantis was in Africa and there's room for a lot of people."

Hübner had no doubt that Plato, through Socrates, had been speaking sincerely at the start of the *Timaeus*. "If the information is not correct, or if Plato has invented the story, it would be extremely improbable that all these criteria would apply to one place. And if he mixed criteria or made a fantasy, it would be very improbable that all these criteria could be found in one place." I couldn't help but think of the Wall Street geniuses who had made millions slicing and dicing mortgages into countless forms of new securities but who had almost wrecked the world economy because their sophisticated statistical models failed to account for the possibility that housing prices might actually fall.

If I didn't quite share Hübner's Platonic faith in numbers, I had to admire his dedication to gathering new data. The next morning the two of us walked around an abandoned lot on the outskirts of Agadir filled with nothing but tree stumps and litter. I watched as he used an old satellite map to search for evidence of a canal that might have once run through what was now an industrial park. Hübner stepped onto one of the taller stumps for a higher vantage point. "If there was a canal here, there might still be moisture in the ground," he explained, turning left and right. We didn't find any. Later, he pulled over on the shoulder of a highway to take a sample from a ten-foot-high wall of sand through which the road had been carved. "This is a good chance to look for foraminifera," he explained through the passenger-side window as he sifted sand between his fingers— foraminifera being nothing but tiny sea creatures whose fossilized presence might indicate an ancient tsunami.

Hübner had two more sites he wanted me to see before I left. Catastrophic flooding was even more on my mind than usual, because a hurricane that had been building for several days on the other side of the Atlantic was headed directly toward my wife, kids, and home near New York City. I'd moved my departure up a day in hopes of beating the storm. I wasn't exactly heartbroken by this prospect. After my run-in with passport control, I had never warmed to Morocco. My unease was not alleviated by Michael's frequent references to Morocco's surveillance state, which along with Atlantis was one of the two subjects he was comfortable talking about.

The first place we stopped was a set of oceanfront caves at a place called Cap Ghir that matched Plato's descriptions of docks carved out of the red, white, and black stone of Atlantis. The caves were, as promised, extraordinary. They could have been airplane hangars chiseled into a cliff face. Fishermen were still using them to shelter their boats.

Nothing I'd seen in Morocco had come close to matching Plato's description of the enormous Atlantis plain. There simply wasn't any fresh water. "Plato said that the most fertile part was the middle of the plain," Hübner told me as we drove through a long series of tiny, dusty towns. It was the second day of Eid al-Adha, and the roads were still crowded with well-dressed people of all ages walking to and from mosque. Skinny boys in djellabas rode sidesaddle on scooters so that two or three might squeeze aboard. The farther we got from Agadir, the more head scarves we saw on women and bushy beards on men. An hour outside of town, women were wearing burqas. Twice, as we drove through dusty villages, young men in T-shirts and shorts spotted us coming and pushed their fully veiled sisters indoors, away from our eyes.

As we passed through yet another town, I was absentmindedly entertaining myself by guessing what the signs in Arabic might say when we suddenly slammed to a stop: A turn had left us unexpectedly blocked by a herd of donkeys. When our honking dispersed them, we faced a tall wall of bamboo stalks, the first green I had seen since we had passed the king's compound near Agadir. We drove on slowly for a few minutes until we found a breach in the barrier. Beyond lay lush fields growing a variety of produce.

"It's an elongated oasis," Hübner said, pulling the Nissan over so we could absorb the incongruously lovely sight and smell of cultivation in the desert. The neat rows weren't Plato's canals, but they were the closest thing I'd yet seen to them. "Maybe this was like an island inside an island. I think maybe this place and the annular structure meld together somehow with the caves at Cap Ghir."

Hübner leaned on the steering wheel with both elbows and asked, "So do you think I have found Plato's Atlantis?"

It certainly wasn't Seven Sigma, but he made a compelling case. "Honestly," I said, "at this point I'm not really sure what I think."

CHAPTER TWENTY-SEVEN

The Sky Is Falling

Between the Moon and New York City

My urgent departure from Morocco attempting to beat Hurricane Sandy to New York was a bust. The storm's grievous day and night of destruction left my family unscathed, but flights into New York were canceled for days. I was trapped in rainy Madrid for almost a week, waiting for my lost luggage to arrive from Casablanca and watching the weather-based drama unfold on the only English-language channel available at my hotel, CNBC. When one Wall Street analyst pointed out that the devastation, while tragic, was also a great opportunity to buy home-supply stocks, I clicked off the TV and turned to the backpack full of unread books I'd lugged up and down the Mediterranean while chasing Atlantis. One seemed particularly appropriate.

Trevor Palmer's *Perilous Planet Earth* is a scholarly overview of catastrophism—the study of how natural disasters have influenced events over millions of years. It is also one of the most terrifying books I have ever read. Palmer is a professor emeritus of life sciences at England's Nottingham Trent University. (He wrote a standard text on enzymes.) What makes his catastrophism book so scary is its very lack of drama; he slowly builds up details about the surprising regularity of devastating volcanic explosions, earthquakes, floods, and extraterrestrial impacts (comets and asteroids striking the earth). Because of humans' ever-shrinking attention spans, natural disasters such as Hurricane Sandy—or the eruption of Mount Vesuvius—often seem like rare events, but they aren't. As of this writing, hurricanes and tsunamis remain hot news topics because they've caused so much trouble in recent years. Nobody's been talking much about volcanoes, because volcanoes have been relatively quiet of late. Historical data shows this peace won't last. According to the volcanic explosivity index (VEI), Mount St. Helens in Washington erupted at VEI 5 in 1980, similar to the blast that buried Pompeii. Such events are estimated to happen about once per decade. Thera and Krakatoa were VEI 6 eruptions, several of which typically occur worldwide each century.[12]

"Although we may try to put it out of our minds, we know with near certainty of forthcoming events which could kill thousands, if not millions, of people," Palmer explains calmly in *Perilous Planet Earth*'s conclusion. "The only question is, 'When?'"

After reading consecutive chapters titled "Modern Views of Atlantis" and "Natural Catastrophes and the Rise and Fall of Civilizations," I called Palmer in Scotland. I imagined him holed up in a waterproof concrete bunker, but he assured me that there was no point in worrying about perishing in an unforeseen natural disaster.

---

12 The last VEI 6 blast was Mount Pinatubo in the Philippines, in 1991. Just two hundred years ago, in 1815, the Indonesian volcano Tambora erupted at VEI 7, pulverizing almost a mile of rock off its crown and spewing so much debris into the atmosphere that temperatures dropped around the world for months afterward, resulting in what historians call 1816's "Year without a Summer." A June 6 storm dumped half a foot of snow on New England; an estimated one hundred thousand malnourished Irish died in the years that followed. Such blasts occur every few hundred years. The picturesque geysers of Yellowstone National Park are visible evidence of an underlying supervolcano that has erupted at VEI 8 three times in the last 2.1 million years. VEI 8s occur about twice every hundred thousand years. The next Yellowstone superblast could bury most of the western United States in thick, heavy ash and blot out the sun for years.

"I tend to take the view that I'm more likely to be struck down by a car the next time I try to cross the road," he said. He then reminded me that Plato, in addition to his interest in watery cataclysms like the Deucalion flood and the sinking of Atlantis, also took seriously the inevitability of extraterrestrial events. In the *Timaeus*, the Egyptian priest tells Solon:

> There have been and will be many different calamities to destroy mankind, the greatest of them by fire and water, lesser ones by countless other means. Your own story of how Phaethon, child of the sun, harnessed his father's chariot, but was unable to guide it along his father's course and so burnt up things on the earth and was himself destroyed by a thunderbolt, is a mythical version of the truth that there is at long intervals a variation in the course of the heavenly bodies and a consequent widespread destruction by fire of things on the earth.

I didn't really give this passage much thought until a few months later, when an undetected meteor suddenly burst into a fireball in the sky of eastern Russia, causing a retina-searing flash and a shock wave that shattered windows. Sixteen hours later an unrelated asteroid that astronomers *had* been expecting passed within 17,200 miles of Earth. Perhaps Plato knew something that we've forgotten.

Palmer had explained that one reason catastrophism has been so slow to catch on with mainstream scientists—beyond the religious taint it still carried from affiliation with stories like Noah's flood—was that catastrophist studies had been hindered by, as he politely put it, "theories put forward that have proved untenable." He might have been describing Atlantology. In at least one sense, he was. In 1883, the year after Ignatius Donnelly launched the modern search for Plato's lost island with *Atlantis: The Antediluvian World*, he published a sequel. In *Ragnarok: The Age of Fire and Gravel*, Donnelly purported to explain how the disappearance of the sophisticated civilization of Atlantis had been caused by the impact of a comet. Donnelly believed the memory of this impact had been encoded in the fiery wipeout of the Phaethon myth.

The bombastic *Ragnarok* was a critical and commercial dud, and in the century that followed the slow-and-steady school of uniformitarianism exemplified by Darwin's theory of evolution became even more entrenched as catastrophism was nudged ever further toward the fringes. Plate tectonics and continental drift, initially ridiculed by geologists a hundred years ago when proposed by the nonspecialist Alfred Wegener, and not taken seriously for another fifty years, are now core uniformitarian principles of the earth sciences.

Perhaps the greatest reason for scientific resistance to catastrophism can be summed up in one name: Immanuel Velikovsky. After studying psychoanalysis under one of Sigmund Freud's disciples, Velikovsky came to New York City prior to World War II and conducted an exhaustive comparative study of ancient myths, legends, and folklore from around the world, which resulted in his hugely popular 1950 book *Worlds in Collision* (a number one bestseller) and its sequel two years later, *Ages in Chaos*. His main argument was that events related in stories such as the Atlantis tale were, in fact, chronicles of ancient natural disasters. Velikovsky's speculations combined aspects of Donnelly's *Ragnarok*, the World Ice Theory beloved by the Nazis, and a spirited game of interstellar croquet: Around 1500 BC, he proposed, the planet Jupiter ejected a mass that took the form of a comet, which zoomed past the earth twice at close range. One loop skimmed near enough to cause intense heat and enormous tides, triggering the general environmental mayhem recorded in the Ten Plagues of Egypt and the Great Flood myths, including that of Atlantis. The hypothetical comet finally collided with Mars and settled into orbit as the planet Venus.

The *very* Freudian analysis Velikovsky gave of the situation was that humankind suffered from a collective amnesia regarding these terrifying events, resulting from repressed memories of ancient trauma. A prime example was the priest at Saïs explaining to Solon that "when, after the usual interval of years, like a plague, the flood from heaven comes sweeping down afresh upon your people, it leaves none of you but the unlettered and the uncultured, so that you become young as ever, with no knowledge of all that happened in old times in this land or in your own."

This calamitous revision of history infuriated scholars in almost every discipline imaginable. (Carl Sagan, among the grooviest and most open-minded of astrophysicists, practically choked on his turtleneck whenever given the chance to denounce Velikovsky's theories.) When the respected German scientist Otto Muck's well-researched but somewhat fanciful book *The Secret of Atlantis* was published posthumously in English in 1978, experts had a good laugh at his cartoonish catastrophist ideas, one of them straight out of the Ignatius Donnelly playbook: that Atlantis had been sunk by a wave that resulted when a six-mile-wide asteroid crashed into the Earth.

The general distrust of giant killer missiles from space was still dominant in 1980, when a team led by Luis and Walter Alvarez—a Nobel Prize–winning physicist father and his geologist son working at the University of California, Berkeley—published a paper that, in synopsis, sounded almost as crazy as Velikovsky's cometary collisions. Why, the two men wondered, did global geologic samples taken at the layer of the Cretaceous-Paleogene boundary (a thin band of clay that dates to around 65 million years ago) show extremely high levels of iridium, an element typically scarce in the earth's crust but plentiful in meteorites and comets? The Alvarezes formulated a radically simple solution: The end of the Cretaceous period—and the extinction of dinosaurs and two-thirds of other animal species—had resulted when a six-mile-wide asteroid crashed into the earth.

The Alvarezes proved one thing almost immediately—that even a Nobel Prize wasn't sufficient to quell doubts from geologists and paleontologists about asteroid-impact theories. But new iridium samples continued to trickle in from around the world, supporting their hypothesis, and a decade later, it was matched with a massive 110-mile-wide crater that oil-company geologists had located beneath several hundred feet of debris on the Yucatán Peninsula. Such an impact would have had a force equivalent to a billion Hiroshima atomic bombs and could have unleashed enough particulate matter into the atmosphere to block sunlight (and life-giving photosynthesis) for months. With this new evidence fresh in their minds, astrophysicists watched in awe through their telescopes in July 1994 as the Shoemaker-Levy 9 comet split apart and crashed into Jupiter at more than one hundred thousand miles per hour. One fragment's impact raised a debris cloud seven thousand miles across. Twenty years later, the collision is still roiling weather on Jupiter.

Among the eclectic list of papers presented at Stavros Papamarinopoulos's first Atlantis conference, one in particular stood out because of the unique scientific credentials of its authors. Members of the Holocene Impact Working Group (HIWG), a loosely affiliated team of scientists working at some of the world's most reputable institutions, had submitted a paper inferring that a fragment of a comet had plummeted into the Indian Ocean east of Madagascar around five thousand years ago, producing a "Shoemaker-Levy type impact" that formed an eighteen-mile-wide depression in the seafloor. The HIWG team named the hypothetical impact site the Burckle Crater.

One member had drawn a plausible link between this catastrophe and the world's flood myths, including that of Atlantis.

The paper had been presented by Dallas Abbott, an expert in marine geophysics at Columbia University's Lamont-Doherty Earth Observatory. After locating the possible crater (and finding nickel deposits that suggested an extraterrestrial origin), she began to look for physical evidence of an impact's aftermath. "Basically, when I found Burckle I realized that if I was right about it, there ought to be something really big in Madagascar," she told me. When Google Earth was introduced in 2005, Abbott almost immediately spotted telltale V shapes in the dunes along Madagascar's eastern edge. Such maritime sand wedges, called chevrons, can be evidence of tsunamis. She visited the island in 2006 to take sediment samples and found deep-ocean marine microfossils more than six hundred feet above sea level, far higher than could have been deposited by a wave of seismic or volcanic origin. If the chevrons were the fingerprints of a postimpact tsunami, their source had been a wave twenty times as tall as the one that demolished Fukushima and powerful enough to produce "megatsunamis in many parts of the world." Abbott suggested that if I wanted to hear about the even more devastating—and Atlantis-like—effects of a deep-water impact, I should speak with her HIWG colleague W. Bruce Masse, who had the original idea to search for a crater in the Indian Ocean.

Masse had recently retired from his day job as an archaeologist and environmental compliance professional at the Los Alamos National Laboratory, where his duties had included keeping tabs on the hundreds of ancient sites on the institution's grounds. I'd seen him on TV describing one of his theories; he was big and goateed and with the sound turned down could have passed for a high school football coach gleefully describing a touchdown against a crosstown rival, rather than a catastrophic event that might have decimated ancient civilization. He may have spent more time pondering the intersection of myth and natural disasters than any person since Velikovsky.

To truly understand the relationship between myth and catastrophe, Masse explained, "you have to be a *classical* classical scholar," someone like Plato or Aristotle, who "knew every natural science there ever was and everything in it." Masse had been trained to trust in the hard evidence of material culture and to doubt the importance of any information transmitted through astronomy, mythology, and, especially, oral tradition. "Basically, as archaeologists and cultural anthropologists we are taught that each generation leaves more potential for loss of information," he said. Masse fell in line with his training completely until the early 1980s, when an elderly oral historian in the Palau archipelago described to him distant villages abandoned during undocumented battles centuries earlier. Masse examined the archaeological record and found evidence of defensive fortifications and shrinking food stocks. "That was my first inkling that something was wrong with my training," he said.

Later, in Hawaii, Masse studied local myths about the volcano goddess Pele. He noticed that battles she'd reputedly fought with real Hawaiian chiefs could be roughly matched to carbon-dated debris from lava flows—an indication that orally transmitted Pele myths contained real historical truths. Masse found that in many cases "accurate details of celestial events" recorded in Hawaiian myths, such as comets, meteor storms, and supernovae, could be "exactly matched with the historic record in Asia, Europe, and the Middle East."

Masse's widening investigations into traditional astronomy and the geological origins of myths inevitably led him to the one "catastrophic event that has universal distribution in virtually all cultures": the Great Flood. He assembled and analyzed 175 different flood myths from around the world and compiled their recurring themes: torrential rains; tsunamis; extended periods of darkness;

hurricane-force winds; and the appearance of elongated celestial creatures such as serpents or fish, likely descriptors of comets. In the ancient Hindu story of Manu, a fish-god instructs the first man to prepare a ship—in one version, he lassoes the fish's prominent horn (likely the comet's tail)—to survive a coming cataclysm that arrives in the form of worldwide fire, apocalyptic rain, and floods. Masse noticed that many of the deluge stories roughly coincided with the transition from the middle to the late Holocene, around 2800 BC, a period when the Earth's climate became somewhat cooler and wetter. Societal convulsions resulted: Populations shrank; major language groups migrated to new lands; other new languages and dialects appeared suddenly. Around the same time, catastrophic events were chronicled in Mesopotamia, Egypt, and China. Masse concluded that a single cataclysm—a comet impact similar to the Shoemaker-Levy collision with Jupiter—had occurred. Such a disaster may have wiped out a quarter of the world's human inhabitants. References to a conjunction of planets in the watery constellation Aquarius and a partial lunar eclipse even allowed him to propose a precise date for the world-changing event: May 10, 2807 BC.

Masse and Abbott agree that much more physical evidence from the Indian Ocean is needed to prove the HIWG Burckle impact-crater hypothesis, and the list of their peers who have cast stones is long and impressively credentialed. "Catastrophism is still the stepchild that no one likes to talk about," Masse says. If HIWG is correct, however, the impact's effects would have been much more complex than the *kerplunk* and splash of a fat kid cannonballing into a swimming pool. A giant, superheated comet slamming into the ocean at one hundred thousand miles per hour would cause immediate skyscraper-tall tsunamis and vaporize huge amounts of seawater, injecting it into the atmosphere. As this water cooled and condensed, likely effects would include cyclonic storms with hurricane-force winds and several days of torrential rainfall, the sorts of incredible deluges described in the tales of Noah, Gilgamesh, Manu, and Deucalion—and in the *Timaeus*, the rains that wash the soil from the Acropolis in Athens.

I turned the subject to Atlantis, and Masse (who had recently had an interview artfully edited in a documentary "proving" Noah's ark was real) prefaced his thoughts with a warning that "everything I'm telling you now I would label as a preliminary but informed opinion."

Masse believes that Solon truly did hear the original Atlantis tale from the Egyptian priest. "Atlantis is a story, a myth, that we know in fragmentary form about an actual catastrophe," Masse explained. The closest correlation he sees is with the Thera blast—in which a prosperous island was destroyed overnight by a natural disaster, turning it into a ring-shaped remnant. But because priests and shamans usually transmitted oral history via performance-based techniques, he said, Solon may have heard an incomplete version of the story that was further distorted or garbled in transmission down to Plato. Somehow, important elements of the Deucalion flood—which Masse equates with the 2807 BC comet event—seem to have been blended into the story.

"The other thing we need to consider is that in the *Timaeus* itself Plato is trying to not only provide bits and pieces of this story, however accurate or faithful, but his own ideas about how the universe works and how knowledge works," Masse said. Plato wrote often of the cyclical repetition of time, what the classical scholar Desmond Lee called "the notion of periodic destructions by natural cataclysm, followed by a slow redevelopment of civilization." In the *Timaeus*, Plato may have been taking the pieces of an incomplete story that had originated in Egypt and using them to explain the order of the universe.

Plato felt so strongly about the oral transmission of stories concerning the periodic deviations of the heavenly bodies that he explicitly addressed them in his final work, the *Laws*, in which three men on a pilgrimage to the birthplace of Zeus on Crete discuss how to create a hypothetical city:

ATHENIAN: Do you consider that there is any truth in the ancient tales?

CLINIAS: What tales?

ATHENIAN: That the world of men has often been destroyed by floods, plagues, and many other things, in such a way that only a small portion of the human race has survived.

CLINIAS: Everyone would regard such accounts as perfectly credible.

Catastrophist hypotheses may be slightly more acceptable than they were twenty years ago, but they're still a long way from "perfectly credible." Masse argues that by ignoring the Saïs priest's warning about periodic destructions, we may be missing the essential scientific point of Plato's Atlantis story: "that current models substantially underestimate the risk and effects of catastrophic cosmic impact."

Plato may have thought he was clear about the devastating consequences of cosmic eruptions, but that doesn't mean anyone listened. Impact craters don't get much attention, because they're rare: Fewer than two hundred confirmed examples have been located on the face of the planet. Some have been worn away over time by erosion, glaciers, floods, earthquakes, and other geophysical processes. Many more have presumably vanished beneath the 70 percent of the Earth's surface that is covered by water and ice. "People still don't have a clue about oceanic impact," Masse told me. "Did you know there has not been an ocean impact crater identified and confirmed for the last 25 million years?"

A few hundred scattered craters over the earth's 4.5 billion years doesn't sound so scary—until you point a telescope at the night sky. As Masse notes in a recent paper, astrophysicists have logged more than forty-two thousand impact craters with diameters of three miles or more on Mars, which has a surface area less than a third of the Earth's. The moon, which has less than a twelfth of the Earth's surface area, "exhibits more than thirty thousand craters greater than one kilometer in diameter," or 0.6 miles across. The moon's lack of an atmosphere and weaker gravitational effects amplify the size of its impact craters, which persist indefinitely due to the absence of erosion. Still, those thirty thousand impacts, if occurring on Earth, would have ranged from *at least* 240 Hiroshima explosions to, in a handful of cases, greater than the cometary collision that killed the dinosaurs.

Some extraterrestrial objects wreak havoc without ever reaching the ground. Plato's rendition of the Phaethon myth, which along with the more detailed version in Ovid's *Metamorphoses* Masse called "a perfect description of an impact event," is one possible example. (Explosions in the sky, like the 2013 airburst in Russia, are classified as impact events.) On June 30, 1908, a meteor exploded a few miles above the ground in a sparsely populated area near the Podkamennaya Tunguska River in Siberia. Indigenous Evenki reindeer hunters reported being knocked down by a sudden wind and witnessing a second sun in the sky—the fireball caused by the exploding meteor. Eight hundred square miles of trees were flattened. In *Perilous Planet Earth*, Trevor Palmer notes that "had the Tunguska object arrived just four hours later, destroying St. Petersburg"—then the center of soon-to-be-revolutionized Russian politics—"the history of the twentieth century could have been very different from what it was." A recent model of a Tunguska-size air burst over modern Manhattan estimates 3.9 million deaths. Masse says the frequency of such events has recently been recalculated at every two hundred years.

On at least one point, catastrophist Donnelly trumps evolutionist Darwin: When catastrophe inevitably strikes, evolutionary laws favoring the survival of the fittest are temporarily suspended. "It's more like survival of the luckiest," Masse said, echoing Plato's claim that only illiterate mountain dwellers survived the great floods. While post-Sandy New York was slowly adjusting to elevated flood dangers from rising sea levels, Dallas Abbott was examining sediment deposits that indicated a sixty-foot-high tsunami, caused by an asteroid impact, might have slammed into Manhattan as recently as 300 BC.[13]

I assumed Masse would blame Velikovsky for scientists' reluctance to share Plato's concerns about catastrophes, but he said that actually, with some Venus-size caveats, he respected Velikovsky's work. While it's true that *Worlds in Collision* was a little kooky, Velikovsky—like Schliemann at Troy—had accomplished two difficult tasks: breaching the wall between natural sciences and myth and capturing the public's attention. It was a skill Plato also possessed—as demonstrated by his use of the Atlantis tale in the *Timaeus*—the ability to take important, complicated ideas and "really pull them together to tell a fascinating story," Masse said.

I told Masse that it was almost time for me to sort through all the conflicting information I'd gathered and reach some conclusions about Atlantis.

"In a sense, you're like Plato," Masse said. "There are nuances in the stuff all of us are telling you, which you have to draw upon to

---

13 The idea that humans might one day disrupt nature's catastrophist cycles by deflecting unwelcome flying projectiles from space probably never occurred to Plato. NASA's Near-Earth Object Program calculates that it has located 95 percent of Earth-threatening asteroids one kilometer (0.6 miles) or wider, but that accuracy plummets as objects get smaller. (The 1908 Tunguska meteoroid, for example, was estimated to be only about two hundred feet in diameter.) An independent group called the B612 Foundation, which includes former astronauts, is raising funds to build a satellite to track smaller objects. Masse, who has seen multiple grant requests to study the Burckle Crater declined, isn't optimistic.

make an informed, knowledgeable story. Are you in denial that you are following in his footsteps?"

The very idea struck me as so ridiculous that I laughed out loud. Aristotle was the sort of person who followed in Plato's footsteps. I couldn't even get through the *Timaeus* without a personal tutor. After thinking about it for a while, though, I realized that I had formulated answers to—or at least plausible explanations for—almost every problem in Plato's Atlantis story: the mountains, the shoals, the circles, the Pillars of Heracles, even the cataclysm. I may have been suffering from the sort of Atlantean overconfidence that invited the wrath of Zeus, but I even thought I might provide something the Atlantis story has always lacked: an ending.

All I had to do first was decipher the meaning of Plato's numbers.

CHAPTER TWENTY-EIGHT

The Plato Code

In the Green Mountains of Vermont

In 1666, the Atlantis tale briefly crossed paths with another unsolved mystery of antiquity in the person of a Jesuit scholar working in Rome. Athanasius Kircher had just published his monumental work of speculative science, *Mundus Subterraneus*, which included his upside-down map of Atlantis that is the most famous ever drawn. (It's the one Rand Flem-Ath had tried to convince me was a dead ringer for Antarctica.) A dying friend sent a gift Kircher had long coveted—an illustrated manuscript, filled with colored drawings of plants, astronomical charts, and naked women. What made the book unique was its minuscule handwritten text, comprised of alphabetic characters never seen elsewhere and thus completely indecipherable. Kircher was not a man who lacked confidence. He claimed, erroneously, to have decoded hieroglyphics almost two hundred years before the discovery of the Rosetta stone. But even he didn't dare to pretend to have broken this mysterious manuscript's baffling code. After Kircher's death, the manuscript vanished until 1912, when it was purchased by the Polish antiquities dealer Wilfrid Voynich. By 1969 what's now known as the Voynich Manuscript made its way to Yale University. There it fell into the hands of a philosophy professor named Robert Brumbaugh.

Brumbaugh, who died in 1992, was not a typical philosophy professor. He had worked as a code breaker in the US Army Signal Corps during World War II. He specialized in translating difficult material, such as Plato's ideas, into simple English that college freshmen could understand. And he was willing to tackle offbeat subjects that made less curious academics uncomfortable. Brumbaugh once floated a hypothesis that the Pythagorean aversion to eating legumes had a hereditary cause, an enzyme debility that sometimes resulted in a deadly reaction to the consumption of fava beans. Brumbaugh's son told me that his father became a little obsessed with deciphering the Voynich, to the degree that his mother, also a former code breaker, "eventually had to sit him down and say, *enough*." Brumbaugh finally concluded that the text might have been a "treatise on the Elixir of Life" and possibly part of a Renaissance con game. He may have been right on both counts—despite his own efforts and subsequent quantum leaps in cryptological computing power, the manuscript still hasn't been decoded.

Considering the amount of online cross-pollination between Voynich fanatics (among whom Brumbaugh is a celebrity) and the fundamentalist Atlantology crowd, I was surprised that no one seemed to have noticed Brumbaugh's attempt to decode another problematic manuscript: Plato's *Critias*. In a little-known 1954 book titled *Plato's Mathematical Imagination*, Brumbaugh noted that for more than two thousand years scholars have been confused by Plato's seemingly baffling use of numbers. Atlantologists, of course, had seized on precise details such as the nine thousand years, the three concentric circles, and the measurements of Atlantis's capital and its enormous oblong plain, contorting the mathematics when necessary to fit a particular hypothesis.

Rather than pausing to wonder what the genius who proclaimed

LET NO ONE IGNORANT OF GEOMETRY ENTER HERE over the entrance to his school might have been up to with all those numbers and forms, scholars have almost universally dismissed passages that contain mathematics as "nonsense or riddles," Brumbaugh noted. Yes, the numerical sections of Plato's works are doubly impenetrable, the most obscure writings of an exceedingly elusive writer. But Brumbaugh saw this as no excuse on the part of scholars to pretend they don't exist. "In literature, it may be allowable to introduce meaningless passages to create an effect of difficulty," he wrote. "In philosophy, it is not."

According to Elizabeth Barber's Silence Principle, storytellers don't bother to give their audiences information they can assume is already known. Anything not stated explicitly in a narrative is likely to be forgotten over time. If two thousand years from now humans are cannibals who have obliterated the earth's forests and live in houses made of gingerbread, the story of Hansel and Gretel will require footnotes. Brumbaugh believed that Plato intended the numbers in the *Critias* not to be taken literally but to conjure up images that, for his audience at the Academy, would add an additional layer of meaning to the text. Illustrated manuscripts did not yet exist in the fourth century BC, so Plato (in Brumbaugh's opinion) included Pythagorean-influenced math that "was intended to be metaphorical."

In one example Brumbaugh cites, near the start of Book VIII of the *Republic*, Socrates mentions "the 4 and 3 joined to the pempad," which scholars generally agree refers to the most famous of Pythagorean diagrams, the 3-4-5 right triangle. Beyond that, those same scholars have mostly scratched their heads about what the heck Plato was trying to say. Brumbaugh points out that book VIII is where Plato considers the five types of leader (in descending order of desirability: aristocrat, timocrat, oligarch, democrat, tyrant). These character types are the products of the three parts of the soul discussed in books II–IV (intelligence, spirit, and appetite), combined with the four ascending levels of understanding described in books V–VII (conjecture, opinion, understanding, reason; we will come back to this in a moment). A passage that the eminent Plato scholar James Adam described as "notoriously the most difficult in his writings" suddenly becomes clearer when drawn out as it might have been on a wax tablet at the Academy:

The Brumbaugh Triangle

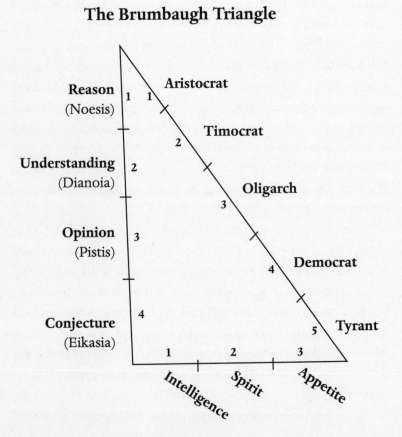

Two of Plato's works containing the most—and strangest—numbers were, of course, the *Timaeus* and *Critias*. The only Atlantis-related figures Plato cites in the *Timaeus* are the dates—eight thousand years since the founding of Egypt, and nine thousand since the destruction of Atlantis and Athens. Critias pauses the story and Timaeus jumps in with his very Pythagorean discussion of numbers and harmonics, the World-Soul, and so on. Brumbaugh notes that in the data-rich *Critias*, only a single number, the twenty-thousand-strong fighting force, is used to describe Athens. Atlantis, on the other hand, is described in the rich numerical detail that has led people to search for the lost city. Brumbaugh homes in on Plato's statement that the kings of Atlantis "met alternately every fifth and every sixth year paying equal honor to the odd and to the even."

In a casual reading, this is the sort of ho-hum detail even an ardent Atlantologist glosses over. For Brumbaugh it was a stop-the-presses moment. Isn't Plato's indifferent attitude about the ratio of fives and sixes a little strange, he asks, coming on the heels of the Steinway-precise tunings of the World-Soul in the *Timaeus*? One of the key tenets of Pythagoreanism was that odd numbers were male and evens were female. In Plato's final dialogue, the *Laws*, the gods of Olympus receive the "superior" honors in odd numbers while those of the underworld are honored by the "secondary" evens. Brumbaugh cites numerous examples of fives and sixes in the text of the *Critias*, both explicit and implied. If one draws a diagram of the three-ringed city and counts the total widths of sea and land, they add up to a ratio of 6:5. The central island is five stades across; the statue of Poseidon has six horses. Poseidon sires five sets of twin sons; six of them must vote in favor if an Atlantean king is to be put to death. Nowhere else in his body of work does Plato use such alternating numbers.

For an Academy audience conversant in Pythagorean concepts,

the idea that odds and evens could be used interchangeably would have been as unthinkable as Le Cordon Bleu students casually substituting vinegar for butter. Brumbaugh concludes that these clashing odds and evens demonstrate that "Plato meant his Atlantis to be a blueprint of a bad society, eventually corrupted by prosperity, disorganization, and a lack of education."

Like a chess grandmaster checkmating a line of novices in succession at a charity tournament, Plato may have been playing several sophisticated numbers games simultaneously with his disciples that are only now coming to light. Stavros Papamarinopoulos had e-mailed me two recently uncovered examples of hidden mathematics in Plato's dialogues. The first was a paper by math scholars Antonis Vardulakis and Clive Pugh, which examined the importance of the number 5040 in the *Laws*, which Plato wrote was the optimum number of families in his ideal city of Magnesia. The number 5040 is the product of $1 \times 2 \times 3 \times 4 \times 5 \times 6 \times 7$ and appears in *Laws* exactly seven times. Buried even more deeply in the dialogue, Vardulakis and Pugh believe, were hidden theorems about consecutive prime numbers and divisibility of composite (i.e., nonprime) numbers—the sorts of sophisticated mathematical concepts that wouldn't have required an explanation for an audience at the Academy.

The other example Papamarinopoulos had mentioned was one I'd heard about on the radio but hadn't given much thought because I wasn't sure if it applied to Atlantis. In 2010, Jay Kennedy, an instructor at the University of Manchester in England, announced that he had discovered a hidden mathematical and musical code in several works by Plato. Kennedy employed a tool known as stichometry, or line counting, to reach his conclusions. He had used a computer program to estimate the number of lines in Plato's original manuscripts and found that within a very small margin of error, they all had line counts that tallied up to multiples of 1,200. (The

Republic, for example, had 12,000.) Kennedy argued that Plato had structured his dialogues in twelve parts, based on the twelve-note Pythagorean harmonic scale.[14] To mark the transition between each of these twelve sections—in other words, at the 1/12 mark, the 2/12 mark, and so on up to the 11/12 mark—Plato inserted a symbolic passage.

What was fascinating about Kennedy's discovery was that Plato seems to have used this twelve-part architecture not simply as an organizing principle, like a harmonic outline, but as a rhetorical device. In several dialogues, at precisely the midpoint (6/12, or a 6:12 ratio), Plato inserted "passages describing the divine wisdom and justice of the philosopher," Kennedy writes. In the *Republic*, this is where Socrates discusses the philosopher-king. In the *Timaeus*, the title character pauses his windy discourse on the four basic elements and their atomic triangles to remind everyone that the Divine Craftsman has arranged these particles in perfect harmony.

The code Kennedy found coincides with the primary ratios of Pythagorean harmony. "According to Greek theory," he wrote in an article for the philosophy and science journal *Apeiron*, "the third (1:4), fourth (1:3), sixth (1:2), eighth (2:3) and ninth (3:4) notes on the twelve-note scale will best harmonize with the twelfth. Passages near these relatively harmonious notes are dominated by positively valued concepts, while passages near dissonant notes (the fifth, seventh, tenth and eleventh) are dominated by negative ones." In the *Timaeus*, Kennedy notes, Plato describes the harmonious creations of the Divine Craftsman at the harmonious eighth and ninth passages. At the disharmonious tenth and eleventh passages, he discusses the physical decay of the body and diseases of the soul.

---

14 On a piano, these twelve notes are represented by the seven white keys of the major scale (ABCDEFG) plus the five black keys, the sharps and flats of the chromatic scale, that fall between them.

Obviously, I was getting warmer. More than once I caught myself daydreaming that I was on the verge of a *Da Vinci Code*–type breakthrough, that like Professor Robert Langdon unscrambling the numbers of Fibonacci's sequence to find the real murderer I could follow Plato's mathematical clues all the way to a solution to the Atlantis riddle. Occasionally, while driving, I silently rehearsed the introduction Steve Kroft would give me on *60 Minutes*: "For more than two thousand years, the mystery of Atlantis has befuddled history's greatest minds. Now, one intrepid reporter has achieved what was once considered impossible . . ."

I'd even found the obscure genius who could help me make the final leap. I hopped a train to Washington, DC, and headed to the apartment of ninety-five-year-old Ernest McClain, a retired music professor who had written a book titled *The Pythagorean Plato*. In it, McClain described the Atlantis tale as "a sophisticated entertainment for Pythagoreans only" and lamented that "for the musically innocent, it is and must remain merely a Platonic fairy tale, incomprehensibly loaded with absolutely meaningless numerical detail."

The book was tough sledding; a leading American musicologist who specializes in Pythagorean harmonics later described it to me as "completely impenetrable." I spent a pleasant four hours nodding my head and listening to McClain weave a word tapestry about the relationship between ancient Sumerian octaves, the *Rig Veda*, the Babylonian base-sixty number system, and the music of the spheres. I sat at his table and briefly held hands in silent prayer with him and his home health care aide before eating a bowl of chicken soup and a sandwich, and returned to Union Station as musically innocent as when I'd arrived. About the only thing I'd understood was McClain's repeated exhortation: "I know you've come for a shortcut, but some things you can't understand until you figure them out for yourself!"

. . .

A few weeks later, I made my way to the Green Mountains of Vermont, where John Bremer had offered to try to untangle all this stuff for me. Bremer was a retired educator; like Plato he had traveled widely and founded an institution of higher learning, Cambridge College, just outside of Boston. He had spent decades thinking about Plato. He knew Ernest McClain personally and considered him brilliant. A half century before Jay Kennedy began his computer stichometric analysis, Bremer was counting syllables of ancient Greek by hand. Like Kennedy, he noticed patterns that seemed too striking to be coincidental.

Still dashing at age eighty-six, with longish hair, a posh British accent, and a peach-colored shirt unbuttoned to his sternum, Bremer continued to wrestle with Plato daily. We met on an unseasonably hot day, so we retreated to his basement, where his large desk sat amid a forest of bookshelves, one devoted entirely to Plato. He called himself a Socratic philosopher, which I supposed meant he asked a lot of questions in order to reach the truth. We assumed the familiar positions of teacher and student, he behind the desk and me across, frantically scribbling lecture notes.

"Have you met Plato's Divided Line?" he asked, as if making introductions at a party.

We were acquainted, the Divided Line and I, though I wouldn't go so far as to say we were friends. Robert Brumbaugh had called Plato's Divided Line "probably the most famous and most often drawn diagram in the whole history of philosophy." It is a deceptively simple geometric image that helps explain one of Plato's most important principles: that knowledge can be classified into four types. The description is spoken by Socrates: "Take a line which has been cut into two unequal parts, and divide each of them again in the same proportion." Each of these sections represents one of Plato's four ascending levels of knowledge. If the line is drawn vertically, it looks something like this:

Divided Line

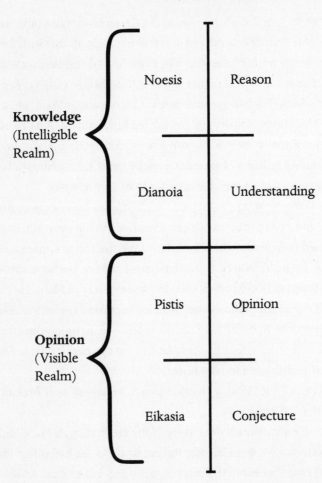

The top two sections of the line represent the intelligible world; the bottom two the visible world. The lowest of the four is *Eikasia*, or conjecture, which Brumbaugh equates with guessing, as in "I guess so"; it is opinion based on hearsay or stories. The next highest level is *Pistis*, or belief "based on first-hand experience," Brumbaugh writes. Above that is *Dianoia*, or understanding, using reason to reach conclusions. Mathematics falls into this category.

The highest level, *Noesis*, moves beyond following rules to reach correct answers to comprehending the true essence of the eternal forms, those perfect examples that exist beyond time and space. Plato says this fourth state is attainable only "by the power of dialectic," or rigorous philosophical discourse. The highest example of this level of knowledge is the form of the good, a concept so abstract that only philosopher-kings can fully understand it. The closest Plato comes to explaining it is by comparison to the role of the sun in the visible world. Instead of illuminating the observable world, the form of the good illuminates truth.

Got all that? I didn't either the first time Bremer explained it, and he was a very skillful explainer. It was only much later that I realized the Divided Line was where the worlds of Plato, Pythagoras, and the *Da Vinci Code* truly did collide.

Bremer pulled out a large sheet of paper filled with columns of neat, tiny handwritten numbers. It looked like a page from the ledger of a particularly prosperous Victorian merchant. On closer inspection I saw it was his hand-counted tally of syllables in the *Republic*. Sometime during the second Eisenhower administration, Bremer had sat down and determined that the *Republic* had taken twelve hours to read aloud during Plato's lifetime, and then broke the dialogue down into 240 units of three minutes each. When he examined the content of each of these sections, he found that Socrates's explanation of the Divided Line fell between the sixty-first percentile and the sixty-third percentile of the *Republic*. Jay Kennedy's computer analysis fifty years later confirmed Bremer's work. Both men's calculations placed Plato's discourse on the Divided Line almost exactly at what is known as the golden section (or golden ratio), a mathematical ratio usually represented by the Greek letter *phi*.

The ratio is approximately 1:1.618, or the equivalent (for our purposes) of 61.8 percent. For a geometer like Plato, obsessed with uncovering the eternal mathematical laws guiding the universe, the golden section must have been like a glimpse into the mind of the Divine Craftsman.

The golden section can be found by dividing a line into two parts, so that the length of the longer section divided by the length of the shorter one is equal to the entire length divided by the length of the longer section. (The ratio should be approximately 0.618:0.382.) If one takes a golden rectangle, a parallelogram whose sides are in proportion to the golden section, and subtracts the area of a square whose sides include one of the shorter sides of the rectangle, the remaining parallelogram will also be a golden rectangle. This process can be repeated forever. (See the diagram on the facing page.)

Another method of reaching the golden ratio is via the Fibonacci sequence. This is a series of numbers in which the sum of any two consecutive numbers adds up to the next number in the sequence: 0, 1, 1, 2, 3, 5, 8, 13, 21, 34, 55, and so on to infinity. As the sequence progresses and the numbers get larger, the result of any number divided by its predecessor edges ever closer to the irrational number 1.618. . . . (Thus: $8 \div 5 = 1.6$; $13 \div 8 = 1.625$; $21 \div 13 = 1.615$; and so on.)

What Bremer determined is that the allegory of the Divided Line, which appears roughly 61.8 percent of the way through the *Republic*, separates the dialogue into two distinct sections. Everything up to that point deals with the sensible world. Everything after it deals with knowledge that exists only in the intelligible realm.

Though Plato doesn't name the golden section explicitly in his works, he quite clearly refers to its perfect proportions in the *Timaeus* when introducing the elemental particles of air, fire, water, and earth. The ratio 1:1.618, like the Pythagorean harmonies, is one

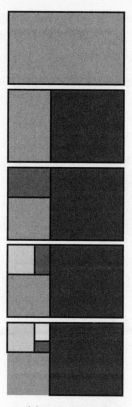

Golden Rectangles

of those cosmic intersections where the natural world and mathematics converge. It appears frequently in nature, most famously in the spiral of a nautilus shell. Its aesthetically pleasing proportions can be found throughout the human body, in everything from the dimensions of a beautiful face to the comparative lengths of your finger bones. The Parthenon and its gigantic statue of Athena were likely designed to adhere to its laws of symmetry.

When Plato lists his five elemental polyhedrons in the *Timaeus*, four of them are matched to the basic elements of fire, air, earth, and water. He singles out the fifth, the twelve-sided dodecahedron, as that "which the god used for embroidering the constellations on the whole heaven."[15]

The faces of a dodecahedron are pentagons; the ratio of any diagonal drawn between two of a pentagon's five interior angles to the length of any of its five sides is the golden section.

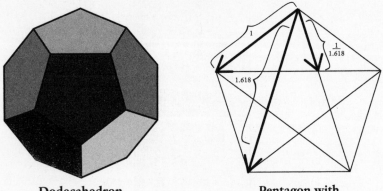

Dodecahedron

Pentagon with Golden Sections

Mephistopheles himself would get bored counting the various golden sections hidden within a Pythagorean pentagram.

In a Platonic dialogue, this might be the point in the conversation at which Socrates raised an important question: So what? Bremer had already provided an answer of sorts in an essay titled "Plato, Pythagoras, and Stichometry." The mathematical patterns he'd uncovered in Plato's works were not "simply a kind of ornamentation, a pleasurable addition to the content of the dialogue, a literary device," he wrote. Instead, they were "an essential, perhaps the essential, part of the dialogue."

Which brings us back to Bremer's basement, and to Atlantis.

"I wanted to mention something to you in the *Critias*," Bremer

---

15 At the risk of piling on, I should note that in 2003, a team of researchers that had studied microwave radiation created shortly after the Big Bang published a paper arguing persuasively, according to *The Economist*, "that the universe is, indeed, a dodecahedron."

said, flipping through the pages of a translation. "Take a look at the paragraph that states 'Now first of all we must recall the fact . . .'"

I had practically memorized the words that follow, since they are some of the most important in Atlantology: ". . . that nine thousand is the sum of years since the war occurred."

"The number of syllables from there to the end of the *Critias* is nine thousand. Nobody in the world—except me, and now you—knows that."

"There's no chance that it's a coincidence?"

"Oh, no, of course not! Plato is far too careful a writer. You must understand that in this stichometric game we're dealing with a text that was sort of established in the sixteenth century, which in turn was based on manuscripts which were written in the ninth and tenth centuries, fifteen hundred years after the death of Plato. So I don't feel very upset if it turns out there are 9017 syllables. With all of my numbers, if it's within 1 percent, it's probably intentional."

What the numbers were not, Bremer said, was a secret code that would lead me to the Temple of Poseidon. Mathematics was simply one method Plato used to convey important information to those prepared to receive it.

"In a way, the *Timaeus* is an invitation to those with a disposition of a certain kind to enter into the inquiry into the nature of the cosmos. What the *Critias* tells you is how far you can go. It ends abruptly. Zeus assembles the gods and begins to address them, and then there's a period. That's all there is! Don't try to go beyond this. It's not the dialogue that's incomplete—it's human knowledge!"

"So don't look for what's not there?"

"Yes. These are the limits of that kind of knowledge. You can't go any further."

In other words, I'd bumped up against my own Divided Line. *Nec plus ultra.* Plato even had a name for this unsatisfactory moment in a philosophical inquiry—*aporia*, or impasse. In the *Meno* Socrates applauds the purgative effect of *aporia*, for only once someone confronts the dead end of his ignorance can he begin to move forward.

"What would you say if someone came in here and told you they'd found Plato's Atlantis by following the numbers from the *Critias*?" I asked.

"What you're describing is what I would regard as a teaching/learning situation," Bremer said, leaning forward and folding his hands. "On the whole there's no point in saying, 'You're loony.' But I think they would be profoundly mistaken."

Bremer's landscaper came to mow the lawn and the buzzing drowned out our conversation. We walked upstairs into the humid late afternoon air and I prepared to drive back home. Bremer walked me to my car, gave directions back to the highway, and, Socratic that he was, left me with a question of his own.

"What fascinates me about what you're doing is why are all these folks devoting untold energy trying to figure out whether this was a historic place or not? What do they think they're up to? What is it that makes them search for this thing, when rationally they must know there are a very large number of people who consider that they are wasting their time?"

Or are they?

CHAPTER TWENTY-NINE

True or False

Atlantis

Tony O'Connell was on the line from Ireland, describing the new house he and Paul had just moved into right outside their village in County Leitrim. "I suppose you could say we're now stumbling distance from both pubs," he said. "Well situated for your next visit."

My Atlantis odyssey finally having ended, I'd called the wise man of Atlantology seeking some guidance on my preliminary findings. Tony was a bit like Socrates—and unlike virtually every other person I'd spoken with about Atlantis over the past two years—in that he was primarily interested in the things he *didn't* know about Plato's lost city. He'd written more than a thousand detailed entries for the Atlantipedia, and while he was as certain as ever that Plato's story was "generally reliable," he still hadn't settled on a single location hypothesis.

We briefly debated the various possibilities for the Pillars of Heracles, but after a few minutes Tony stopped short and said, "Mark, you should be perfectly happy to come up with your own conclusions whether they agree with mine or not. There's no one dealing with this subject who isn't speculating."

Speculation doesn't have to devolve into theories based on alien visitors or secret rooms beneath the Sphinx's paw; after all, the *Timaeus* is largely a speculative work. Tony suggested a jurisprudential image to illustrate the burden of proof Atlantologists needed to meet. Because the evidence for Atlantis is "at best circumstantial," he said, its existence cannot be proved beyond a reasonable doubt, as it would need to be in a criminal case. In a civil court, however, the legal standard is whether something is more likely to be true than not true. By that measure it should be possible, Tony said, to build a convincing case "for the time and location of Atlantis" from largely circumstantial evidence.

Following Tony's lead, I decided that to reach a verdict about Atlantis, five general points needed to be addressed:

- Plato's numbers, especially the nine thousand years
- The island's physical characteristics, including its concentric rings, mountains, large plain, and canals
- The conflict between Atlantis and Athens
- The Pillars of Heracles and the impassable shoals of mud beyond
- The cataclysmic event that destroyed Atlantis

Plato's numbers were exhibit A, since they are essential to almost every location hypothesis. If some future Heinrich Schliemann ever uncovers a three-ringed coastal city with a central island five stades across and a temple of Poseidon that matches Plato's precise 2:1 dimensions, the Atlantis case will be closed.

I think that's extremely unlikely to happen.

The *Timaeus* and *Critias* are dripping with Pythagorean influence. The dialogues begin with Socrates making a reference to the sacred tetractys: 1, 2, 3, 4. The speaker Timaeus is a Pythagorean who explains to his friends how all matter can be broken down into minuscule right triangles. In the cosmology he lays out, the heavenly bodies move according to the same mathematical harmonies that Pythagoras supposedly discovered in a blacksmith's shop. About the only thing that could make the *Timaeus* and *Critias* more Pythagorean would be for Poseidon to carve the words DON'T EAT BEANS into the Atlantean plain with his trident.

The philosophical meaning of Plato's Atlantis numbers has been lost to nongeometers, possibly forever, unless a copy of his *Critias* lecture notes turns up beneath a swing set in the Athens park where the Academy once stood. What hasn't been lost is Aristotle's reminder that to the Pythagoreans, numbers were not just amounts but *things*. Robert Brumbaugh's conjecture that Plato's opposition of evens and odds symbolized Atlantis's degeneration, like a black hat on a villain, makes much more sense to me than the idea that such specific numbers had been passed down through the millennia like a land surveyor's report.

The three-ringed city was almost certainly intended as a geometric metaphor. Plato *loved* circles, which exemplified the otherworldly perfection of his eternal forms. In the *Timaeus*, the world is a sphere because that is the ideal shape. Both the individual human soul and the soul of the living cosmos—the circles that the Divine Craftsman scissors out of the World-Soul like a chain of paper rings—are said to move in a circular motion. That doesn't necessarily mean Plato didn't have a real-world model in mind. Santorini's rough bull's-eye shape could have inspired the concentric circles of Atlantis, and Michael Hübner's giant stone donut in Morocco was certainly intriguing. Better matches could have been found in the ancient Mediterranean, though. Carthage was famous for its annular naval harbor, constructed around a circular center island, with a single entrance like that of Atlantis. Plato would have been quite familiar with Carthage, since his tyrannical host in Syracuse, Dionysius, was at war with the Carthaginians. But if you want my honest opinion—and if you've read this far, you presumably do—I think Plato just had a thing for circles.

Viewing Plato's numbers and geometric shapes as symbols instead of raw data allowed me to avoid the explanatory gymnastics required to squeeze the key figure of nine thousand years into any hypothesis. With a stroke, some of Atlantology's biggest problems vanished: the lack of evidence for a Paleolithic Athens; the reliance on Egyptian lunar calendars;[16] the parsing of Plato's words to mean *seasons* instead of *years*. The complicated interpretations required to reconcile nine thousand years with dates like 2200 BC in Malta and 1500 BC for the Thera blast simply disappeared. *Poof.* When did Atlantis sink? *We don't know.* Or rather: We don't know *yet*.

Removing the numbers alleviated the headache of accounting for checkerboard canals that supposedly covered an area as large as Nebraska, but it didn't bring me any closer to understanding their purpose in the Atlantis story. Tony reminded me that Critias pauses to comment on how unrealistic Solon's measurements seem—*I know this may sound crazy!*—and his skepticism indicates this piece of information really did come from Egypt, since such doubt would otherwise make Plato's book *less* believable. The channel's perimeter totals ten thousand stades, or a *myriad*, the largest number for which Greeks of Plato's time had a written character. Perhaps Solon's assistant was using shorthand. Or maybe Rainer Kühne was right, and Plato was making a math-nerd joke. The canals remain an *aporia*.

Erasing the canals and numbers from my list of clues felt so satisfying, like a thorough spring cleaning, that I couldn't resist hunting for other criteria to purge. Skimming through the various location

---

16 Feeling a little uncertain about this conclusion, I again e-mailed Janet Johnson, the Egyptologist at the University of Chicago who'd explained how 900 and 9,000 looked similar. This time, she was unequivocal. "The Egyptians used two different lunar calendars and a solar calendar. The lunar calendars were used for calculating religious festivals. The Egyptians knew very well how to convert from one calendar to another. If an Egyptian priest had said 9,000 years, he would not have meant 9,000 months."

hypotheses, I noticed that many of the identifying details in Plato's story are so common throughout the world known to the Athenians as to be almost useless in identifying a single location. Hot and cold springs, tricolored stone, and relics from ancient bull ceremonies are almost as common around the coastal Mediterranean as middle-aged men in Speedos. (Admittedly, Santorini has a *slight* quantitative advantage in all four categories.) Other descriptions Plato used seem of relatively minor importance—he may have employed terms such as *triremes* or *chariots* to describe less sophisticated war machines. The meaning of Atlantis being "greater than Libya and Asia put together" is uncertain enough to strike from the record, and the definition of *nesos* as any sort of land that touches water, rather than a solitary island, is so broad as to be almost meaningless.

Once I'd scrubbed away several layers of Atlantean chaff, I had a brief moment of panic. How big a kernel of truth remained? To my relief, I saw the outlines of a pretty big one.

The Athens half of Plato's story—the physical description of the Bronze Age city, the earthquake that blocked the springs on the Acropolis, the loss of literacy—rings historically true. Plato could not have invented so many accurate details. In fact, as the historian Eric Cline demonstrates in his recent book *1177 B.C.: The Year Civilization Collapsed*, the rapid, well-documented end of the Late Bronze Age throughout the eastern Mediterranean coincided with a near-simultaneous "'perfect storm' of calamities": famines, drought, climate change, and a fifty-year-long series of earthquake storms caused by an unstable fault line slowly "unzipping" as it released pressure. The whole region, including Athens, was shaken up, figuratively and literally.

The year 1177 BC is when the Sea Peoples, probably driven from their homelands by this convergence of disasters, launched their second and more devastating invasion of Egypt. Since the kingdoms of the eastern Mediterranean were interconnected by the sort of trade seen in the cargo of the Uluburun wreck, word would have filtered back to Egypt that the same swarms of mysterious attackers who had been repulsed by Ramses III had annihilated some of its commercial partners. This information could have been twisted—by Plato, Solon, the Saïs priest, or some earlier Egyptian chronicler—into a tale of a mighty naval power attacking from a land far, far away. (This was the period when the Greeks were tinkering with the transition from myth to a radical new information technology, recorded history.) Assuming that Solon really did visit the temple at Saïs—and it seems to me he did—it's logical that a fascinating war story chronicled by an esteemed ancestor would have been passed down through the generations to Plato.

As I sifted again through the various possibilities for the Pillars of Heracles, their location came into sharper focus. Unless the Pillars that Critias described were a metaphor for the end of the known world, they were almost certainly the Strait of Gibraltar. Herodotus describes the Pillars at Gibraltar several times in his *Histories*. Critias places them near Gadeira, the Carthaginian port just beyond the blockaded mouth of the Mediterranean. (Pindar, the greatest of Greece's lyric poets, wrote a century before Plato's time, "Westward of Gadeira none may pass / Turn back ship's tackle to Europe's land!") Plato likely heard Carthaginian propaganda in Syracuse, which would have emphasized the dangers of sailing beyond Gibraltar; it seems impossible that such tales would not also have been carried to a major seaport such as Athens.

What about the impassable muddy shoals mentioned by both Plato and Aristotle? The likeliest candidate is the sailing dead zone Herodotus described on the West African coast, citing the Carthaginians as his source. Stories filtering back eastward from this unknown territory could account for the blue vestments worn by the Atlantean kings (tinted with the indigo snail dye from the island of

Mogador), as well as the elephants, which the Carthaginians first spotted in the coastal marshes near Senegal around 500 BC.

The last major item on my checklist was the most famous of all, the cataclysm that destroyed Atlantis. Many of the geologists and mythologists I'd spoken with equated the Thera explosion with the earthquakes and floods the Saïs priest describes. I suspect the Thera blast—and the Minoan Hypothesis—appeals to experts because there's a great deal of physical evidence that *something* terrible happened. Since the effects of the disaster are still largely mysterious, specialists feel safe speculating there might be some connection between the Minoans and Plato's story. But Plato took his catastrophism pretty seriously, and unlike Hesiod's *Theogony*, there's nothing in the *Timaeus* or *Critias* about volcanoes—no loud explosion, no magma boiling under the sea, no ash cloud, no volcanic lightning.

Unless there was a mix-up on the Egyptian end—admittedly, a possibility—Thera was most likely an accessory to the story of Atlantis's sinking rather than the perpetrator: perhaps the cause of one of the three other great floods the priest mentions. Which means the experts who endorse the Minoan Hypothesis for Atlantis are probably mistaken.

Helike's disappearance would have been another likely model for what Spyridon Marinatos called the "one fundamental fact" of the Atlantis story, that "a piece of land becomes submerged." The sequence is identical—earthquake, flood, sinking—and unless Plato was deep in a cave testing ideas for the *Republic*, he must have heard about the disaster. I e-mailed Dora Katsonopoulou to check on her dig, which she confirmed was progressing—*slowly*. If the city buried there is half as wonderful as described in ancient accounts, Katsonopoulou will one day be as famous as Schliemann, and Helike will almost certainly supplant Santorini as the leading establishment candidate for Atlantis. (This is speculation, of course; the only absolute certainty is that its discovery will launch a thousand ships carrying cable-channel documentary crews.) But Helike was not at war with Athens, hadn't conquered most of the Mediterranean, wasn't anywhere near the various purported Pillars of Heracles, and certainly didn't vanish prior to Solon's visit to Egypt. Its destruction probably colored Plato's account, and perhaps even reminded him of an old family story. But the event doesn't seem to be his primary source.

If Atlantis were to be found on the basis of sheer enthusiasm, Anton Mifsud's argument for Malta would be difficult to beat, yes? Yes! But the more I thought about it, the more his essential source, the manuscript from Eumalos of Cyrene, seemed just a little too convenient to be true—antiquity's equivalent of a *Scooby-Doo* confession when Shaggy yanks off the villain's monster mask. Malta has no mountains and hasn't been attached to any sort of plain for a very long time, and while no one can say definitively what the cart ruts were (grooves worn by hauling sledges seems the most probable explanation), they definitely weren't irrigation canals, unless Malta was also the original Lilliput. I would gladly let Dr. Mifsud remove my child's appendix, but I can't agree with his Atlantis conclusions.

Michael Hübner's Morocco hypothesis was the most convincing on paper: the mountains matched perfectly; the spot where the Persian sailor Sataspes's ships had stuck fast in the water—likely inspiration for the muddy shoals—was nearby. The location was not too far south of the likeliest Pillars of Heracles. Even the name *Gadir* seemed to match. Once I subtracted the Pythagorean numbers from Plato's story, though, Hübner's logic instantly became less compelling. Like a beguiling online dating profile that fizzles at first sight, the precision of Hübner's Seven Sigma correlations didn't begin to match the real-world evidence. The ringed structure he found, while intriguing, sits several miles inland, in the foothills of the Atlas

Mountains, at an elevation that even Dallas Abbott's six-hundred-foot-high Madagascar wave couldn't reach.

In the end, my conclusion was inescapable. Plato stated pretty clearly where the island that Solon called Atlantis was located: Poseidon's second son ruled over "the cape of the island facing the Pillars of Heracles opposite what is now called the territory of Gadeira," or Gades/Cádiz. The Greeks were quite familiar with an island city in Gades: Tartessos, the trading port famous for its precious metals.

Tartessos is a good, if imperfect, match with Atlantis. The shiny orichalcum of Plato's city could be related to the region's famous copper and tin, which were mixed into Tartessian bronze. The Sierra Morena protect the Andalusian plains from northerly winds, and if they don't fit exactly like a puzzle piece, as Stavros Papamarinopoulos suggests, they strongly resemble Plato's description. The impassable mud shoals and elephants of Africa are close enough to Tartessos to have been co-opted into Carthaginian propaganda meant to dissuade curious Greeks from exploring the strange and dangerous world beyond the Pillars. The Azores-Gibraltar Transform Fault has demonstrated repeatedly its ability to unleash earthquakes and tsunamis that could wipe out a city overnight.

Are the concentric rings and temples of Atlantis buried under the sand and clay of Doñana National Park? I doubt it, no matter what Werner Wickboldt sees in his satellite photos. Such details seem like Platonic embellishments. Papamarinopoulos's natural circular craters, while fascinating, are what Donald Rumsfeld would call known unknowns: They may have existed; if they did exist, they might help explain the rings of Atlantis; and if they were ever discovered, I'd be on the first plane to Seville to check them out. But they're a long shot.

The biggest issue with identifying Tartessos as the original Atlantis is the date of its destruction. The city seems to have still existed in Solon's time, disappearing from the historical record around

500 BC. Wickboldt suggests that the Tartessos known to the Greeks was built on top of the ruins of a destroyed Atlantis, or whatever the island was originally called. Papamarinopoulos has a similar idea, except he thinks the predecessor was an "elder prehistoric Tartessos," one that now lies buried under the mud and clay of the Guadalquivir River. He believes the war between Athens and Atlantis may be a "parallel history within the turbulent twelfth century BC, unknown to science so far." Considering what we know of the general chaos of the Sea Peoples era, that seems about as close to an explanation—and a date—as we can hope for without further evidence.

Because it is so entertaining and so different from his other writings, Plato's tale of a lost city is often mistakenly dismissed as a one-off novelty created by an otherwise brilliant artist: philosophy's answer to Bob Dylan's Christmas album, with a little Athenian political theory sprinkled on top. Plato knew well the power of stories, which is why he used the account of Atlantis's rise and fall as the bridge linking two of his most ambitious works. Having wrestled with some of the heaviest questions faced by humanity (What is knowledge? How does one lead a good life?), the *Republic* ends with Socrates telling the story of a soldier who learns the secrets of the human soul's indestructibility and the circular design of the eternal cosmos. The *Timaeus* is Plato's attempt to give a Pythagorean account of all that exists, from the tiniest triangular atom to the music of the spheres. The irresistible Atlantis story that Critias tells, with its enigmatic numbers and cyclical destructions, was—and still is—Plato's invitation to engage in the only activity that could hope to make sense of it all: philosophy.

The question everyone wants answered about Atlantis is, was it real? If I may channel Plato for a moment, I guess that depends on the definition of *real*. I think Plato took elements of the Sea Peoples story that Solon heard in Egypt, combined them with stories about ancient Athens that had been passed down orally, and blended that with accounts he'd heard of a lost city beyond the Pillars of Heracles.

My conclusions were similar to those of Rainer Kühne, onetime believer in the historical Atlantis, who'd changed his mind after writing his *Antiquity* article to conclude that Plato's story was fiction, based on some true events. Stavros Papamarinopoulos, using almost the same information, concluded that Plato's story was a bricolage of true myths based in history, mixed in with some made-up stuff and mathematical codes. Werner Wickboldt, *also* employing a similar thought process, thought the Atlantis tale was more or less factual. You say *Puh-lay-toh*, I say *Puh-lah-toh*.

"Aren't there two kinds of story, one true and the other false?" Socrates asks in the *Republic*. When discussing Atlantis, those usually seem to be the only two choices: Either Plato made it up, or he didn't.

Plato loved mathematics because it provided definite answers, but his genius was demonstrating that everything else in the universe was worth taking a guess at, including the universe itself. After stating the binary nature of fact versus fiction in the *Republic*, Socrates concedes that there are stories that "are false, on the whole, though they have some truth in them." At the risk of correcting the intellectual hero of the greatest philosopher who ever lived, I'd reverse that order. There are stories—"likely accounts," in the words of Timaeus himself, clearing his throat before unleashing his wild cosmic speculations—that may contain some false information, though they are true on the whole.

Plato's Atlantis story is one of them.

Acknowledgments

A number of people were extremely helpful in writing this book. Tony O'Connell fed and sheltered me in County Leitrim and Malta in addition to answering hundreds of queries before, during, and after my visits, even though he disagreed with my conclusions. (His hospitality was abetted by Paul Gordon, Claire Armstrong, and Dai Konieczny.) Several busy people were kind enough to share their expertise in person: Brian Johnson in New York City; Patrick Coleman in Saint Paul; Richard Freund in Hartford; Juan Villarias-Robles in Madrid; José María Galán at Doñana Park; Rainer Kühne and Werner Wickboldt in Braunschweig; Anton Mifsud in Malta; David Gallo and William Lange at the Woods Hole Oceanographic Institute; George Nomikos and Christos Doumas in Santorini; Dora Katsonopoulou in Athens; Stavros Papamarinopoulos in Patras; and John Bremer in Vermont.

Michael Hübner, who was particularly generous with his time in both Bonn and Morocco, died in a bicycling accident in December 2013. Ernest McClain passed away in April 2014, at age ninety-five.

Those who kindly provided essential knowledge and guidance included Dallas Abbott, Corby Anderson, Elizabeth Barber, Anthony Beavers, Robert Brumbaugh Jr., Rand Flem-Ath, Joscelyn Godwin, Michael Higgins, Laura Hoff, Janet Johnson, Alice Kehoe,

Alexander MacGillivray, Bruce Masse, Floyd McCoy, Gregory McIntosh, Trevor Palmer, and Duane Roller.

An incomplete list of those owed gratitude for assistance personal and professional: Ryan Bradley; Steve Byers; Alex Chepstow-Lusty; Caryn Davidson; Gillian Fassell; Christiane and Peter Hübner; Joy Kerluke and Dimitris Hamalidis; Chelo Medina; Mary Anne Potts; Robert Sullivan; Charlie and Jen Baker Vanek; Donovan Webster; and everyone at the extraordinary Westchester Library System, especially Claudia Gisolfi and Patricia Perito.

Special thanks to David Adams and Mary McEnery, Fred and Aura Truslow, Natividad Huamani, and Veronica Francis. Belated gratitude is also owed to the Borgstrom and Kunkel families.

Jason Adams, Maura Fritz, Laura Hohnhold, and David McAninch, gifted editors all, were kind enough to read and comment on early drafts. My agent, Daniel Greenberg, was, as always, stalwart in his support. Brian Tart and Jessica Renheim at Dutton once again provided essential editorial guidance.

My dear wife, Dr. Aurita Truslow, somehow manages to keep the household together when I go off on these strange adventures, which is but one reason I love her with all my heart. Alex, Lucas, and Magnus: You encircle my life with a joy as perfect as Plato's concentric rings.

A Few Notes on Sources

Plato was not the only Greek artist-in-residence at Dionysius I's court. The poet Philoxenus of Cythera, invited to hear some lines of verse his host had composed, gave an honest—and scathing—assessment for which he was condemned to hard labor in Syracuse's infamous mines. He was soon liberated and summoned to a second recitation, after which the tyrant again asked Philoxenus for his opinion.

"Carry me back to the mines," he said.

A modern Philoxenus asked to evaluate the Atlantis canon could spend several lifetimes swinging a pickax. Thousands of books have been written about Plato's lost city; most of them are terrible. Something about Atlantis seems to invite the suspension of both critical thinking and generally accepted rhetorical standards. Many hypotheses about Atlantis are similar, and the purpose of this book is not to determine who originated any particular idea. However, if you spot a factual error or have a question about something, feel free to e-mail me at mmiatlantis@gmail.com. If you have theories based on clairvoyant readings, alien visitors, or other such "evidence," please keep them to yourself.

I have quoted Plato's works from several published translations; in each instance I chose the one that I felt most clearly conveyed Plato's message or imagery. The best-known translations of the *Timaeus* and *Critias* are those by Benjamin Jowett (available free online), R. G. Bury, and Desmond Lee. The more recent *Plato: Complete Works*, edited by John M. Cooper, includes perhaps the clearest renderings available of the *Timaeus* (translated by Donald J. Zeyl) and *Critias* (translated by Diskin Clay) as well as everything else Plato wrote.

Anyone interested in learning more about Atlantis and related topics will find the following sources useful:

Atlantipedia.ie
> Tony O'Connell's comprehensive website. Also available in hardcover and eBook editions.

The Atlantis Hypothesis: Searching for a Lost Land: Proceedings of the 2005 International Conference, edited by Stavros Papamarinopoulos
> Of particular interest are the essays by Papamarinopoulos, Christos Doumas, Dora Katsonopoulou, Werner Wickboldt, A. N. Kontaratos, Floyd McCoy, and Dallas Abbott et al.

The Atlantis Hypothesis: Proceedings of the 2008 International Conference, edited by Stavros Papamarinopoulos
> Of particular interest are the essays by Papamarinopoulos, Wickboldt, Kontaratos, and Thorwald Franke.

> An edition of papers from the 2011 conference is forthcoming.

Lost Continents: The Atlantis Theme in History, Science, and Literature, by L. Sprague de Camp

Imagining Atlantis, by Richard Ellis

The Sunken Kingdom: The Atlantis Mystery Solved, by Peter James

> The best historical overviews of the search for Atlantis. Sprague de Camp and Ellis conclude that Plato's lost island was fiction; James places it in Turkey.

Plato's Mathematical Imagination: The Mathematical Passages in the Dialogues and Their Interpretation, by Robert Brumbaugh
> A surprisingly readable account of Plato's enigmatic use of numbers.

When They Severed Earth from Sky, by Elizabeth Wayland Barber and Paul T. Barber
> A terrific introduction to the formation and interpretation of myths.

Lost Atlantis: New Light on an Old Legend, by John V. Luce
> The most scholarly and engaging account of the Minoan Hypothesis.

Some Words About the Legend of Atlantis, by Spyridon Marinatos
> A thin volume that may be the most important book in Atlantology.

Atlantis: The Antediluvian World, by Ignatius Donnelly
> The book that launched Atlantology.

Beyond the Pillars of Heracles: The Classical World Seen Through the Eyes of Its Discoverers, by Rhys Carpenter

Through the Pillars of Herakles: Greco-Roman Exploration of the Atlantic, by Duane W. Roller

> Fascinating histories of early sea exploration by an eminent classics scholar.

Selected Bibliography

Abrahams, Edward H. "Ignatius Donnelly and the Apocalyptic Style." *Minnesota History*, Fall 1978.

Amos, H. D., and A. G. P. Lang. *These Were the Greeks*. Chester Springs, PA: Dufour Editions, 1982.

Annas, Julia. "The Atlantis Story: The *Republic* and the *Timaeus*." In *Plato's Republic: A Critical Guide*, edited by Mark McPherran. New York: Cambridge University Press, 2011.

———. *Plato: A Very Short Introduction*. New York: Oxford University Press, 2003.

Aristotle. *Meteorology*. Translated by E. W. Webster. Accessed via classics.mit.edu.

Armstrong, Karen. *A Short History of Myth*. New York: Canongate, 2005.

Barrientos, Gustavo, and W. Bruce Masse. "The Archaeology of Cosmic Impact: Lessons from Two Mid-Holocene Argentine Case Studies." *Journal of Archaeological Method and Theory* 21 (2014): 134–211.

Bellamy, Hans. *The Atlantis Myth*. New York: Faber and Faber, 1948.

Bonsor, Jorge Eduardo. *El Coto de Doñana*. Madrid, 1922.

Bremer, John. "Some Arithmetical Patterns in Plato's *Republic*." *Hermathena* 169 (Winter 2000).

Brumbaugh, Robert S. *The Philosophers of Greece*. Albany: State University of New York Press, 1969.

———. *Plato for the Modern Age*. New York: Crowell-Collier Press, 1962.

———. "Plato's Atlantis." *Yale Alumni Magazine*, January 1970.

Carpenter, Rhys. *Discontinuity in Greek Civilization*. Cambridge: Cambridge University Press, 1966.

Castleden, Rodney. *Atlantis Destroyed*. London: Routledge, 1998.

Cline, Eric. *1177 B.C.: The Year Civilization Collapsed*. Princeton, NJ: Princeton University Press, 2014.

Cohn, Norman. *Noah's Flood: The Genesis Story in Western Thought*. New Haven, CT: Yale University Press, 1996.

Cornford, Francis. *Plato's Cosmology: The* Timaeus *of Plato*. New York, Harcourt, Brace, 1937.

DeMeules, Donald H. "Ignatius Donnelly: A Don Quixote in the World of Science." *Minnesota History* 37, no. 6 (June 1961).

Donnelly, Ignatius. *Ragnarok: The Age of Fire and Gravel*. New York: D. Appleton and Company, 1883.

Feder, Kenneth. *Frauds, Myths, and Mysteries: Science and Pseudoscience in Archaeology*. New York: McGraw-Hill, 2013.

Flem-Ath, Rand, and Rose Flem-Ath. *Atlantis Beneath the Ice: The Fate of the Lost Continent*. Rochester, VT: Bear & Company, 2012.

Fox, Margaret. *The Riddle of the Labyrinth: The Quest to Crack an Ancient Code*. New York: Ecco, 2013.

Franke, Thorwald C. *Aristotle and Atlantis: What Did the Philosopher Really Think About Plato's Island Empire?* Norderstedt: Books on Demand, 2012.

Freund, Richard. *Digging Through History: Archaeology and Religion from Atlantis to the Holocaust*. Lanham, MD: Rowman and Littlefield, 2012.

Frost, K. T. "The *Critias* and Minoan Crete." *Journal of Hellenic Studies* 33, no. 189 (1913).

Galanopoulos, Angelos G., and Edward Bacon. *Atlantis: The Truth Behind the Legend*. Indianapolis: Bobbs-Merrill, 1969.

Gill, Christopher. "The Genre of the Atlantis Story." *Classical Philology* 72, no. 4 (October 1977).

Godwin, Joscelyn. *Atlantis and the Cycles of Time: Prophecies, Traditions, and Occult Revelations*. Rochester, VT: Inner Traditions, 2011.

Hapgood, Charles. *Maps of the Ancient Sea Kings: Evidence of Advanced Civilization in the Ice Age*. Philadelphia: Chilton Books, 1966.

Herodotus. *The Histories*. Translated by George Rawlinson. Accessed via classics.mit.edu.

Higgins, Michael Denis, and Reynold Higgins. *A Geological Companion to Greece and the Aegean*. Ithaca, NY: Cornell University Press, 1996.

Hübner, Michael. "Circumstantial Evidence for Plato's Island Atlantis in the Souss-Massa Plain in Today's South Morocco." 2012. Accessed from Hübner's website at asalas.org.

Hübner, Michael, and Sebastian Hübner. "New Evidence for a Large Prehistoric Settlement in a Caldera-Like Geomorphological Structure in Southwest Morocco." 2012. Accessed from Hübner's website at asalas .org.

James, Jamie. *The Music of the Spheres: Music, Science, and the Natural Order of the Universe*. New York: Grove Press, 1993.

Johnson, Janet H. *The Demotic Dictionary of the Oriental Institute of the University of Chicago*. Chicago: Oriental Institute, University of Chicago, 2001.

Joint Association of Classical Teachers. *The World of Athens: An Introduction to Classical Athenian Culture*. New York: Cambridge University Press, 1984.

Jordan, Paul. *The Atlantis Syndrome*. Stroud, England: Sutton, 2001.

Kehoe, Alice Beck. *Controversies in Archaeology*. Walnut Creek, CA: Left Coast Press, 2008.

Kennedy, J. B. "Plato's Forms, Pythagorean Mathematics, and Stichometry." *Apeiron* 43, no. 1 (2010).

Kühne, Rainer. "A Location for 'Atlantis'?" *Antiquity* 78, no. 300 (June 2004).

MacGillivray, Joseph Alexander. *Minotaur: Sir Arthur Evans and the Archaeology of the Minoan Myth*. New York: Hill and Wang, 2000.

———. "Thera, Hatshepsut, and the Keftiu: Crisis and Response." In *Time's Up!: Dating the Minoan Eruption of Santorini*, edited by D. Warburton. Athens: The Danish Institute at Athens, 2009.

Masse, W. Bruce. "The Archaeology and Anthropology of Quaternary Period Cosmic Impact." In *Comet/Asteroid Impacts and Human Society*, edited by P. Bobrowsky and H. Rickman. Berlin: Springer, 2007.

———. "Earth, Air, Fire, & Water: The Archaeology of Bronze Age Cosmic Catastrophes." In *Natural Catastrophes During Bronze Age Civilisations: Archaeological, Geological, Astronomical, and Cultural Perspectives*, edited by B. J. Peiser, T. Palmer, and M. E. Bailey. British Archaeological Reports International Series. Oxford, England: Archaeopress, 1998.

Masse, W. Bruce, Elizabeth W. Barber, Luigi Piccardi, and Paul T. Barber. "Exploring the Nature of Myth and Its Role in Science." In *Myth and Geology*, edited by L. Piccardi and W. B. Masse. London: Geological Society of London, 2007.

Mavor, James. *Voyage to Atlantis*. New York: Putnam, 1969.

McClain, Ernest. *The Pythagorean Plato: Prelude to the Song Itself*. York Beach, ME: Nicolas-Hays Inc., 1978.

McIntosh, Gregory. *The Piri Reis Map of 1513*. Athens: University of Georgia Press, 2000.

Mifsud, Anton, Simon Mifsud, Chris Agius Sultana, and Charles Savona Ventura. *Malta: Echoes of Plato's Island*. The Prehistoric Society of Malta, 2001.

Miles, Richard. *Carthage Must Be Destroyed: The Rise and Fall of an Ancient Civilization*. New York: Viking, 2011.

Montgomery, David R. *The Rocks Don't Lie: A Geologist Investigates Noah's Flood*. New York: W. W. Norton, 2012.

Muck, Otto. *The Secret of Atlantis*. New York: Times Books, 1978.

Nur, Amos, with Dawn Burgess. *Apocalypse: Earthquakes, Archaeology, and the Wrath of God*. Princeton, NJ : Princeton University Press, 2008.

Nur, Amos, and Eric Cline. "Poseidon's Horses: Plate Tectonics and Earthquake Storms in the Late Bronze Age Aegean and Eastern Mediterranean." *Journal of Archaeological Science* 27, no. 1 (January 2000): 43–63.

Palmer, Trevor. *Perilous Planet Earth*. Cambridge: Cambridge University Press, 2003.

———. "Science and Catastrophism, from Velikovsky to the Present Day." Unpublished paper.

Papamarinopoulos, Stavros. "Atlantis in Spain: I–VI." *Bulletin of the Geological Society of Greece* 43, no 1 (2010).

Pellegrino, Charles. *Unearthing Atlantis: An Archaeological Odyssey*. New York: Random House, 1991.

Pringle, Heather. *The Master Plan: Himmler's Scholars and the Holocaust*. New York: Hyperion, 2006.

Ramage, Edwin, et al. *Atlantis: Fact or Fiction?* Bloomington: Indiana University Press, 1978.

Ridge, Martin. *Ignatius Donnelly: The Portrait of a Politician*. Chicago: University of Chicago Press, 1962.

Rodríguez-Ramírez, Antonio, Enrique Flores, Carmen Contreras, Juan J. R. Villarias-Robles, Sebastián Celestino-Pérez, and Ángel León. "Indicadores de actividad neotectónica durante el Holoceno Reciente en el P. N. de Doñana (SO, España)." In *Avances de la geomorfología en España, 2010–2012: Actas de la XII Reunión Nacional de Geomorfología, Santander, 17–20 Septiembre 2012*. Santander, Spain: PUbliCan, Ediciones de la Universidad de Cantabria, 2012.

Russell, Bertrand. *A History of Western Philosophy*. New York: Simon & Schuster, 1972.

Schulten, Adolf. *Tartessos*. Madrid: Espasa-Calpe, 1945.

Spanuth, Jürgen. *Atlantis of the North*. New York: Van Nostrand Reinhold Co., 1980.

Taylor, A. E. *Plato: The Man and His Work*. London: Methuen, 1960.

———. *Ages in Chaos*. Garden City, NY: Doubleday, 1952.

Velikovsky, Immanuel. *Worlds in Collision*. Garden City, NY: Doubleday, 1950.

Vermeule, Emily. "The Promise of Thera." *The Atlantic*, December 1967.

Vidal-Naquet, Pierre. *The Atlantis Story: A Short History of Plato's Myth*. Exeter, England: University of Exeter Press, 2007.

Zangger, Eberhard. *The Flood from Heaven: Deciphering the Atlantis Legend*. New York: Morrow, 1992.

Index

If you liked **MEET ME IN ATLANTIS**, see what happens when an unadventurous adventure writer tries to re-create the original expedition to Machu Picchu. Mark Adams's *New York Times* bestselling **TURN RIGHT AT MACHU PICCHU** is a fascinating and funny account of his journey through some of the world's most majestic, historic, and remote landscapes.

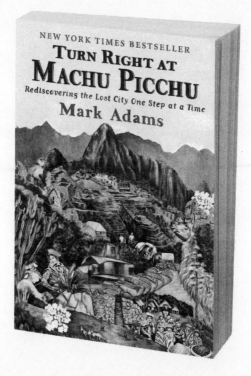

"An engaging and informative guide to all things Inca."
—*Entertainment Weekly*

TURN THE PAGE FOR AN EXCERPT

ONE

The Man from Oz

Cusco, Peru

As the man dressed head to toe in khaki turned the corner and began racewalking uphill in my direction, I had to wonder: had we met before? It certainly seemed unlikely. John Leivers was in his late fifties and spent most of his time exploring in remote parts of the Andes, machete in hand, searching for ancient ruins. The overdeveloped pop-culture lobe of my brain noted his passing resemblance to Crocodile Dundee—John wore a vest and a bush hat, and greeted me on the sidewalk outside my hotel with a cheery "Hallo, Mark!" that confirmed deep Australian roots—but there was something else strangely familiar about him.

"Sorry about the delay," he said as we shook hands. "Just got back to Cusco last night."

In a general sort of way, John Leivers reminded me of the professional explorers I'd encountered over the years while working as an editor at various adventure travel magazines in New York City—the kind of men and women who drove dogsleds to the South Pole and combed the ocean floor for sunken treasure. John was extremely fit; dressed as if ready to clamber up the Matterhorn though it was a cloudless, seventy-degree day; and about as unattached as a man could be in the twenty-first century. He had no wife, no children, no permanent mailing address, just a cell phone and a Gmail account. He'd been recommended to me as one of the best guides in South America, and it had taken weeks to reach him. But now that he was finally here, sitting down to a late breakfast at my tiny hotel in Cusco, an old colonial city in the middle of the Peruvian Andes, I wasn't quite sure where to begin. Because I didn't exactly have a plan.

We ordered coffees, and John started to tell me about himself, occasionally stopping in the middle of a sentence—"When you're traveling alone, you've got to be absolutely, um, *seguro* . . . sorry, it's been a little while since I've spoken English"—then patting his ear like a swimmer dislodging water, as if a tenacious Spanish verb were stuck in there. John had started coming to Cusco twenty years ago, when he was working as an extreme-trip leader, driving fearless globe-trotters across four continents in an open-back truck. "Back then the shops were still closed on Sundays and you could go months without seeing an American," he said. During the last decade, a period during which the number of visitors to Cusco had multiplied exponentially because of its position as the gateway to Machu Picchu, John had seen interest in serious adventure dwindle.

"People used to be *travelers*, Mark," he said, stirring his coffee. "Now they're *tourists*. People want hotels, cafés, the Internet. They won't even camp!"

"You're kidding!" I said, a little too loudly. I had already checked my e-mail at an Internet café twice that morning. The last time I'd slept in a tent was in 1978, when my father brought an imitation teepee home from Sears and set it up in our backyard.

And that, more or less, was why I was in Cusco. After years of sitting at a computer in New York and sending writers off on assignment to Kilimanjaro and Katmandu—places John knew firsthand—I wanted an adventure of my own. I figured that my near-total lack of outdoor experience was a subject that John and I could discuss once I'd decided whether to go through with this.

"So what sort of trip did you have in mind?" John asked. "Paolo says you're thinking about going after Bingham."

"Yeah, I think so. Something like that."

For most of his life and many decades after his death in 1956, Hiram Bingham III was known as the discoverer of Machu Picchu. The story he told in his adventure classic *Lost City of the Incas*—knockoff editions of which were available in most of the stores that catered to tourists (even on Sundays) in the center of Cusco—was one of the most famous in the annals of exploration. Bingham was a Yale University history lecturer who happened to be passing through Cusco in 1909 when he learned of a four-hundred-year-old unsolved mystery. When the Spanish conquistadors had invaded in the sixteenth century, a group of Incas withdrew to a hidden city high in Peru's impenetrable cloud forest, carrying with them the sacred treasures of their empire. This city and its inhabitants had vanished so long ago that as far as most serious scholars were concerned, legends of its existence were about as credible as tales of Atlantis. Bingham thought the experts were wrong, and he scoured obscure texts and maps for clues to its location. In the dramatic climax of *Lost City of the Incas*, he was on the hunt for this final Inca refuge on July 24, 1911, when he stumbled across the geometric splendor of Machu Picchu instead. The ruins he discovered were so unexpected, so incredible that he wondered, "Will anyone believe what I have found?"

As the hundredth anniversary of Bingham's achievement approached, the explorer was suddenly back in the news. I'd been introduced to John via e-mail through his friend Paolo Greer, an obsessive amateur researcher with an encyclopedic knowledge of Inca history. Paolo also happened to be a retired Alaskan pipeline worker who lived alone in an off-the-grid cabin in the woods outside of Fairbanks. He had found what he claimed was a rare map indicating that someone may have beaten Bingham to the top of Machu Picchu by forty years or more. Just months after Paolo's map made headlines around the globe, Bingham's name began popping up again. The former first lady of Peru had ignited an international incident by demanding that Yale return artifacts that Bingham had excavated at Machu Picchu, on the grounds that the explorer—she preferred the term "grave robber"—and his employer had violated a legal agreement. Yale and Peru had originally planned to jointly open a new museum in Cusco to celebrate the centennial of Bingham's feat. As the hundred-year mark approached, they were suing each other in U.S. courts instead.

In the avalanche of news coverage that followed the filing of Peru's lawsuit, questions kept popping up: Had Bingham lied about discovering Machu Picchu? Had he smuggled artifacts out of the country illegally? A woman in Cusco was even claiming that her family still owned the land on which Machu Picchu sits; was it possible that both Yale and the government of Peru were wrong?

As a magazine editor, I knew the revised version of Bingham's tale had the makings of a great story: hero adventurer exposed as villainous fraud. To get a clearer idea of what had really happened on that mountaintop in 1911, I took a day off and rode the train up to Yale. I spent hours in the library, leafing through Bingham's diaries and expedition journals. While holding the little leather-covered notebook in which Bingham had penciled his first impressions of Machu Picchu, any thoughts of the controversies fell away. Far more interesting was the story of how he had gotten to Machu Picchu in the first place. I'd heard that Bingham had inspired the character Indiana Jones, a connection that was mentioned—without much evidence—in almost every news story about the explorer in the last twenty years. Sitting in the neo-Gothic splendor of Yale's Rare Books and Manuscripts Room, the Indy-Bingham connection made sense for the first time. Bingham's search had been a geographic detective story, one that began as a hunt for the Lost City of the Incas but grew into an all-consuming attempt to solve the mystery of why such a spectacular granite city had been built in such a spellbinding location: high on a secluded mountain ridge, in the misty subtropical zone where the Andes meet the Amazon. Fifty years after Bingham's death, the case had been reopened. And the clues were still out there to be examined by anyone with strong legs and a large block of vacation time.

"What's your take on Bingham?" I asked John.

"Bit of a martini explorer," he said, employing what I later learned was a euphemism for a traveler who fancies himself tough but who really expects a certain level of comfort. "Not very popular in Peru at the moment. But you can't argue with the things he found."

Like every serious explorer in Peru, John had all but memorized Bingham's published accounts of his 1911 expedition. During that summer, Bingham had made not one but *three* incredible archaeological discoveries, any one of which would have cemented his reputation as a world-class explorer. In his spare time during that visit, he had managed to squeeze in the first ascent of Peru's twenty-thousand-foot Mount Coropuna, thought at the time to be the highest unclimbed peak in the Western Hemisphere. Bingham found so many ruins during his three major Peru expeditions that many had since been reclaimed by the wilderness. John had helped organize an expedition a few years earlier to *rediscover* a site that Bingham had found within view of Machu Picchu, which had gone missing again for ninety years.

As John sipped his coffee, I floated my idea to him. I wanted to retrace Bingham's route through the Andes on the way to discovering Machu Picchu. I also wanted to see three other important sites that he had visited: the mountaintop citadel of Choquequirao, now considered by many to be Machu Picchu's twin city; Vitcos, site of one of the holiest shrines in the Inca empire; and Espiritu Pampa, the long-lost jungle city where the Incas made their last stand against the Spaniards. Exactly how we were going to accomplish this—buses? trains? llamas?—was a detail I hadn't thought through very well.

"Maybe we could hike the Inca Trail," I said. "That way I could get a taste of Bingham's experience, you know, following the road that leads to Machu Picchu." I had mixed feelings about the Inca Trail. For trekkers, hiking it was like making the hajj to Mecca; you had to do it once in your life. But every story I'd read about the Inca Trail—and when you work at an adventure travel magazine, you read a *lot* of stories about the Inca Trail—made it sound as crowded as the George Washington Bridge at rush hour. The best parts of Bingham's books were those sections describing Peru's natural beauty, and I was hoping to get a sense of Peru as Bingham had seen it, if such a thing still existed.

"You know, Mark, *all* Inca roads lead to Machu Picchu," John said. He reached across the cluttered tabletop for a jam jar. I couldn't help but notice how different our hands were. His had square-cut nails and looked like they'd spent a lifetime hauling lines on a trawler. Mine looked like I'd just visited the salon for a mani-pedi. "If this is Machu Picchu"—here he placed the jar at the center of the table—"and this is Choquequirao"—he aligned the sugar bowl—"then these are Vitcos and Espiritu Pampa." He moved the salt and pepper shakers into position. The four pieces formed a Y shape with Machu Picchu at the bottom.

"There are no roads to most of these places, only trails," John said. "You can still walk pretty much everywhere Bingham went." He reached into one of his vest's many pockets and pulled out a little blue notebook with a plastic cover. "I buy these in Chile—they're essential for traveling in wet areas.

"Now, let's see. You'll need three days in Cusco to acclimatize to the altitude. One day to drive to the trailhead for the hike to Choquequirao. Two days' walk to the ruins. It's not very far but it is a bit steep. Incredible views. We'll have a look around, then continue on to Vitcos—that's about four more days of walking. We'll take a good look at the White Rock, a *very* important religious site that Bingham spent a lot of time trying to figure out. Serious country out there, *serious* Inca trails. You'll need a good sleeping bag because we'll be spending one night near fifteen thousand feet. Might get snowed in.

"We'll take a day or two of rest near Vitcos. Then we go down to the jungle, quite a ways down, actually, toward the Amazon basin. Maybe three more days to get there, depending on the weather, which can be a *little* unpredictable. We get to Espiritu Pampa and walk down the staircase to the old capital of the Inca empire, which Bingham made it to, though he never really understood the importance of what he'd seen. You'll want at least two days there." John paused for a second. "Presumably you want to see Llactapata, too."

"Huh?"

"Llactapata. It's the site Bingham found when he came back to Peru in 1912. I was up there a few years ago. You can look right across the valley to Machu Picchu. Just incredible. It's like what Machu Picchu used to be like before it was cleaned up—hardly been excavated."

"Of course, *that* Llactapata," I said, trying to guess how the name was spelled so that I could look it up later. *"Definitely* can't miss that."

"It'll help you get an idea of how the Inca engineers and priests aligned all these sites with the sun and stars. Brilliant stuff."

If John didn't look like a cum laude graduate of the French Foreign Legion, I'd have sworn we were tiptoeing into New Age territory. Cusco was a magnet for mystics. You couldn't swing a crystal without hitting someone wearing feathers who called himself a spiritual healer. The big draw, of course, was Machu Picchu itself. Something about the cloud-swathed ruins in the sky had a dog-whistle effect on the sorts of New Agers who went in for astrological readings, sweat lodges, and Kabbalah bracelets. Travel brochures that arrived in my magazine office always seemed to imply that the stones of Machu Picchu practically glowed with positive energy. There was no single explanation for *why* the citadel Bingham had found was sacred ground, but that didn't stop thousands of spiritual pilgrims from flocking to the site each year, hoping to experience a personal harmonic convergence.

"All right. So we walk up to Llactapata, come down the far side, and we can either take the train to Aguas Calientes"—he looked at me over his notebook—"that's the town at the base of Machu Picchu. Or we can walk along the rails and save the train fare."

"Is that legal?"

"Well, you know how things work in Peru, Mark. It all depends on who you ask."

"Do a lot of people sign up for this sort of trip?"

"We used to get a few people every year—*serious* travelers. Hardly anyone does it anymore."

"How long would it take?"

"About a month. Maybe less if the weather cooperates."

Represented by jars of breakfast condiments, the trip didn't look especially daunting. About a hundred miles of walking, by my rough calculations. From the sound of what John had described, we'd go north, cut through the mountains, bear left toward the jungle, then double back toward Cusco. For the big finish, all we had to do was follow the river and turn right at Machu Picchu. This last part sounded like a pleasant afternoon stroll, something to kill a few hours and work up an appetite for dinner.

"I know it's a lot to take in," John said. "Any questions so far?"

I could only think of one. "Is this harder than the Inca Trail?"

For a split second, John looked like he didn't understand me. "Mark, this trek is a *lot* harder than the Inca Trail."

TWO

Navel Intelligence

Cusco, continued

John and I agreed to meet the next day for breakfast to coordinate our schedules. He had tentative plans to spend several weeks hiking out to someplace that sounded like it was on the dark side of the moon, and I had commitments of my own. As I was starting to stand up to leave, I felt one of those commitments place a hand on my head. I looked up to see my thirteen-year-old son, Alex, standing over me. This trip to Cusco was both a reconnaissance mission and a father-son adventure. Though we'd both been to Peru many times because Alex's mother is Peruvian (and I suppose by the law of matrilineal descent, so is he), we'd never been to the famous capital of the Inca empire.

"I thought you were going to be down here for half an hour," he said. "That was two hours ago. I'm *starving*."

We walked down to the Plaza de Armas, which had once been the center of pre-Columbian Cusco. The name of the Incas' holiest city translates as "navel of the world." From the plaza four roads led out toward the four regions of Tawantinsuyu—literally, "four parts together"—as the Incas called their empire. At its height from 1438 to 1532, Cusco had been the heart of a kingdom that ruled ten million subjects and stretched twenty-five hundred miles up and down the Andes. In this city so sacred that commoners were expelled each night had stood the Koricancha, the gold-plated temple of the sun. The great nineteenth-century historian William Prescott called it "the most magnificent structure in the New World, and unsurpassed, probably, in the costliness of its decorations by any building in the Old." The absolute ruler of it all was the Sapa Inca, a hereditary monarch whose power derived not only from his parentage but from his religious status as the son of Inti, the sun god. So divine was the Inca's person that everything he touched—whether the clothing he wore only once or the bones of meat he'd consumed—was ritualistically burned each year. Any stray hair that fell from his head was swallowed by one of his beautiful female attendants. Being a god, the Sapa Inca was considered immortal. When he died, his body was mummified, and he continued to reside in the palaces he'd inhabited while alive, providing imperial guidance through special interpreters when needed.

Visitors to Machu Picchu are advised to spend a day or two in Cusco to adjust to the altitude, but it's also a good place to acclimatize to the strangeness of the Andes. Like Hong Kong or Beirut, Cusco is an in-between city where cultures have collided, in this case those of the Incas and the Spaniards. Several epochs now clashed in the plaza where the Incas had once celebrated their military victories by stepping on the necks of their vanquished foes. Vintage VW Beetles cruised the square, passing in front of a McDonald's advertising lattes and Wi-Fi, next to a seventeenth-century Spanish church built with stones cut by Inca masons before Spain existed. (Two blocks away the Koricancha sun temple was now the Santo Domingo monastery.) Small packs of stray dogs jogged through the tight alleyways of an ancient street grid, appearing and disappearing like ghosts. The only certainty was that no matter what restaurant, café, taxi or pharmacy Alex and I entered, some awful song from the 1980s would be playing. When we heard Quiet Riot's "Cum on Feel the Noize" for the third time, Alex turned to me with a pained look and asked, "Is this really what music used to sound like?"

We met John early the following day at a fake English pub.

His "martini explorer" comment had unnerved me a little—compared to Bingham, I was a white-wine spritzer explorer—so before committing to anything, I thought I should mention that it had been a while since I had slept outdoors. What came out of my mouth instead was "I might not be completely up-to-date on the latest tent-erecting methods."

"That's all right," John said. "We'll need mules for a trip like this and the *arrieros*—the muleteers—can set up the tents. How do you feel about food?"

"Sorry?"

"You like cooked food?" John asked. I admitted that I did, in fact, have a weakness for victuals prepared over heat.

"Right. When I travel solo, I usually prepare my own cereal mix and carry that with me. Fantastic stuff—all the nutrition you need. You're going to need a lot of calories out there, maybe twice as many as usual, because the body starts breaking down after three days." John was a serious clean-your-plate man; he'd finished his enormous breakfast, polished off the toast that Alex and I couldn't get down, scraped the remaining yogurt out of everyone's serving dishes and poured all the leftover dairy products into his coffee before downing it.

"So let's say we bring a cook. Shouldn't be too expensive. We'll need maybe four mules to carry the food and gear. Now, do you need a toilet, or can you go in the bush?"

"You go to the bathroom in a bush?" Alex asked, his attention suddenly diverted from CNN's *World Business Today*, the first television he'd seen in a week.

"No, in *the* bush," John said. "Like the forest."

"Oh man, that's gross," Alex said.

I sensed that this was not the correct answer.

"No, no. I can go outside," I said.

Alex's facial expression made clear that this, alternative was no less gross.

"Good! Because a toilet means an extra mule and chemicals sloshing around all over the place. How's your health? Any history of heart trouble, or stroke? People think if you get into trouble out there that you can just pull out the satellite phone and call in a helicopter. They're kidding themselves. That's tough, tough country. You break a leg, even two days from the nearest hospital, and you're walking out."

I assured him that other than a little thickness around the midsection and occasional sore knees, my health was fine.

"You've got about six weeks between now and the time we leave. You've *got* to exercise. Focus on your core, your upper back and your joints. Your body's going to take a lot of abuse on this trip."

When John excused himself for a minute, I turned to Alex. "What do you think of John?"

"I guess he's a little intense. But I like him. And he sure knows a lot more about Peru than you do."

On the way back to the hotel, John dictated a long list of equipment that I needed to buy for our excursion: drip-dry clothing for day, warm clothing for night, walking stick, rain gear, headlamp, sleeping bag liner, rip-proof daypack, waterproof cover for daypack. My pen ran out of ink. We stopped at a stationery store off the plaza to buy a new one. The shopkeeper, standing over a glass display case holding copies of *Lost City of the Incas*, stared at John—dressed, as I soon learned he always was, in full explorer garb—as if she'd seen him before.

"You know who your friend looks like?" she asked me as I handed over my money. "Hiram Bingham."